AF471184

DRONE
THE AUTOMATED IMAGE
EDITED BY PAUL WOMBELL

LE MOIS DE LA PHOTO À MONTRÉAL

KERBER PHOTO ART

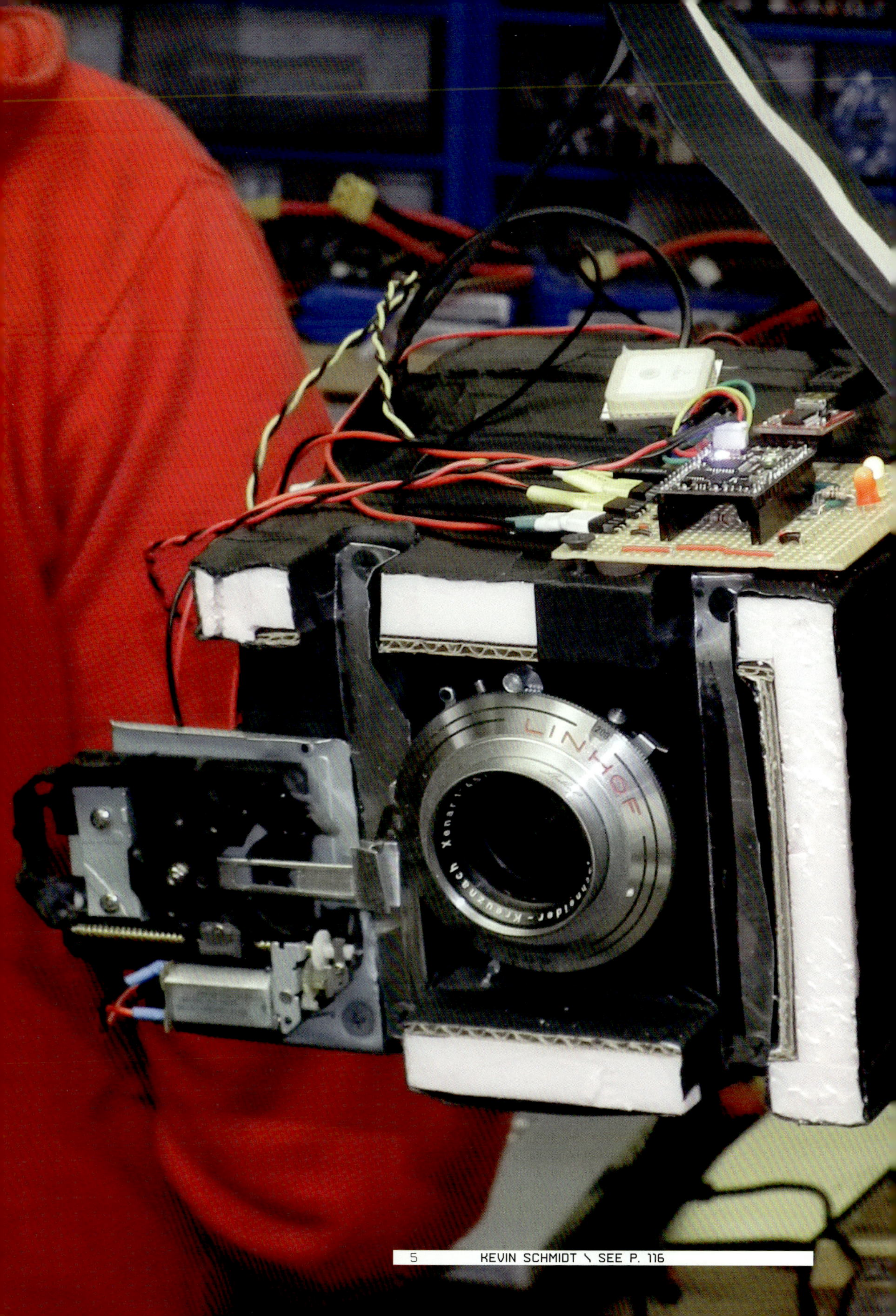

 KEVIN SCHMIDT \ SEE P. 116

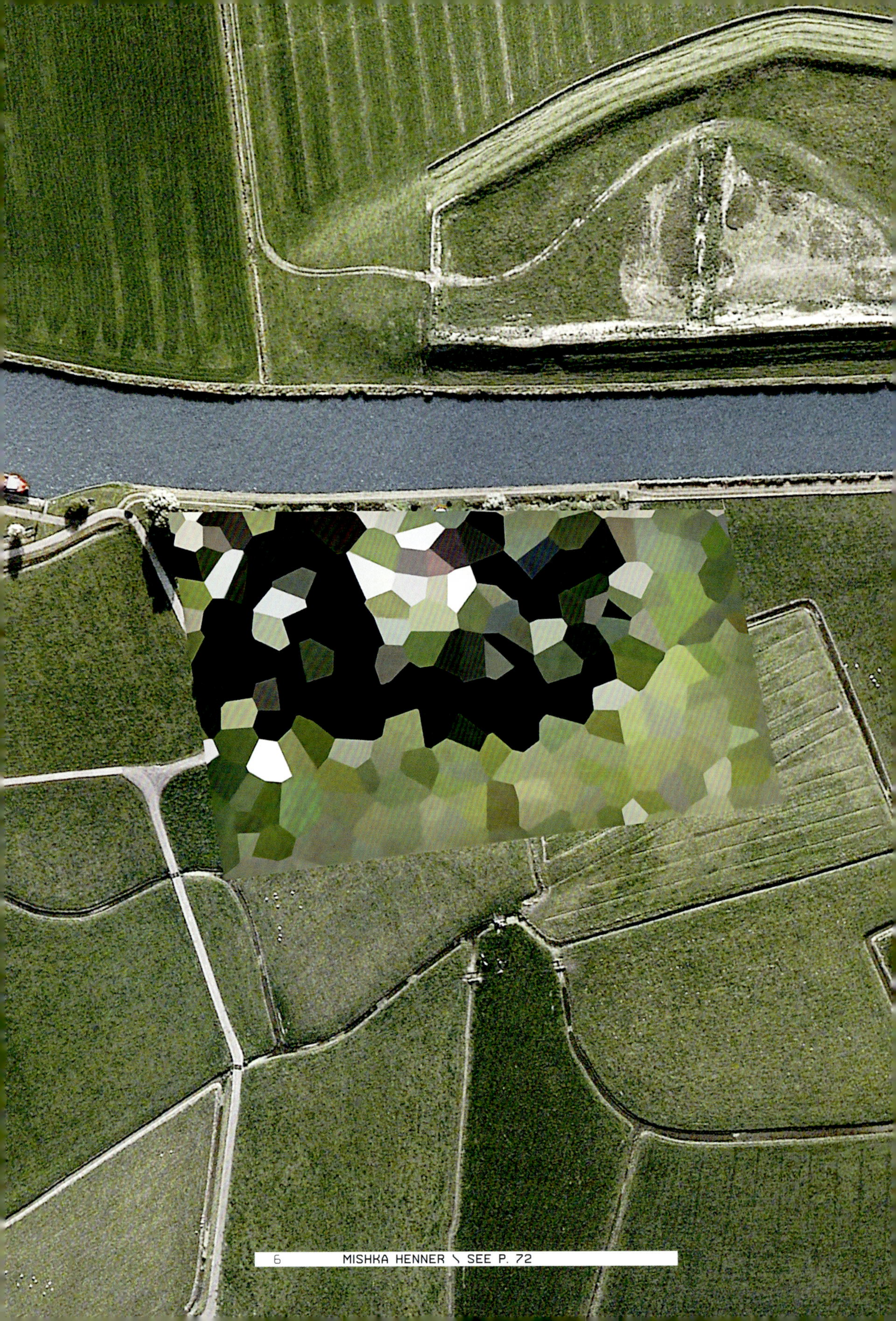

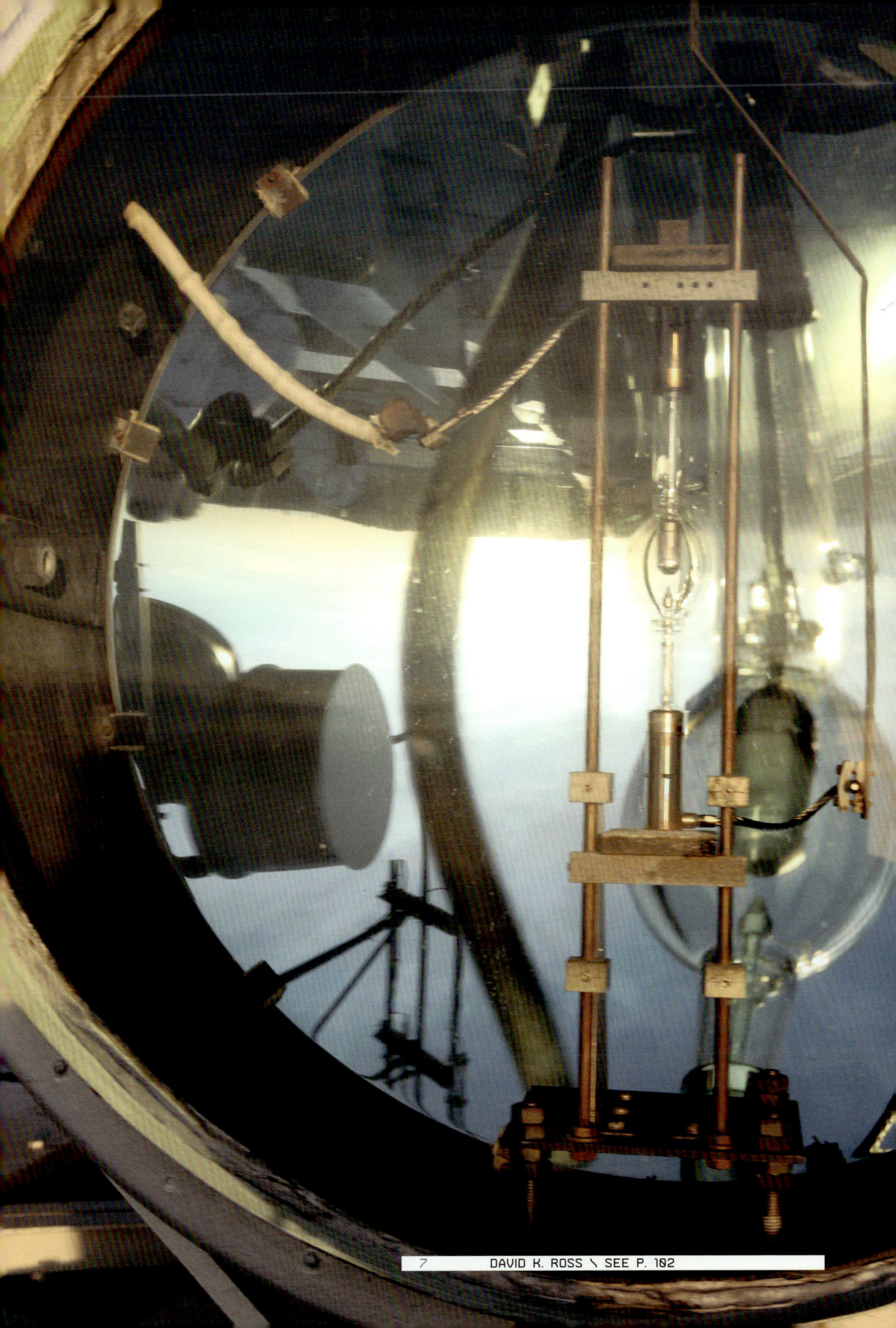

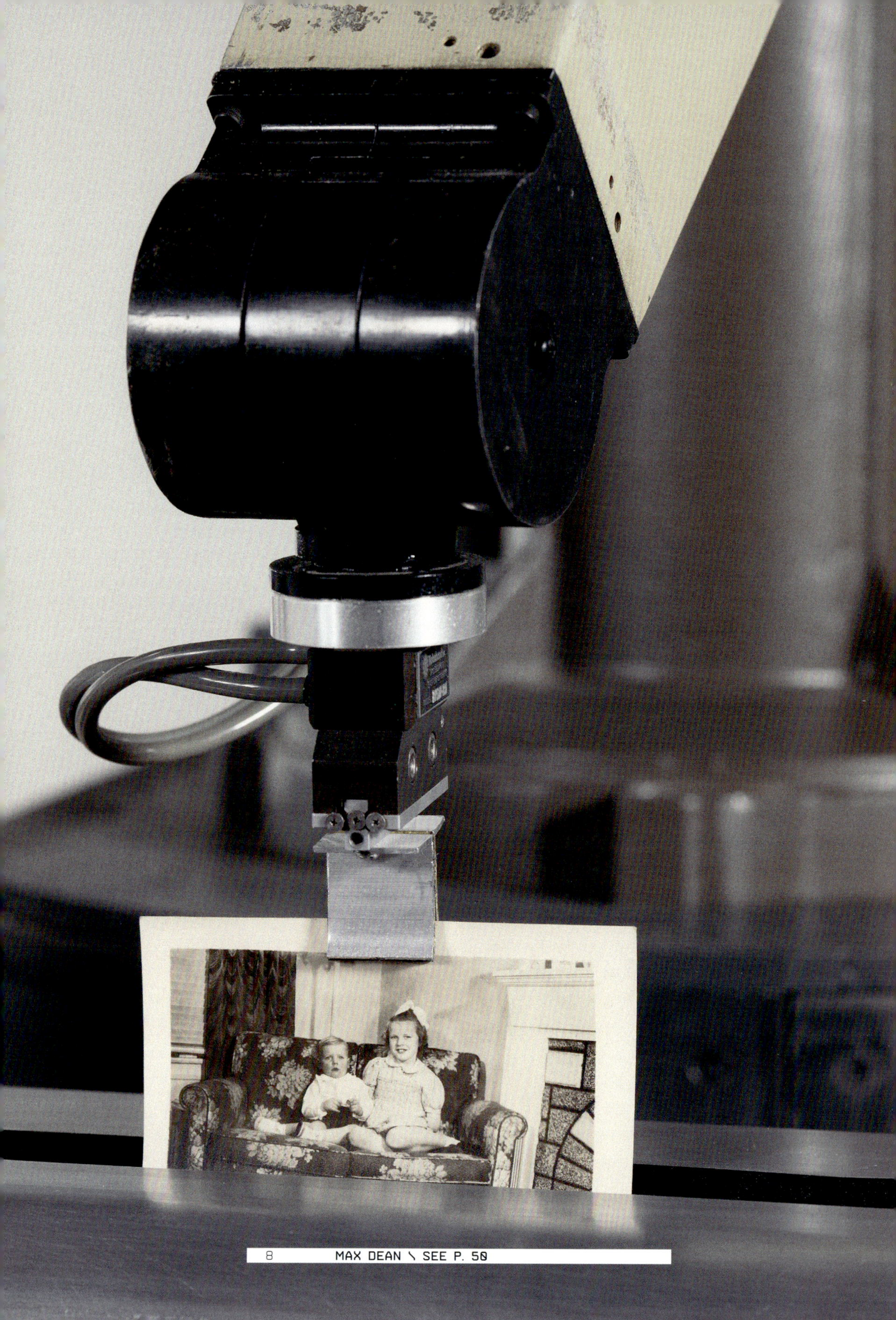

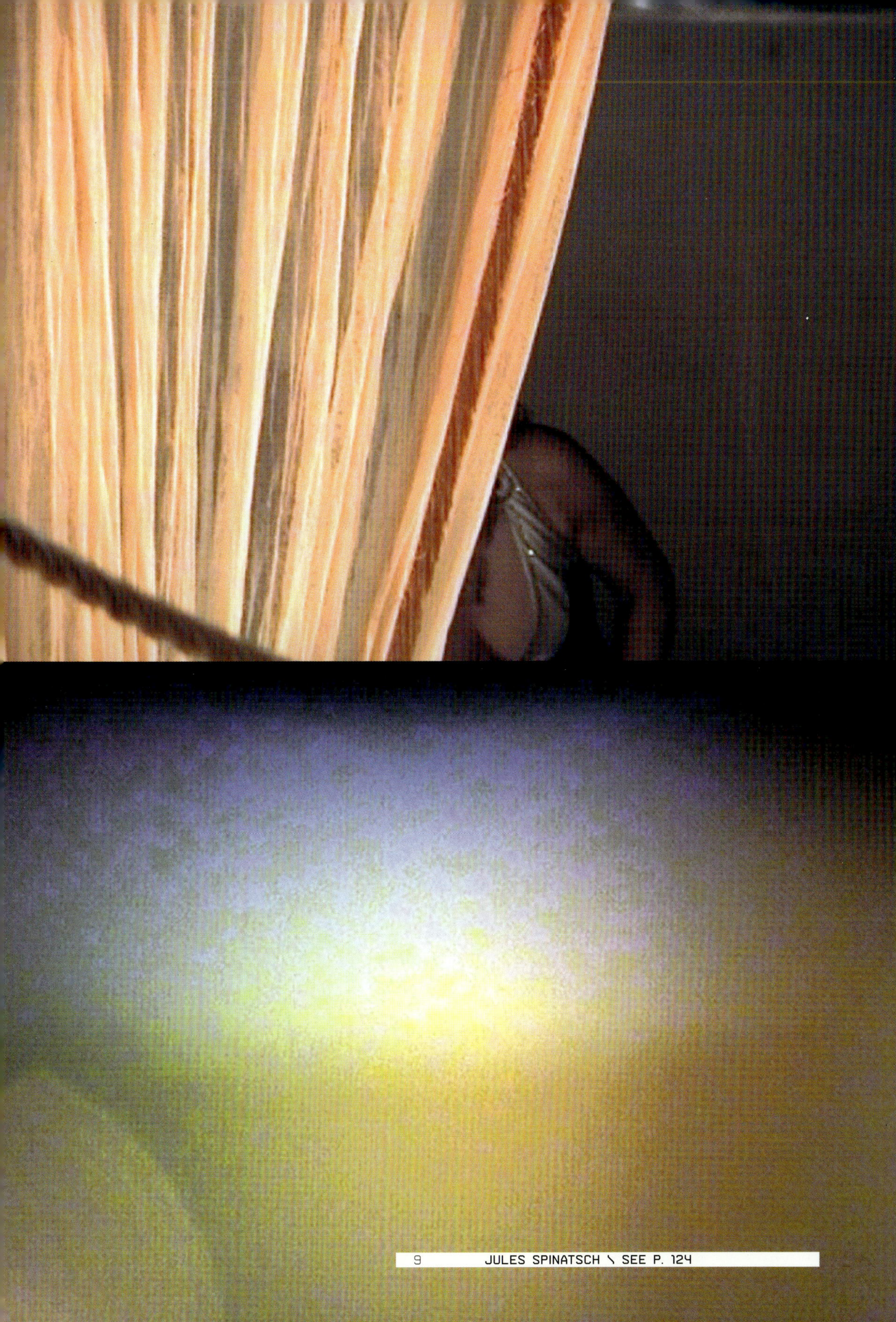

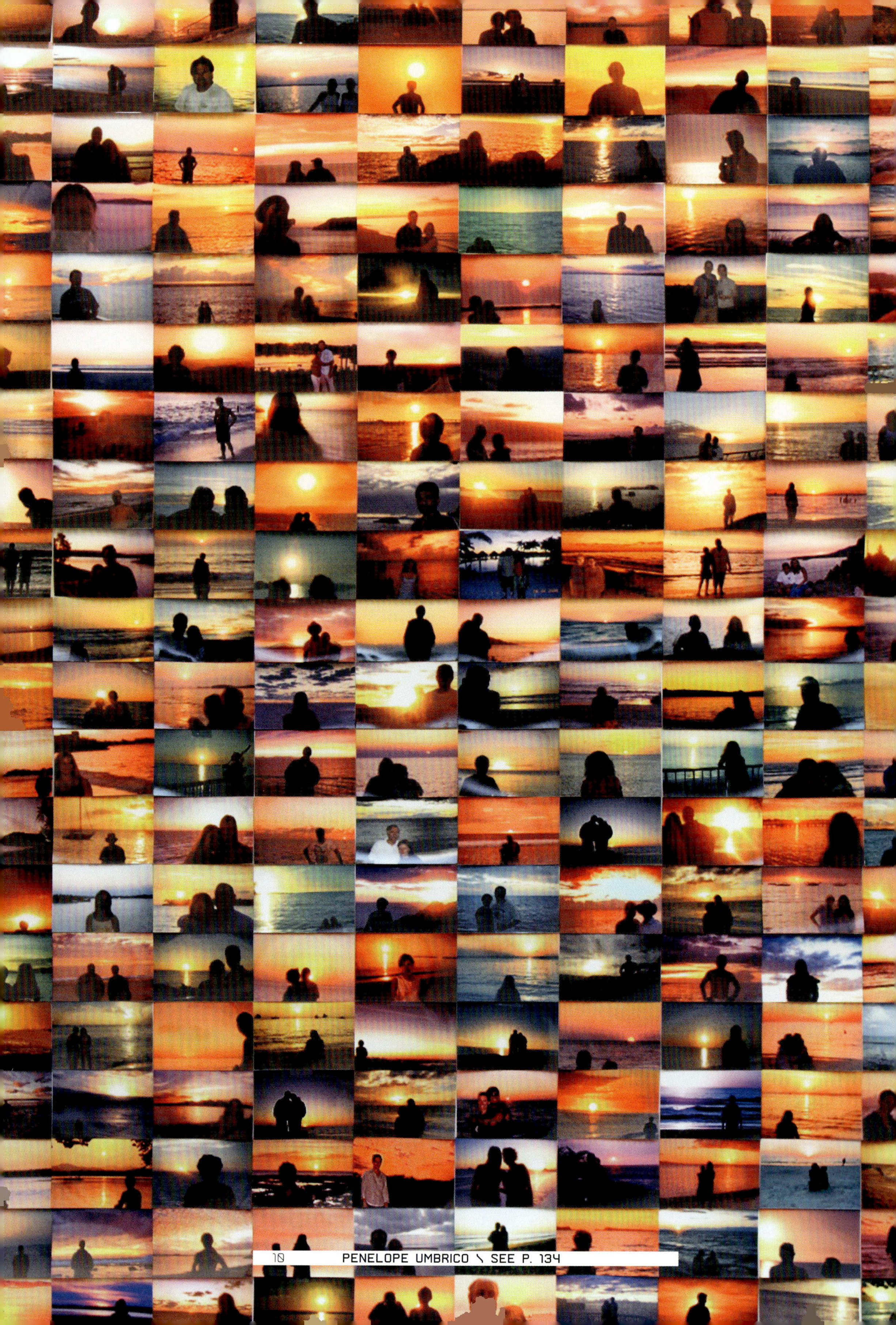

 PENELOPE UMBRICO ＼ SEE P. 134

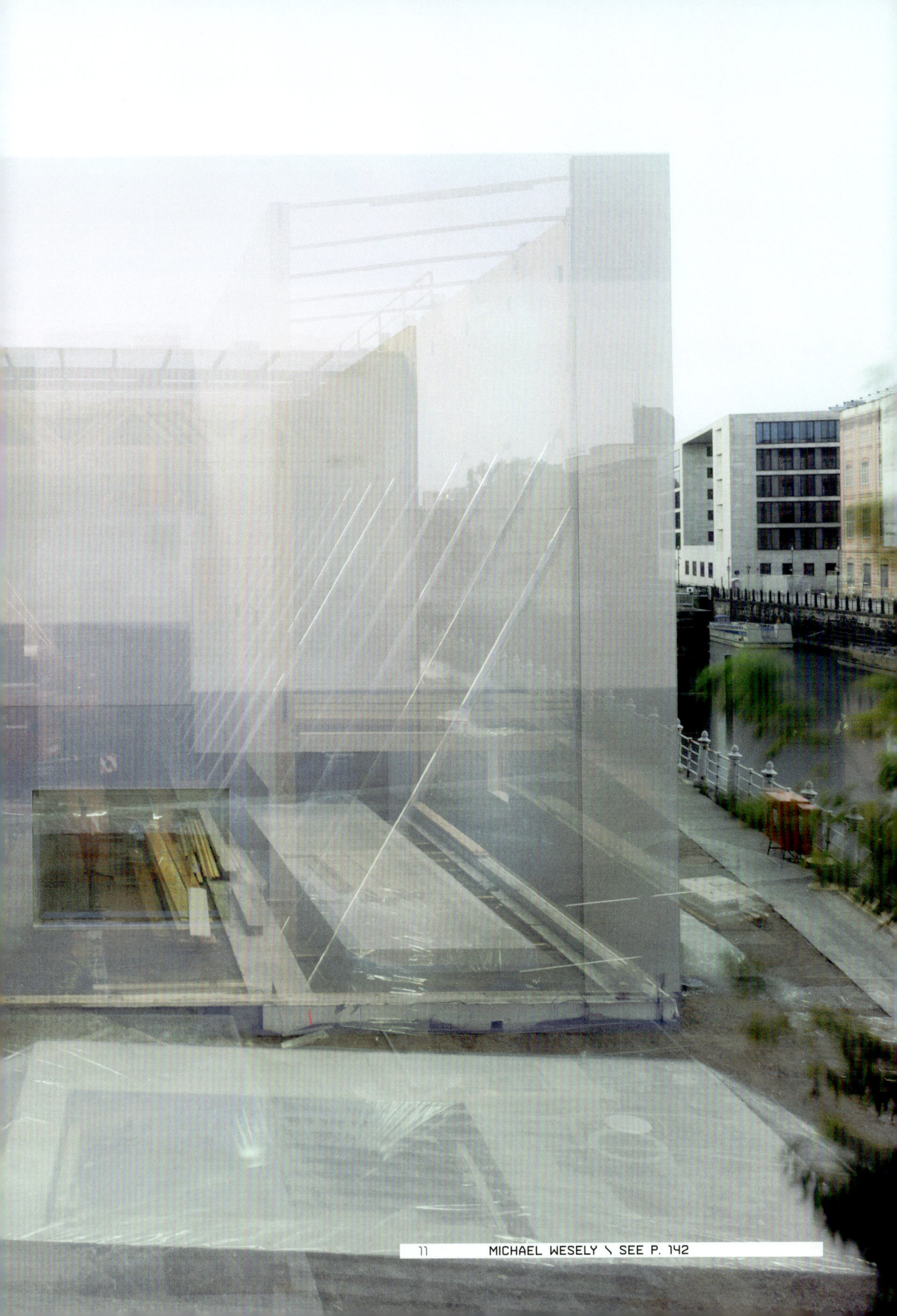

 MICHAEL WESELY \ SEE P. 142

PAUL WOMBELL

BLACK BOX

No photographer, not even the totality of all photographers, can entirely get
to the bottom of what a correctly programmed camera is up to. It is a *black box*.[1]
Vilém Flusser

Some villagers in Sikhim betrayed a lively horror and hid away whenever the lens
of a camera, or "the evil eye of the box" as they called it, was turned on them. They
thought it took away their souls with their pictures, and so put it in the power of the
owner of the pictures to cast spells on them, and they alleged that a photograph
of the scenery blighted the landscape.[2]
L. A. Waddell

1. Vilém Flusser, *Towards A Philosophy of
Photography* (London: Reaktion Books, 2000), 27.

2. Laurence Austin Waddell, *Among the Himalayas*
(New York: Amsterdam Book Co.; Westminster:
A. Constable & Co., 1899), 85.

The account in this epigraph is taken from the book *The Golden Bough* by J. G. Frazer, which I found on the document-sharing Web site Scribd.[3] As I scrolled down the site, an advertisement announced, "I AM A NIKON D3200." This Nikon camera had a voice and said, "I AM ALIVE." This camera is your friend, part of the family; it will remember the important events in your life, take photographs in the dark, record sound, and shoot remotely. This camera is alive.

One of the recurring stories in the history of photography is that in some so-called primitive societies there was a belief that photography could capture the soul. This photographic encounter from the late nineteenth century might seem, from a distance, to be more about anthropology and colonialism, which it is. However, the villagers in Sikhim were aware of something more profound: the changing relationship between the human and technology. This box might well have power over the subject, but the box also has power over the photographer. Many photographers have the perception that the camera is just an object over which they have complete mastery and control, an object that they can pick up and spontaneously use to take their photographs. The political theorist Langdon Winner has suggested that technical devices are not somehow separate and autonomous bits of machinery, but require social coordination and training: "We do not use technologies so much as live them. One begins to think differently about tools when one notices that the tools include persons as functioning parts."[4] We are socialized to use the camera both formally and informally. Family, friends, manuals, education, and advertisements all play a part in passing on the skills required to take photographs. More recently, the camera has become the active partner in transmitting these skills.

Cameras are complex instruments that transform three-dimensional space into miniature two-dimensional form by controlling space, light, and time. Whereas at one time the photographer had some control over the calculations used to make the final exposure, by the 1960s low-cost electronic internal components were commonplace and the actions required to take the photograph became automated. Cameras were equipped with exposure meters to adjust the aperture and shutter speed for the light conditions, autofocus sensors to determine the distance from the lens, and self-timing devices to set the exposure so that the photographer could move from behind the camera to be included in the picture. With the advent of the Internet and

3. James George Frazer, *The Golden Bough: A Study in Magic and Religion, Part II, Taboo and the Perils of the Soul*, 3rd ed. (London: MacMillan, 1919), http://www.scribd.com/doc/18067818/Frazer-Taboo-and-the-Perils-of-the-Soul-The-Golden-Bough-part-II.

4. Langdon Winner, *Autonomous Technology: Technics-out-of-Control as a Theme in Political Thought* (Cambridge, Mass.: MIT Press, 1977), 202.

Wi-Fi, images can now be instantly shared across social media platforms and stored on image libraries that are accessed via computers, mobile phones, and other cameras. The camera has taken on a life of its own, requiring little or no human involvement: it is part of the family, our friend, fully integrated technology, connected to other machines, an object of desire that makes images of our desires. But what kind of desire does the camera have for us? As the novelist J. G. Ballard said,

> The Church of England has lost a lot of its authority, so has the monarchy. So what we have is consumerism. I'm not suspicious of consumerism, but the problem arises when it's all there is left. I mean, if you go out in the London suburbs, away from our great museums and Houses of Parliament and art galleries, theatres and the like, into a world where all you have are retail outlets . . . there's nothing other than a new range of digital cameras, or what have you, to sustain one's dreams . . .[5]

This view of authority being eroded by consumerism and, more importantly, the influence of technology on human imagination and desires are recurring topics in Ballard's novels, and also fundamental themes in *Drone: The Automated Image*. However, it is in museums and art galleries that artists have investigated the different multiple uses that the camera has today, and its transformation into an object that can inspire dreams.

We shall start our investigation into the life of the camera with the work of artists Penelope Umbrico and Cheryl Sourkes, and their connection to themes of consumerism and suburbia desire. **Penelope Umbrico** appropriates existing images from Web sites or from the printed pages of catalogues that sell consumer goods. The *TVs From Craigslist* (2009–12) project shows images of second-hand televisions that the artist found on Craigslist. The use of the digital camera's automatic settings produced visual results that inadvertently reflected the flash on the television screen, revealing the ghostly image of the sellers and their interior domestic space. Umbrico wrote about this series, "Believing in ghosts assumes that the ghost is 'other,' but maybe we are (or at least verging on becoming) the ghost if our relationship to our identification with nonmaterial digital representation and presence defines large aspects of our world. It's like we've found a way to leave the cave and have left our bodies behind."[6]

5. From a BBC Radio 4 interview with J. G. Ballard by James Naughtie in Simon Sellars and Dan O'Hara, eds., *Extreme Metaphors: Selected Interviews with J.G. Ballard 1967–2008* (London: Fourth Estate, 2012), 481.

6. Penelope Umbrico, "From Narcissus to Narcosis," in *Penelope Umbrico (photographs)* (New York: Aperture, 2011), 9.

In his book *Haunted Media*, Jeffrey Sconce writes about the electronic media and their connection with the paranormal and the widely held belief in the 1950s that technologies such as television were "alive."[7] He draws an uncanny parallel between late-nineteenth-century *spirit photography* and late-twentieth-century cyberspace, and the idea of *cyberspirits*. His use of the Freudian concept of the uncanny makes reference to the familiar becoming strange or to fear of being taken over by external forces that can articulate hidden repressed tensions. The automatic settings of the camera are central to Umbrico's work *Sunset Portraits from 12,193,606 Flickr Sunsets on 4/25/13* (2013), in which she uses pictures found on the photo-sharing Web site Flickr. The images depict people standing in front of a sunset, but because the cameras are set on automatic, the exposure compensates for the bright light of the sun by underexposing the people standing in foreground. Both sets of Umbrico's works might be seen as bad photography with wrong exposures, but the mechanics of the camera have overridden the intentions of the photographers, displaying their own rules and behaviours.

Cheryl Sourkes evokes the domestic and the automatic in her works *Everybody's* P. 120 *Autobiography (2012), Facebook Albums* (2010), and *BRB* (2010). At some point in the mid-1990s, the once-private world of the home became more visible in a way that even Ballard could never have imagined. It became possible to connect a video camera to the computer and communicate with other people by the way of the screen. This system was to be called webcams. This transformation was part of a wider development of placing autonomous cameras both in private and public locations to watch traffic moving along streets, animals in zoos, or even people undressing and performing sexual acts.[8] Webcams have become ubiquitous and integrated into our daily life. Sourkes may be one of the first artists to engage extensively and imaginatively with this extraordinary development. Using her computer to find material from live webcams and Web sites, she selects and edits from thousands of screen grabs and then organizes the images into typologies. Like Umbrico, Sourkes explores the role played by the camera in redefining the relationship between the public and the private to a point at which the most intimate moments are freely available to view by anyone with access to a computer and the Internet.

7. Jeffrey Sconce, *Haunted Media: Electronic Presence from Telegraphy to Television* (Durham, N.C.: Duke University Press, 2000).

8. This aesthetic recalls Andy Warhol's early experimental films made in the 1960s, such as *Sleep, Eat, Screen Tests,* and *Empire.*

In 1942, the first closed-circuit television (CCTV) system was installed in Germany on the test range for the V2 rocket. The design and installation of this system were undertaken by the engineer Walter Bruch;[9] the aim was to watch at close quarters the launch of the first long-range ballistic rockets. Since the 1960s, the countdown has become one of the visual icons of space exploration. Today's high-definition CCTV cameras, connected to computers that make it possible to identify and track anything and anyone in their field of vision, are omnipresent in public spaces.

P. 124 In 2003, **Jules Spinatsch** started his Surveillance Panorama Projects utilizing CCTV in public spaces. His work *Vienna MMIX 17352/7000, Speculative Portrait of a Society* (2009–11) was made on February 19, 2009 during the annual Vienna Opera Ball, attended by over seven thousand people. The work was made using images generated from two computer-controlled CCTV cameras with a telephoto lens that scanned the event over a period of eight and a half hours. The cameras made two full rotations on their axis, while recording a picture every three seconds, and made 17,352 single images. Because of the automatic nature of the cameras, there is no hierarchy of subjects, no distinction between chandeliers, dust, curtains, and humans. Spinatsch took his inspiration from Josef Haslinger's book *Opernball* (Opera Ball),[10] a political thriller that tells the story of thousands of guests attending the Vienna Opera Ball being killed with poison gas due to a neo-Nazi terrorist attack.

In addition to webcams and CCTV, the other widely recognized automatic cameras are those used by Google Inc. for its Google Earth and Google Street View services. Google Earth, created by Keyhole Inc., was originally called Earth Viewer 3D.[11] Google now has over twenty satellites in operation that it uses for networking, mapping, and communication purposes.

P. 148 **Donovan Wylie**'s project *The Maze* (2003–09) is a photographic survey of the Northern Ireland prison that played a key role during what was called the Troubles. Wylie was the only photographer granted official and unlimited access to the prison. He describes its architecture as a Russian nesting doll – one space leading into another

9. Walter Bruch would later play an important role in the development of television broadcasting.
10. Josef Haslinger, *Opernball* (Frankfurt: Fischer, 2003).

11. Founded in 2001, Keyhole was a software company specializing in geospatial data visualization applications, and it was partly funded by the CIA. The name Keyhole is a reference to the KH reconnaissance satellites that were operated by the CIA and the U.S. Air Force in the 1960s. Google bought Keyhole in 2004.

space. Once he understood that the prison is a machine that controls the human body, he found the visual direction to pursue. He realized that he had to become a "machine" by systematically photographing the uniform nature of the prison. One of the defining architecture elements was the H-block buildings, which housed the cells that Wylie meticulously recorded. In 2006, he returned to capture the demolition of the prison. Though Wylie thought at the time that he was the only one with a camera at the Maze site, he realized some weeks later that Google Earth had been watching him photographing the Maze. The photographer found himself observed from a camera in the sky, by a satellite panopticon. He was caught inside another "machine," the vision machine. In 1930, Ilse Bing had undertaken a similar project to Wylie's, photographing the newly built Henry and Emma Budge-Heim social housing project for elderly people in Frankfurt. Taking inspiration from Le Corbusier's idea that a house is a "machine for living," this modernist building was also based on the H-block structure, with individual rooms located on the longer wings and services placed in the central connecting link. Bing starts her survey by giving an overall exterior perspective of the building, then moves inside corridors and rooms, and ends with a microscopic view of details within the building. These photographs are part of an album in the collection of the Canadian Centre for Architecture.

By searching Google Earth and other freely available visual data on the Web, **Mishka** P. 72 **Henner** makes his landscape works based on patterns and marks inscribed on the surface of Earth. Although Google Earth gives the impression that the surface of the world is available to view without constraints, national governments use visual strategies to censor what they define as sensitive information. In his work *Dutch Landscapes* (2011), Henner found the strange pixelated colour abstractions that the Dutch government uses to hide security-sensitive buildings and installations. Looking more like viruses under a microscope, this "pixelation infection" is replicating itself across the body of Google Earth. The writer Giampaolo Bianconi draws the connection between Henner's work and sixteenth-century Dutch paintings that depicted landscapes from a high angle.[12] This view from above also has affinity with abstract expressionism. For *The Fields* (2012–ongoing), Henner downloaded high-resolution image files of oil fields to make extraordinarily detailed images that verge on the abstract and bear a resemblance to the work of Jackson Pollock

12. Giampaolo Bianconi, "The Golden Age of Dutch Aerial Landscapes," *Rhizome*, June 12, 2012, http://rhizome.org/editorial/2012/jun/12/digital-dutch.

and Barnett Newman. In the late 1960s and early 1970s, the City of Montreal commissioned an aerial photographic survey of the terrain of the city and outlying districts. This survey could be seen as a precursor to Google Earth. One of the by-products of the survey was black-and-white photographic glass plates that were used by cartographers in the production of maps. The plates show the city from varying heights, at slightly different angles, and were made in a series of flights across Montreal. The process is called aerotriangulation. These glass plates are now in the photographic collection of the McCord Museum in Montreal. They show the city from over forty years ago in extraordinary detail: the site of Expo 67 and the recently built Place Ville Marie and Champlain Bridge.[13]

P. 96 In 2007, Google introduced Google Street View by sending out an army of hybrid electric automobiles, each bearing nine cameras on a single pole. Armed with a global positioning system (GPS) and three laser range scanners, this fleet of cars began an endless quest to photograph every highway and byway around the world. **Jon Rafman** is one of a small group of artists that has engaged with the Google Street View archive by collecting screen grabs, which he uses to make prints and films. His *The Nine Eyes of Google Street View* (2008–ongoing) is a selection of images of events that the automatic camera recorded while on the road. Seemingly impartial and detached from human involvement, the camera system creates results that seem surreal. These kinds of images, in which the everyday becomes mysterious and strange, question any rational understanding of the world.

P. 108 For some years, **Thomas Ruff** has been searching the Web and using freely available images and data to compose his works. His most recent series, *ma.r.s.* (2010–ongoing), is based on NASA's archival materials from the Mars Reconnaissance Orbiter. Using cameras, spectrometers, and radar, the mission collects data on the atmosphere and surface conditions of Mars and transmits these data back to Earth. One of these instruments is the high-resolution HiRISE camera. The black-and-white images generated constitute Ruff's starting point in the production of his work. He adds colour to accentuate the physical characteristics of the landscape and changes the perspective to give the impression that the viewer is in a spacecraft orbiting Mars and looking down at the planet's terrain.

13. During the Cold War, aerial photography was extensively referenced in the media. An American U-2 reconnaissance aircraft was shot down over the Soviet Union in 1960, and aerial photographs played an important role during the Cuban missile crisis in 1962.

Mars also plays a central role in the work of **Pascal Dufaux**. He remembers watching P. 68 in 2004 the images broadcast from the cameras mounted on the Mars Exploration Rovers as they searched for clues of past water activity on the planet. For Dufaux, it seemed that the limits of landscape art were being pushed forward and that this vision from so far away was now part of everyday life on Earth.[14] This understanding prompted him to construct his own robotic optical machine, *The Cosmos In Which We Are* (2009–11) – similar to the Mars Rovers, but designed to view life on Earth. Equipped with CCTV, mirrors, aluminum, and Plexiglas, the machine views the world around it as if it were a strange and distant planet. Continually moving in slow rotation, like the motion of the planet Mars, the device captures images from its own locality and projects them with a time lapse onto a screen. Thus, the ordinary world is transformed into a vision of an extraordinary dream state.

Whereas in the past only government agencies were sending cameras into space, today artists can also do this. With the aid of a weather balloon and working with amateur radio operators, **Kevin Schmidt** sent a large-format camera to take one P. 116 4" x 5" transparency photograph of the stratosphere. Connected to a computer to calculate the correct height and time to release the shutter, the camera was attached to the balloon and dispatched 35,000 metres above Earth. The resulting transparency is then presented as a large projection in the gallery. The viewer standing between the projector and the image of *High Altitude Balloon Harmless Amateur Radio Equipment* (2013) becomes part of the aerial scene as a silhouette, evoking the nineteenth-century Romantic painting by Caspar David Friedrich *Wanderer Above the Sea of Fog* (1818) and the idea of the sublime.[15]

The technological sublime can be seen in **David K. Ross**'s film *Le Phare* (2012). Built P. 182 in 1962, 1 Place Ville Marie is one of the most distinctive buildings in Montreal. On its roof, 190 metres above street level, there is a rotating beacon with four separate light beams; fully automated, it starts its own performance every day at sunset and continues until one o'clock in the morning. In *Le Phare*, a camera attached to the rotating unit follows the beams as they illuminate the sky. Ross brings into view what is rarely seen: the lighting apparatus with its mechanically rotating turntable on which the four light fixtures with mirrors and high-intensity bulbs are mounted. Although devoid of the practical role of forewarning of danger, it has nevertheless become one of the recognizable symbols of Montreal – a monument to the unconscious hovering above while the city sleeps.

14. Pascal Dufaux, Artist's Statement, "Vision Machines," http://pascaldufaux.com/en/info_e.html.

15. See David E. Nye, *American Technological Sublime* (Cambridge, Mass.: MIT Press 1994). Nye develops the concept of the sublime from the nineteenth century to the present. He posits that the sublime has a history – that sublime experiences emerge from new social and technological conditions, and that each new experience to some extent undermines and displaces the older versions of the sublime. The natural sublime of the landscape is surpassed by the power and scale of technology.

P. 142 **Michael Wesely** reconstructs the camera to allow single exposures with a duration of up to twenty-six months. The results are photographs that constantly remake themselves with different layers of changing light and weather conditions. Each photograph is a living memory of time; newly erected buildings become ghostly outlines; the movement of the sun leaves light lines across the sky. Thus, for Wesely each image acquires an extra dimension: "Basically photography for me is about three-dimensional. It is also about the camera, how the camera works."[16] One of his major projects has been on recent urban developments in Germany, particularly in Berlin. Starting in 1997, he has placed cameras around the Potsdamer Platz to record the transformation of the city since the reunification of East and West Germany. The images trace the construction of a new city centre and the changes in light over the seasons.

P. 32 Over the last twelve years, **Elina Brotherus** has produced an extensive body of work that interweaves art history with autobiographical references. Her photographic project *Suites françaises 2* (1999), part of the series *12 ans après* (1999–2012), is based on her experience of moving from Helsinki to Paris and reflects on her difficulties in adapting to a new country and acquiring a new language. Yellow Post-its are placed on her body and on domestic objects identified by their corresponding French name. She writes out descriptions of objects and, sometimes, short texts revealing her thoughts at the time that the self-portraits were taken. Her video *Artists at Work* (2010) revolves around the theme of the artist working in the studio, both as physical presence and as symbolically embedded in a long art-historical tradition of artists' self-representation. This video depicts the artist herself modelling for two male painters, who eventually change roles and become models for her. Regardless of who the protagonist might be, the camera is always silently watching and recording.

P. 92 Using multiple cameras connected to a radio-controlled release system that simultaneously triggers the shutters, **Barbara Probst** creates visually complex works. They take one particular moment in time and dissect it into different points of view: "The camera angles are often overlapping, therefore cameras photograph each other while they are photographing. However, when the cameras are apparent in the images, it unmasks the process of photography, and I am interested in that."[17] *Exposure #55: Munich, Waisenhausstrasse 65, 01.17.08, 1:55 p.m.* (2008) comprises

---

16. Interview with Michael Wesely by Sarah Hermanson Meister, in *Michael Wesely: Open Shutter* (New York: The Museum of Modern Art, 2004), 24.

17. Interview with Barbara Probst by Nicole Padulka, "Split Second," *The Morning News*, June 30, 2008, http://www.themorningnews.org/gallery/split-second.

twelve images, with wide-angle views, close-ups, and oblique angles. Set within a domestic space, a woman looks at her wristwatch, a child faces the viewer, and cameras are mounted on tripods – a visual puzzle that frustrates any easy understanding of what might have happened.

Michel Campeau has been making a photographic study of material culture. Using P. 38 the tools of archaeology – searching for the remains of activity, surveying sites, excavating, identifying objects, making classifications, and developing visual surveys – Campeau has set out to find the remnants of a dying visual technological process known as analog photography. *Industrial Splendour and Fetishism: The Bruce Anderson Collection* (2013) includes images of cameras manufactured over the last hundred years, made using various film formats. Each image emphasizes the different materials used to construct the camera, as well as the range of accessories, such as lens and flash units.

The **ExpVisLab** collective (George Legrady, Marco Pinter, and Danny Bazo), on the other P. 66 hand, looks toward the future of the camera, taking inspiration from the Esper machine camera featured in the science fiction film *Blade Runner* (1982) and from the area of technological development called computational photography. ExpVisLab is engaged in a research project on interactive cameras that explore and respond to their locations and to movement, a kind of living camera that translates human behaviour into machine vision. Their installation *Swarm Vision* (2013) delves into the widening gap between the cultural meaning of the photographic image and the development of highly sophisticated robotic cameras that take, edit, and store the image without human involvement.

Using the camera to track motion has a particular reference in the history of photography. In 1872, Eadweard Muybridge made his famous photographic study of the horse Occident galloping to prove that briefly all four feet were simultaneously off the ground. This established that photography could see what the human eye could not. It was achieved by placing cameras in a line along the edge of the racetrack with each device attached to a thread so that when the galloping horse passed the cameras, its legs would trigger the shutter release to record a sequence of exposures. Although Muybridge set up the apparatus to take the photographs, in the conventional sense the photographer was the horse.

P. 128

P. 54

P. 80

This relationship between technology and animal agency can be seen in the work of Jana Sterbak, Véronique Ducharme, and Craig Kalpakjian. **Jana Sterbak**'s multi-screen video installation *From Here To There* (2003) was made by mounting a camera on a Jack Russell terrier called Stanley. Equipped with a tiny video camera that transmitted pictures and sound, Stanley filmed his vision of the world from thirty-five centimetres above the ground. The viewer is therefore obliged to adopt his four-legged view as he moves along the banks of the St. Lawrence River, the gateway through which the first French explorers arrived in Canada in the sixteenth century. This work is not just a voyage defined by jerky and unpredictable movements, but an investigation of the relationship between animals and technology grounded on a range of senses that are "natural" and "mechanical." For her project *Encounters* (2012–13), **Véronique Ducharme** used a special remote-control camera that hunters employ to collect visual information about potential prey. Ducharme located the camera in the forests of the Laurentians region, north of Montreal. With a night-vision device and infrared illumination, the animals can be observed without being aware of the camera. Their movement or the heat from their bodies triggers an exposure that generates ghostly images as they move around without fear of human presence. The work is presented as an installation, using automatic slide projectors to give the impression that the viewer – inadvertently transformed into potential prey – might be triggering the image.[18] **Craig Kalpakjian**'s *Black Box* (2002–13) places a Sony AIBO (Articial Intelligence roBOt) robotic dog inside a sealed box for the duration of the exhibition. This robot is one of several types of autonomous robot pets manufactured by Sony for predominantly domestic use as "entertainment robots." It can walk, see via a camera, and recognize spoken commands. Due to lack of stimulation in the sealed box, the robotic dog often goes to "sleep"; however, it periodically wakes up, explores its habitat, and takes photographs. Every day these black-and-white photographs are placed on the gallery wall.

In his essay "Why Look at Animals?" John Berger writes about the marginalization of animals, their disappearance from daily life, and their return as images and toys and placement in segregated farms that we call zoos.[19] Whereas in the past we endowed animals with magical functions and mythical powers, today we give these powers to technology. Guard dogs become CCTV units, pets become robots, and bees become unmanned aerial vehicles (UAVs), more commonly known as drones.

18. These remote-control cameras designed for hunting are also used by groups in the U.K. and the U.S. to attempt to record paranormal events such as ghosts. See http://www.project-reveal.com and http://www.ghoststop.com.

19. John Berger, "Why Look at Animals," in *About Looking* (New York: Vintage Books, 1991), 3–28.

Drones are male honeybees hatched from unfertilized eggs, so they cannot sting or produce honey. They are characterized by large eyes, have a body size greater than that of worker bees, and are fast enough to accompany the flight of the queen bee. These sight and movement characteristics have been assigned to UAVs. However, the machine drones do have a sting: they can fire missiles. They are used to perform reconnaissance and attack missions for the military and can fly autonomously under remote control.[20] Drones overcome the limitations of the human body – such as the fixed position of the human eye and the need to rest, take refreshments, and have some form of shelter – as they are able to travel to difficult and remote locations and can see at all times, even in limited light. With their artificial sensing, they convey the impression that they posses an intent or agency of their own. Drones are the robots of seeing. In *The Vision Machine*, Paul Virilio called the reliance on technologies of vision such as cinema, television, and computers the *industrialization of vision*.[21] Since 2004, drones have been used extensively by the U.S. to target militants in Pakistan, particularly in the North Waziristan tribal region. The stories told by innocent survivors of drone attacks uncannily echo the stories told by non-Westerners when they first encountered photography: "People are afraid of dying . . . Children, women, they are all psychologically affected. They look at the sky to see if there are drones."[22] More recently, the U.S. government started using drones over Mexico to gather intelligence on drug cartels. Drones also have many civil applications, such as fire fighting, security work, and pipeline surveillance, and there is growing amateur interest in building and flying them for recreational use. They have become the focus of a wide debate on the ethics of using UAVs to kill humans and on their use for public surveillance.[23]

Both Trevor Paglen and Raphaël Dallaporta engage with the use and the implications of drone technology. Crossing disciplines as diverse as geography, journalism, and fine art, **Trevor Paglen** seeks out the hidden world of military technology in the "black world" in his photographic work. Pushing the limits of the visibility of the photographic process, he explores the U.S. government's technology of warfare, surveillance, and communications and investigates the military use of drones. Making reference to the work of Eadweard Muybridge, Timothy O'Sullivan, and Alfred Stieglitz, Paglen questions how we understand photography by situating it in the history of surveillance

P. 88

20. One of the first surveillance drones ever produced was by Canadair in the 1960s. The CL-89 was a joint project with Britain and West Germany and was used by NATO in Eastern Europe. Canadair was based in Montreal; in 1988 it became part of Bombardier Aerospace.
21. Paul Virilio, *The Vision Machine* (Bloomington: Indiana University Press; London: British Film Institute, 1994), 59.

22. Firoz All Khan, interview, Islamabad, Pakistan, February 26, 2012. In "Living Under Drones," *Sanford/NYU Report*, September 2012, http://www.livingunderdrones.org.
23. See Medea Benjamin, *Drone Warfare: Killing by Remote Control* (New York and London: OR Books, 2012); and Drone Wars UK, http://dronewarsuk.wordpress.com.

and the conquest of space. Stieglitz's clouds become the background for Predator drones, O'Sullivan's landscapes become sites of military installations, and Muybridge's studies of animal movement become studies of drone flights. **Raphaël Dallaporta** is one of a few artists who have directly used a drone in the production of his work *Ruins* (2011). In the autumn of 2010, he travelled to northern Afghanistan to join a group of French archaeologists who were researching threatened archaeological sites. Because of its strategic importance, Afghanistan has been repeatedly invaded. The most famous sites in the Valley of Balkh Ab, associated with Alexander the Great, have been pillaged many times. Following the 9/11 attack on the World Trade Center, Afghanistan yet again became a war zone. Dallaporta flew a specially adapted six-propeller drone equipped with a camera over the landscape, seeking visual evidence of previous invasions and the possibility of finding new archaeological sites. Each image taken by the drone resembles a microscope picture as it looks down on the landscape to see the marks of military activity left over thousands of years ago.

Medical photography is also a form of reconnaissance – reconnaissance of the human body. Using different imaging technology devices, Mona Hatoum and Suzy Lake explore their own bodies through themes of invasion and the human landscape. **Mona Hatoum**'s video installation *Corps étranger* (1994) consists of a tall oval-shaped space with two entrances and a video projection onto the floor. The video was made with endoscopic technology when Hatoum placed a medical camera inside her body. The images show close-ups of human skin and of the inner cavities of the body as the camera circles around orifices, enters, and explores subterranean tunnels with moist and hairy surfaces. The narrow space of the installation almost forces the viewer to stand on the projected images, while continuous heartbeat and breathing sounds generate a rather suffocating ambience. The camera has inserted the viewer inside a human body, a place that is simultaneously near and far away. **Suzy Lake**'s self-portraits *Reduced Performing* (2008–09) were made by placing her body on a flatbed scanner. The scanner uses a light source to illuminate an object positioned on a horizontal plane and converts the reflected light into digital signals, which can then be made into prints. This process is based on wirephoto or telephotography, an early form of technology used to transmit halftone photographs electronically over telephone lines. Lake wore different clothes but assumed a similar position on the

P. 44
P. 70
P. 84

flatbed for each scanned image; the scanner took seven minutes to complete its trace across her body. Thus each image is a performance between the artist and the scanner. The result is a strange image that captures a living body that is breathing, blinking, and sometimes crying, but that at the same time remains still.

Performance and self-portraiture were central to photo booths, the first automatic photographic machines introduced in public places. Catering to the need to cheaply and quickly produce identity photographs for travel documents such as passports and other official documents, photo booths are part of the urban fabric and can be found in any major town and city. However, these devices also created something more interesting – an autonomous space, a kind of private studio where desires could be acted out and performed. Both Tomoko Sawada and WassinkLundgren have used this private studio in the city in the production of their work. **Tomoko** P. 112 **Sawada**'s first major work, *ID400* (1998), was made while she was a student in Kobe, Japan. Using different make-up, clothing, and hairstyles, Sawada created over four hundred different photographic identities: a panorama of multiple, conflicting identities that directly subverts the role of the photo booth in making one permanent photographic portrait for official documents such as passports. *Don't Smile Now... Save it for Later!* (2008) by Dutch duo **WassinkLundgren** (Thijs groot Wassink and P. 138 Ruben Lundgren) is a set of photographic views recording the surroundings of photo booths located in London. Each exposure is triggered by placing a mirror inside the photo booth, keeping the curtain open, and inserting money into the machine. The resulting images are slightly overexposed and out of focus, giving the impression that the camera hesitates as people pass by and are not interested in having their pictures taken. WassinkLundgren has given a new life to the photo booth, transforming it into a machine that can view its own location. Thus the photo booth has achieved subjectivity now that it has been set free from the task of picturing only the human face.

Max Dean's robotic work *As Yet Untitled* (1992–95) centres on the viewer's decision P. 50 to either save a photographic print or have it destroyed. A robotic arm has been programmed to pick up a photographic print from a hopper, present it to the viewer, and wait several seconds for a response. If the viewer covers the hand silhouettes, the image will be deposited in an archival box and so be saved. Should the viewer choose not to intervene, the robot will place the photograph in a shredder and this photographic memory will be destroyed. This work anticipates the end of the analog print, the moment when images became files, and the increased automation of the photographic process.[24]

The artists in *Drone: The Automated Image* are investigating the relationship between humans and non-humans. In their works, humans share the stage with technology, sometimes taking a more prominent role and other times a subservient one. However, the artists' focus is the complex exchanges that are developing between the camera and the human, emphasizing the functions and the intelligence of the camera, which in their work is not confined to the conventional understanding of a handheld instrument. The camera mutates into different configurations that involve robots, CCTV, computers, photo booths, satellites, remote-controlled devices, and drones. The artists are excavating the history of the camera technology and also looking into its future. An important question is raised: do cameras have their own life? This has much wider implications for our understanding of technologies. We are irrevocably connected with machines, instruments, and cameras. We cannot live without them.

Cameras are not simply extensions of human sight that extend vision into places where the human cannot travel, because of either distance or danger. We have little understanding of what it means to use a camera, not to mention the implications of the changes that have taken place over the last fifty years, which have increased the automation of the camera. Do cameras have a soul; do they take away life from the human? The political philosopher John Gray implies yes: "As machines slip from human control they will do more than become conscious. They will become spiritual beings whose inner life is no more limited by conscious thought than ours. Not only will they think and have emotions. They will develop the errors and illusions that go with self-awareness."[25] We need to know a little more about what happens in the "black box." The media theorist Friedrich A. Kittler warned, "Increasingly, data flows once confined to books and later to records and films are disappearing into black holes and boxes that artificial intelligences are bidding us farewell on their way to nameless high commands."[26] The camera might be our friend, but it might also be our enemy and have hostile intent.

24. Digital cameras with liquid crystal display (LCD) and that could be connected to a home computer became more readily available during the 1990s.
25. John Gray, *Straw Dogs* (London: Granta Books, 2002), 187.

26. Friedrich A. Kittler, *Gramophone, Film, Typewriter*, trans. and intro. by Geoffrey Winthrop-Young and Michael Wutz (Stanford: Stanford University Press, 1999), xxxix.

\ **Paul Wombell** is an independent curator and writer on photography living in London (U.K.). He has been director of Impressions Gallery, York (1986–94), director of The Photographers' Gallery, London (1994–2005) and festival director of the Hereford Photography Festival (2006–07). Since 2007 he has curated exhibitions for the annual photographic festival PHotoEspaña in Madrid and for FotoGrafia Festival Internazionale di Roma. Most recently, he organized the one-person exhibition *Calves and Thighs: Juergen Teller* (2010) and the group exhibition *Bumpy Ride: The Prophecies of Photography* (2010). He regularly writes for international photographic publications. He has edited eight books on photography, the most recent being *End Times: Jill Greenberg* (TF Editores/D.A.P., 2012), and *The 70s: Photography and Everyday Life* (La Fábrica, 2009) co-edited with Sergio Mah.

WORKS

Exhibited Works

Artists at Work, 2010
HD video, 41 min 11 s, 16:9, colour, stereo, dialogue in Finnish with English subtitles.

12 ans après, 1999–2012 (selection)
Pigment ink prints on Fine Art Baryta rag paper from analog and digital originals, variable dimensions.

There are two recurring subjects in Elina Brotherus's video *Artists at Work* (2010) and her photographic series *12 ans après* (1999–2012): the artist herself and the camera. Given her long-time interest in the representation of artist as model, Brotherus features predominantly in virtually all of her photographs and videos. The self-portraits picture her in expansive landscapes or in claustrophobic rooms, portraying a range of different emotions, from melancholy to anger, from perplexity to serenity. The other subject is the camera. Sometimes the cable release can be seen winding along the floor toward her hands, leaving the camera off image. In more recent works, the camera is present in her photographs, sharing the space with the artist.

Born in 1972 in Helsinki, Elina Brotherus divides her time between France and Finland, where she obtained an MA in photography at the University of Art and Design Helsinki in 2000. Her works have been in solo and group exhibitions around the world, including at The Photographers' Gallery in London (2013); the Lianzhou Photography Festival (2012); the Musée d'art moderne et d'art contemporain in Liège (2012); the Louisiana Museum of Modern Art in Humlebæk, Denmark (2012); BOZAR, Centre for Fine Art in Brussels (2012); the Sørlandets Kunstmuseum in Kristiansand, Norway (2011); the Bloomberg Space in London (2010); the Finnish Museum of Photography in Helsinki (2009); and the National Art Center in Tokyo (2008). She has received numerous grants and awards and her works are in major public collections. Brotherus is represented by gb agency in Paris, The Wapping Project Bankside in London, and Martin Asbæk Gallery in Copenhagen. \ www.elinabrotherus.com

From the series *12 ans après*:
p. 33 \ *Le Chemin*, 2011, 90 x 120 cm
p. 34 \ *Dans le brouillard*, 2011, 90 x 120 cm
p. 35 \ *En novembre*, 2011, 90 x 117 cm
p. 36 \ *Nu aux bottes de randonnée*, 2011, 90 x 110 cm
p. 37 \ *Exercice d'équilibre*, 2011, 90 x 120 cm

Courtesy of the artist

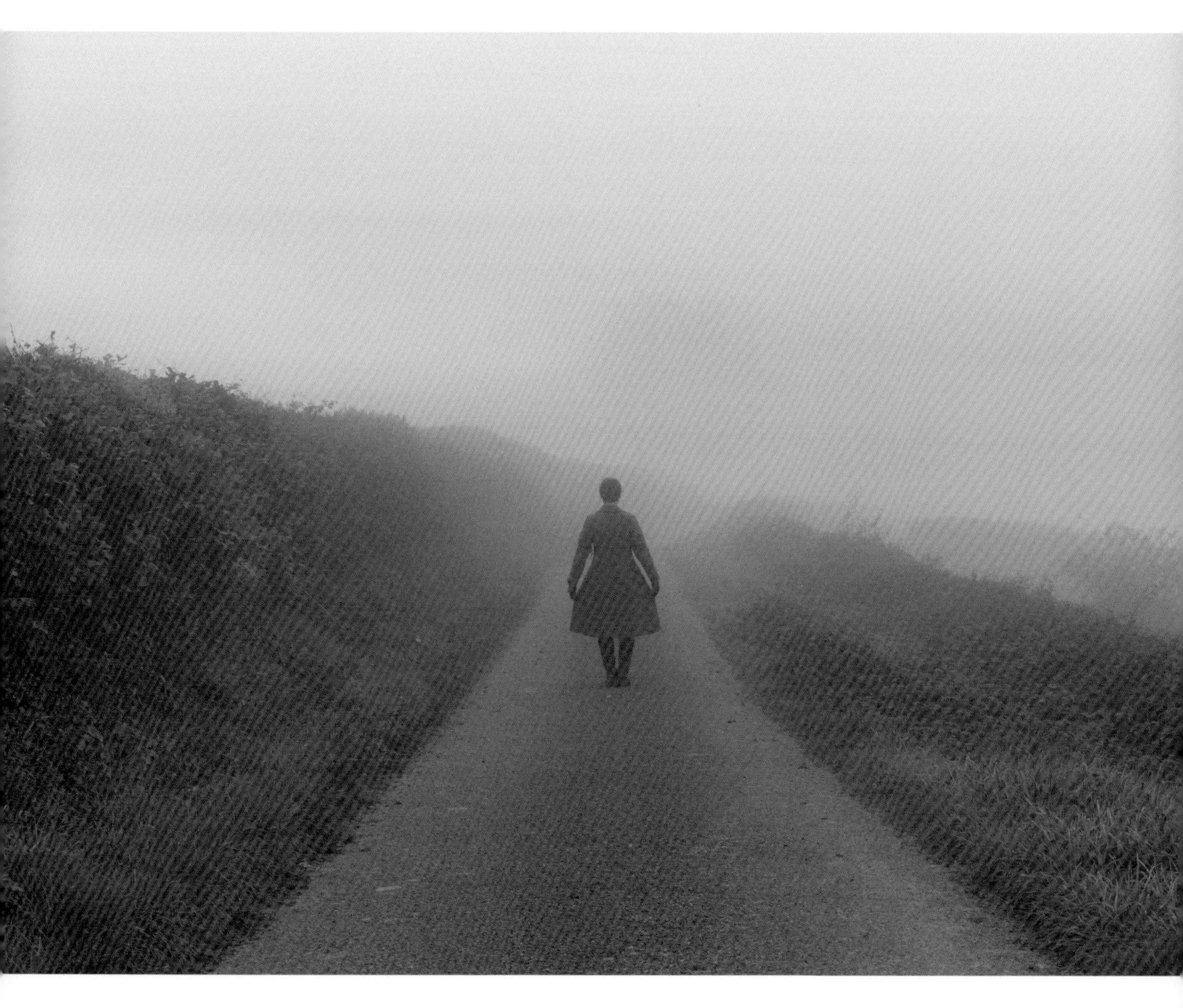

33   ELINA BROTHERUS

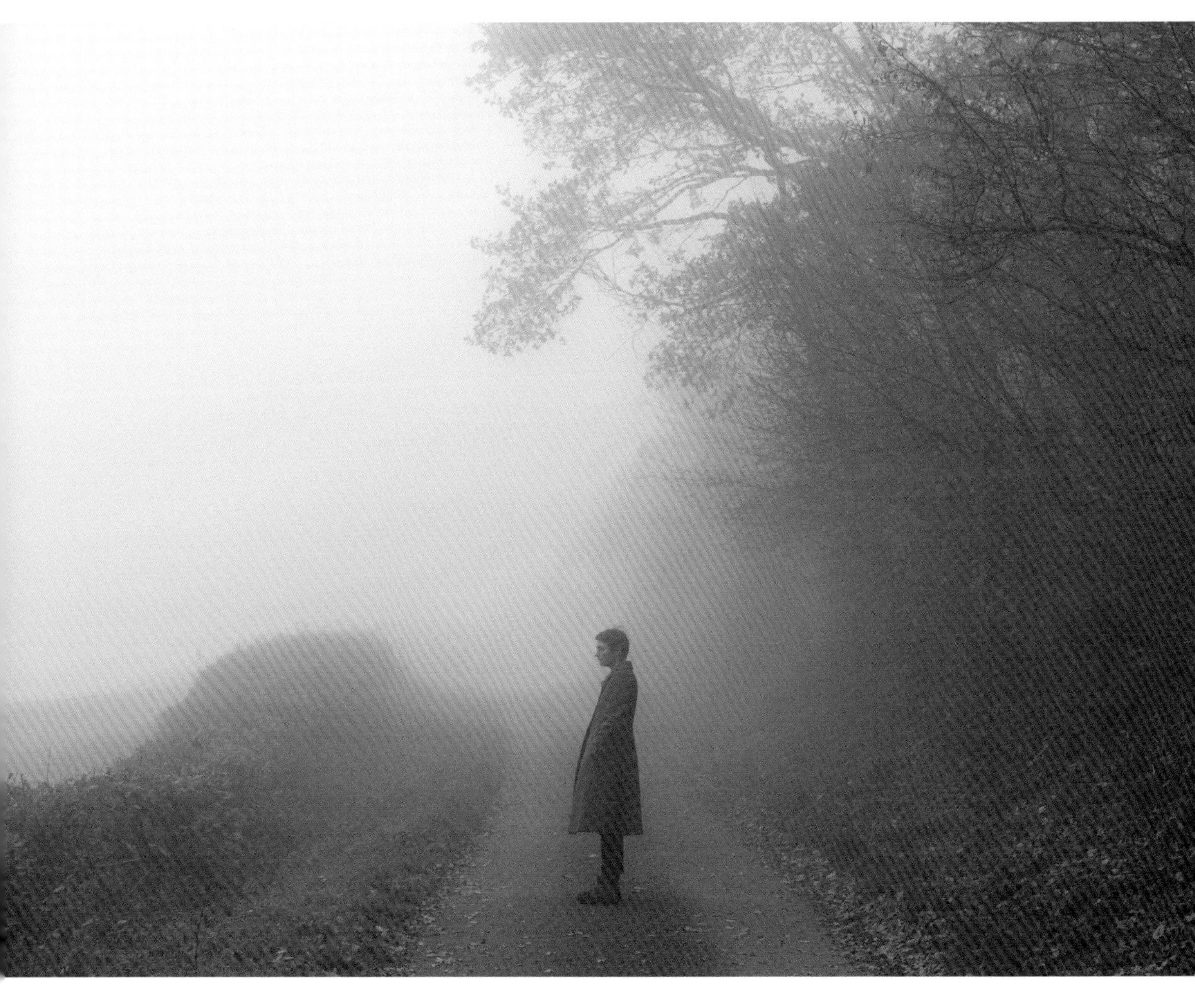

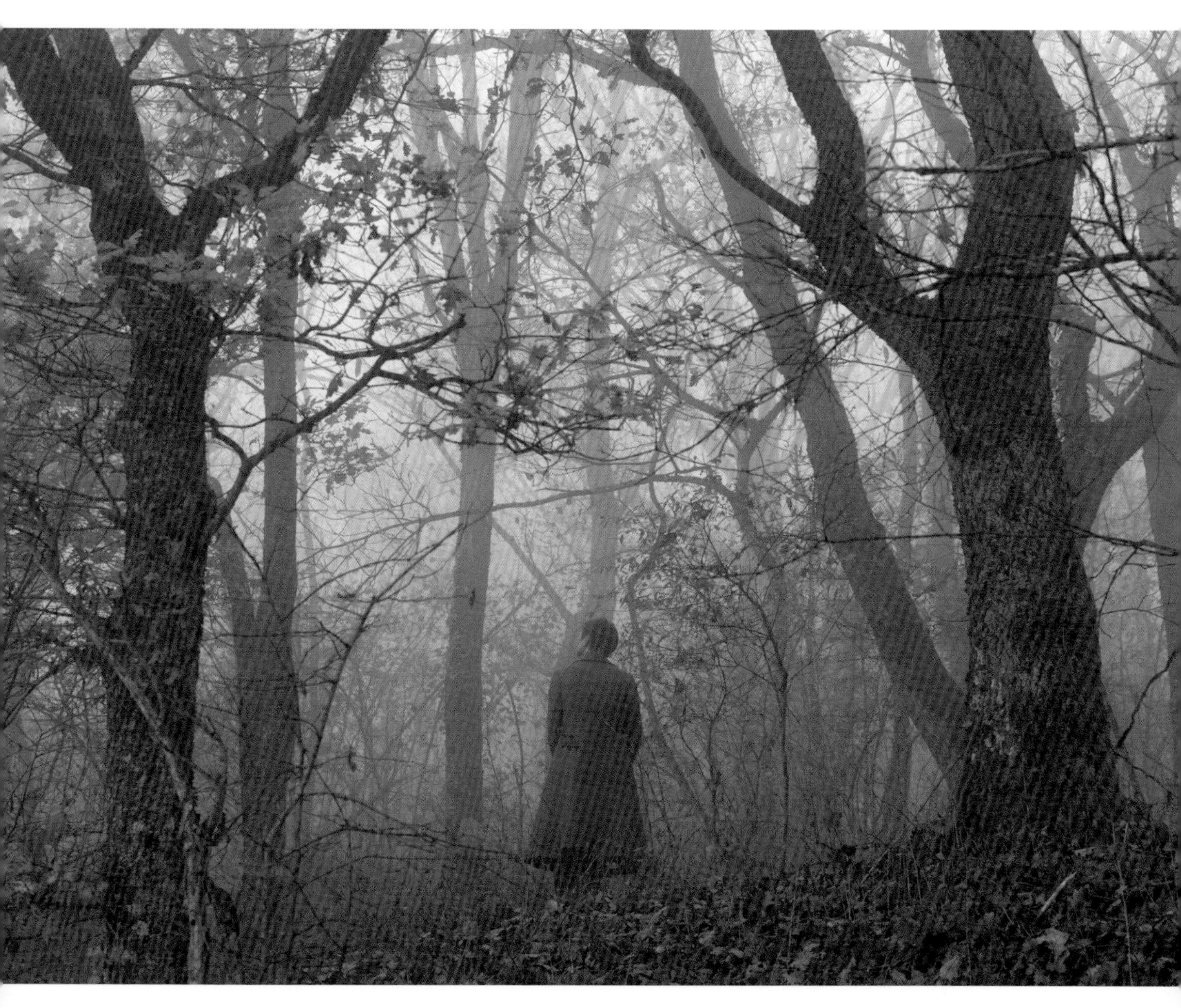

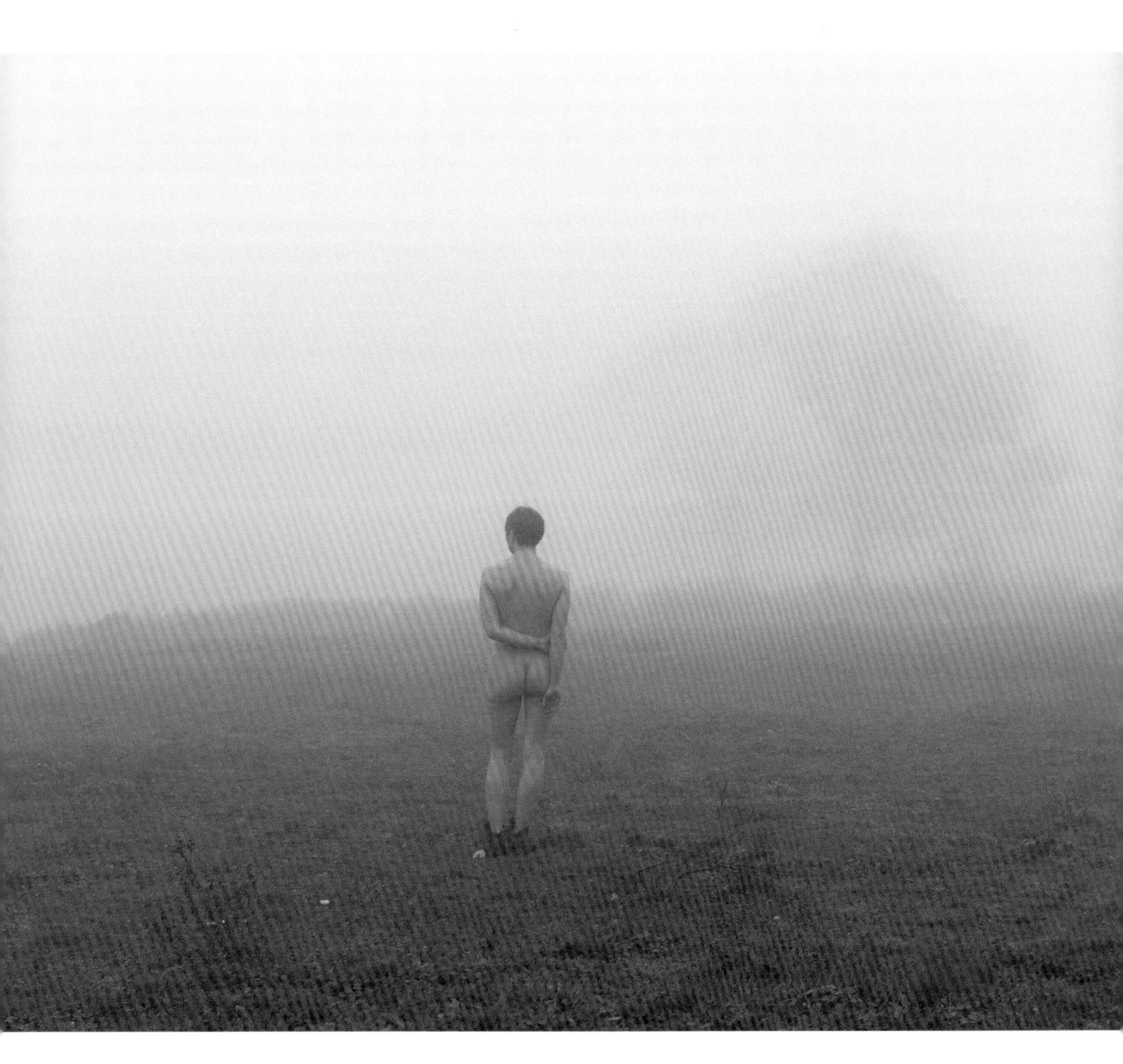

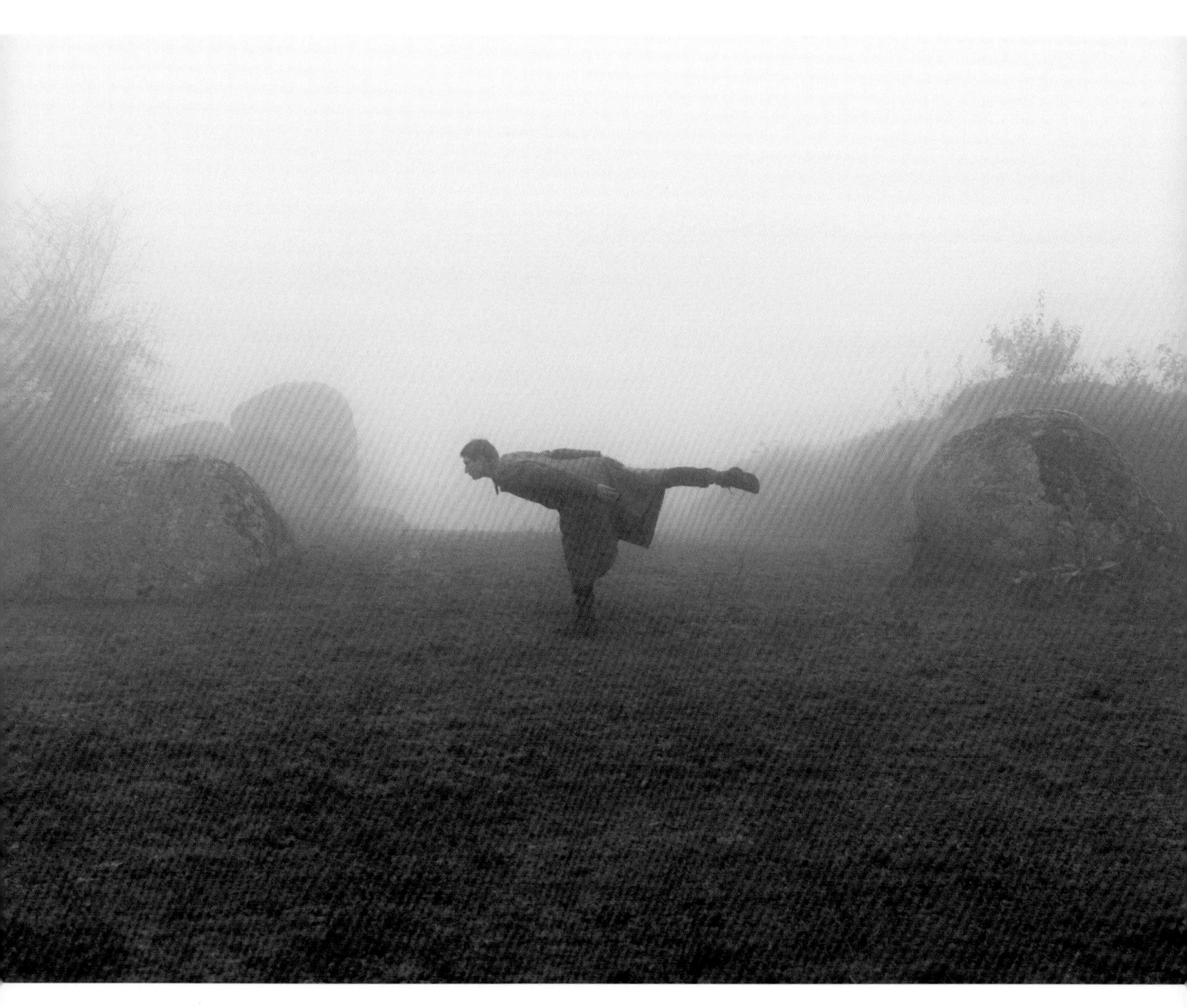

37   ELINA BROTHERUS

Exhibited Work

Industrial Splendour and Fetishism: The Bruce Anderson Collection, **2013**
Digital colour photographs, inkjet prints, 74.3 x 99.1 cm or 99.1 x 74.3 cm, each.
Edition of 8.

Michel Campeau's most recent project, *Industrial Splendour and Fetishism: The Bruce Anderson Collection* (2013), is a photographic study of cameras held in a private collection in Montreal. It is part of a wider project that Campeau is undertaking on the demise of analog photography. His photographs highlight the different materials used in construction of the camera, such as wood, metal, and plastic, as well as various attachments that augment its body, such as lenses and flash units. Each camera is photographed to emphasize the model names and its individual design traits.

Michel Campeau was born in 1948 in Montreal, where he still lives and works. With a photographic career that spans five decades, he has received prestigious awards, among them the Duke and Duchess of York Prize in Photography in 2010 and the Jean-Paul-Riopelle Career Grant in 2009. His *Darkroom* exhibition was presented from 2008 to 2012 at the Musée Nicéphore Niépce in Chalon-sur-Saône, France; the Robert Morat Gallery in Hamburg; Paris Photo; Ffotogallery Cardiff; Les Rencontres d'Arles; and the New York Photo Festival. Some of his works are in permanent collections in Canada and worldwide, including the Montreal Museum of Fine Arts, the National Gallery of Canada in Ottawa, and the Centre national des arts plastiques in Paris. Michel Campeau is represented by Galerie Simon Blais in Montreal. \ www.campeauphoto.com

p. 39 \ *Argus C-Four, Ann Arbor, Michigan, USA, 1951–57*
p. 40 \ *Sinclair Traveller Una, London, England, 1927*
p. 41 \ *Plaubel Makina II, Frankfurt, Germany, 1933–39*
p. 42 \ *Revere Eyematic EE 127, Chicago, Illinois, USA, 1958*
p. 43 \ *Ilford Advocate, Ilford, England, 1949–52*

Courtesy of the artist and Galerie Simon Blais, Montreal
© Michel Campeau / SODRAC (2013)

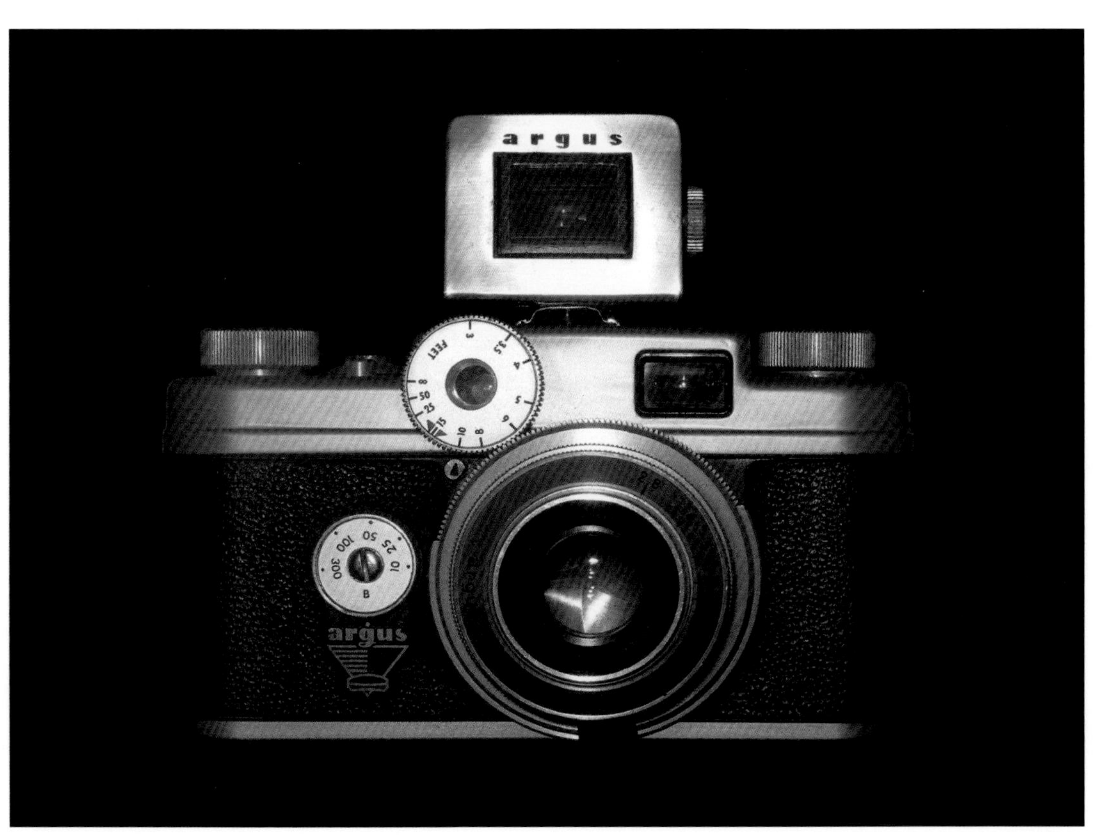
argus
argus

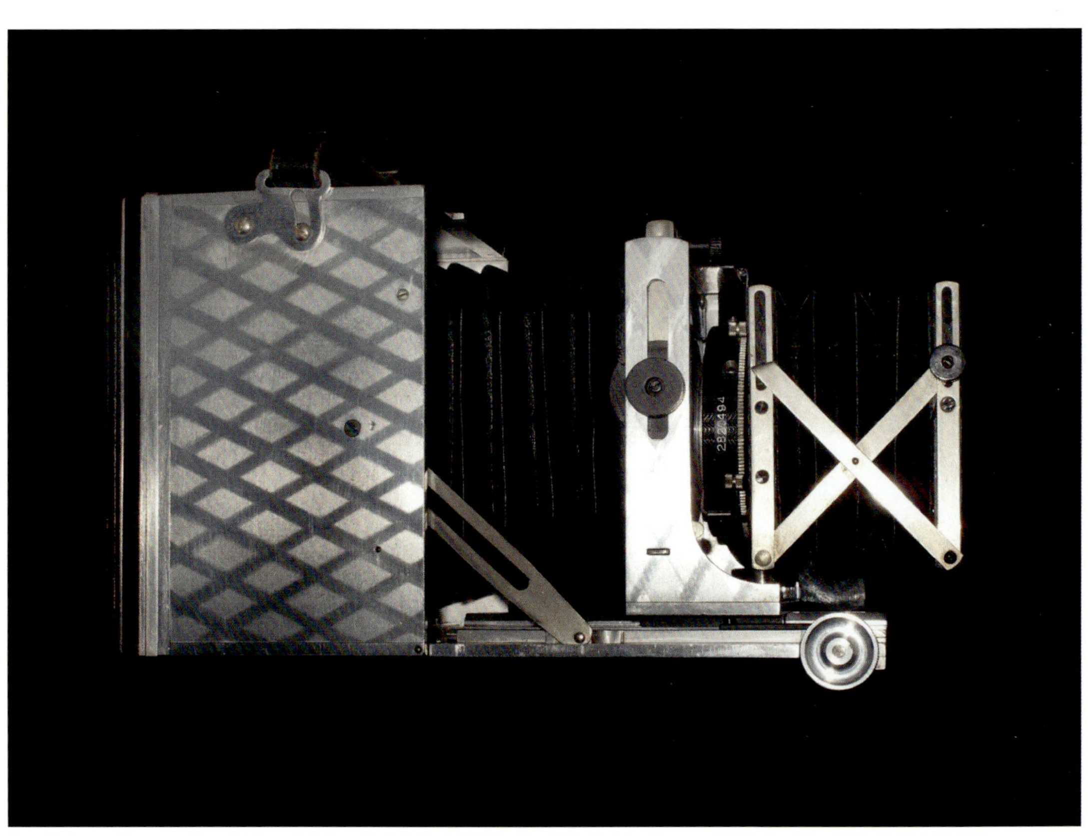

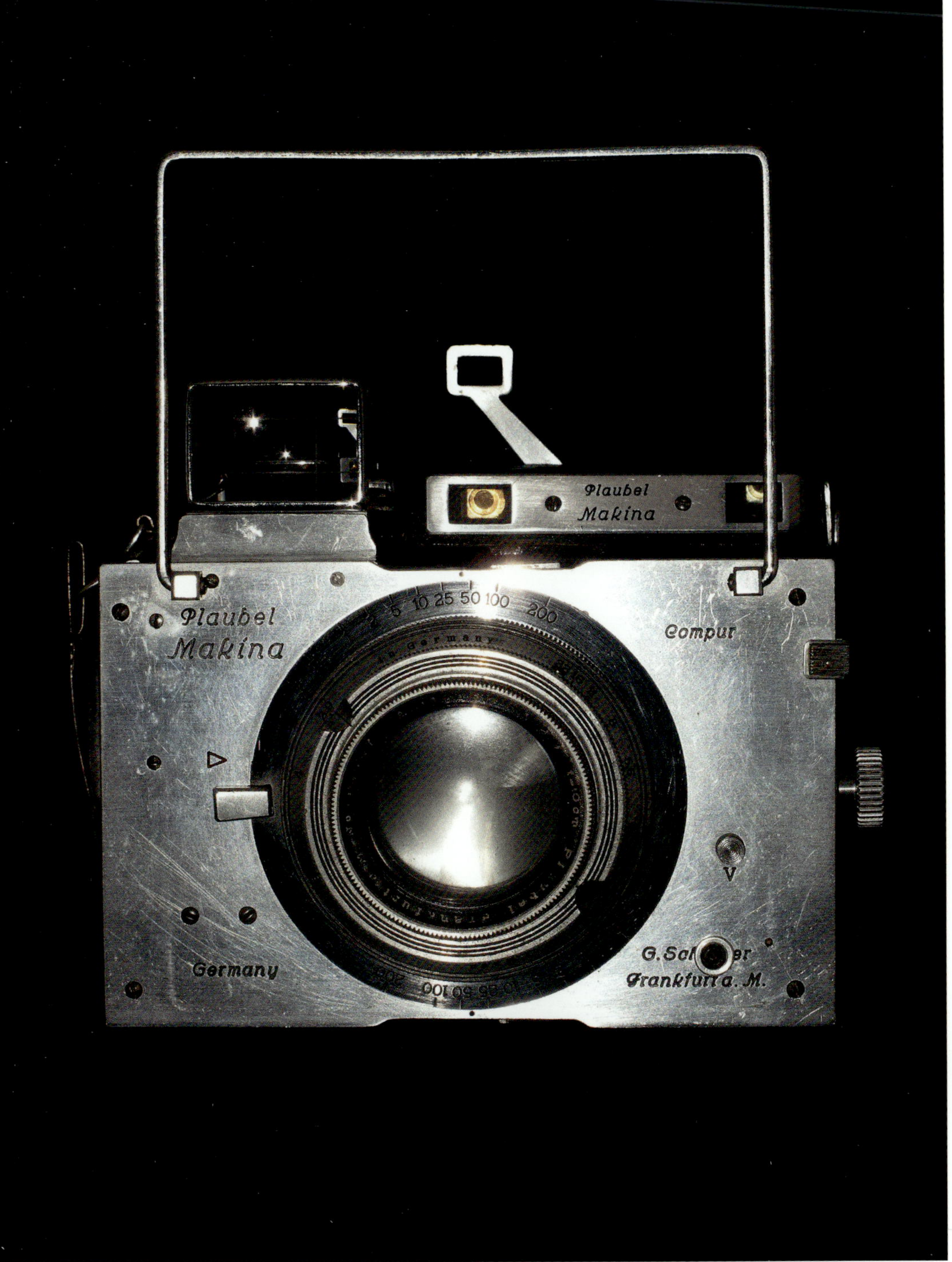
Plaubel
Makina
Plaubel
Makina
Compur
Germany
G. Schneider
Frankfurt a. M.

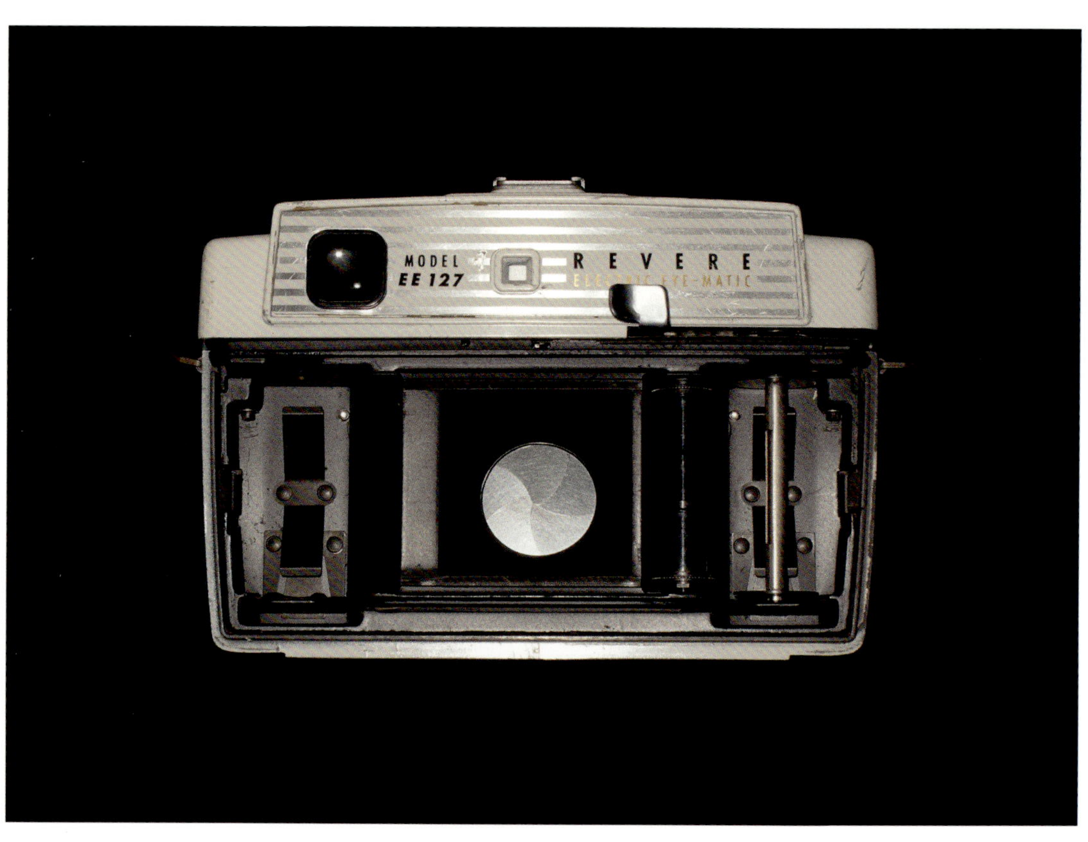

MODEL
EE 127
REVERE
ELECTRIC EYE-MATIC

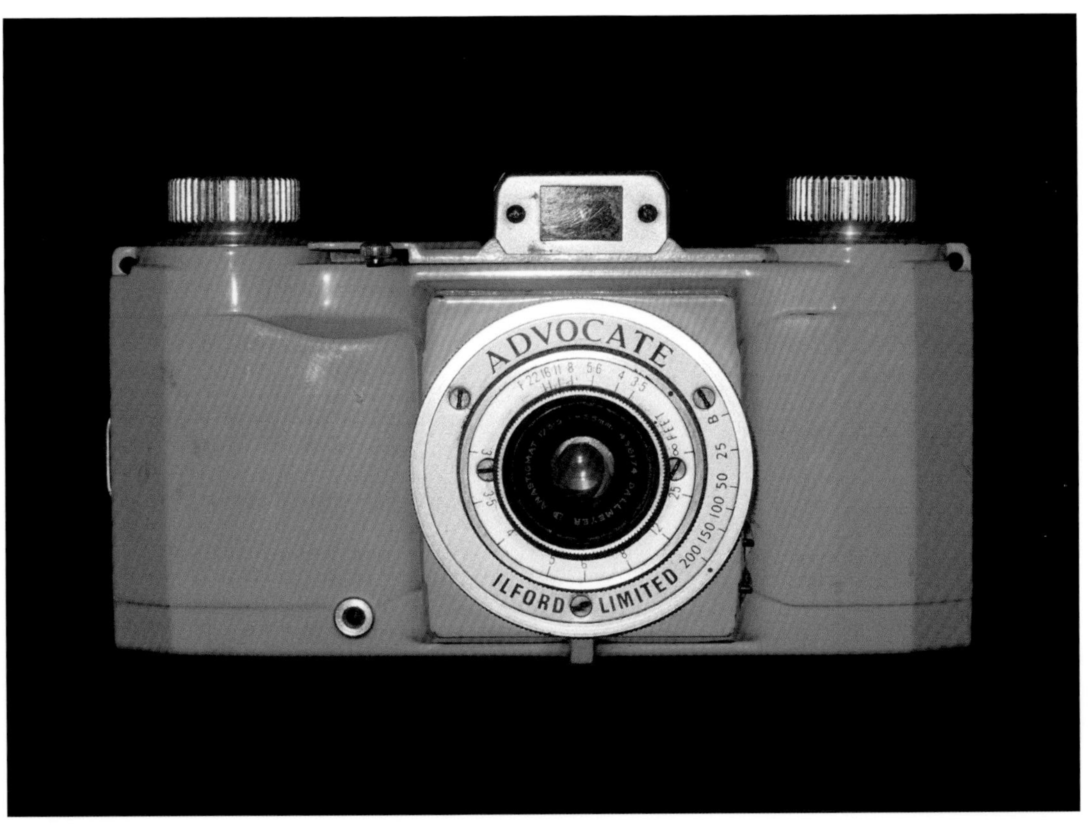
ADVOCATE
ILFORD LIMITED
FEET
B

Exhibited Works

Ruins, 2011
Chromogenic prints on Dibond, 120 x 150 cm each.

Checkpoint Tangui, 2012
Video installation, 8 min 55 s, colour, loop.

In 2010 Raphaël Dallaporta travelled to Afghanistan to assist a team of French archaeologists with compiling a visual inventory of that country's national heritage. Many of these historical sites are endangered by pillage, and the new war that started in 2001 has caused further damage to important monuments. Dallaporta was able to fly a specially adapted drone over the Afghani landscape to take pictures of historical sites. From this survey he made the work *Ruins* (2011). With their jagged edges that break the symmetry of the rectangle, the images reflect on the state of deteriorating remains and convey the fragile nature of the archaeological sites.

Raphaël Dallaporta was born in 1980 in Dourdan, France. He lives and works in Paris, where he graduated from Gobelins, l'École de l'image. He is the recipient of the Foam Paul Huf Award (2011) and the Young Photographer ICP Infinity Award (2010). He has had solo exhibitions at the Musée Nicéphore Niépce in Chalon-sur-Saône, France (2012); the Foam Fotografiemuseum in Amsterdam (2011); the Musée de l'Élysée in Lausanne (2010); and the New York Photo Festival (2008). His series *Ruins* was presented for the Prix découverte at Les Rencontres d'Arles in 2011. His works are in major public collections, including the Fonds National d'Art Contemporain and the Maison Européenne de la Photographie in Paris.
\ www.raphaeldallaporta.com

From the series *Ruins*:
p. 45 \ *CHESME SHAFA*. Fortification Wall. Balkh Province, Afghanistan.
Achaemenid period (6th–4th century BC)
p. 46 \ *CHESME SHAFA*. Balkh Province, Afghanistan.
From the Achaemenid period (6th–4th century BC) to the Ghorid period (12th–13th century AD)
p. 47 \ *KAFIR QALA*. Citadel. Balkh Province, Afghanistan.
From the Achaemenid period (6th–4th century BC) to the Ghorid period (12th–13th century AD)
p. 49 \ *SHAH TEPE, SOUTH-WEST*. Samangan Province, Afghanistan.
From the first Iron Age (late 2nd–early 1st millennium BC) to Timouride (15th century)

Courtesy of the artist

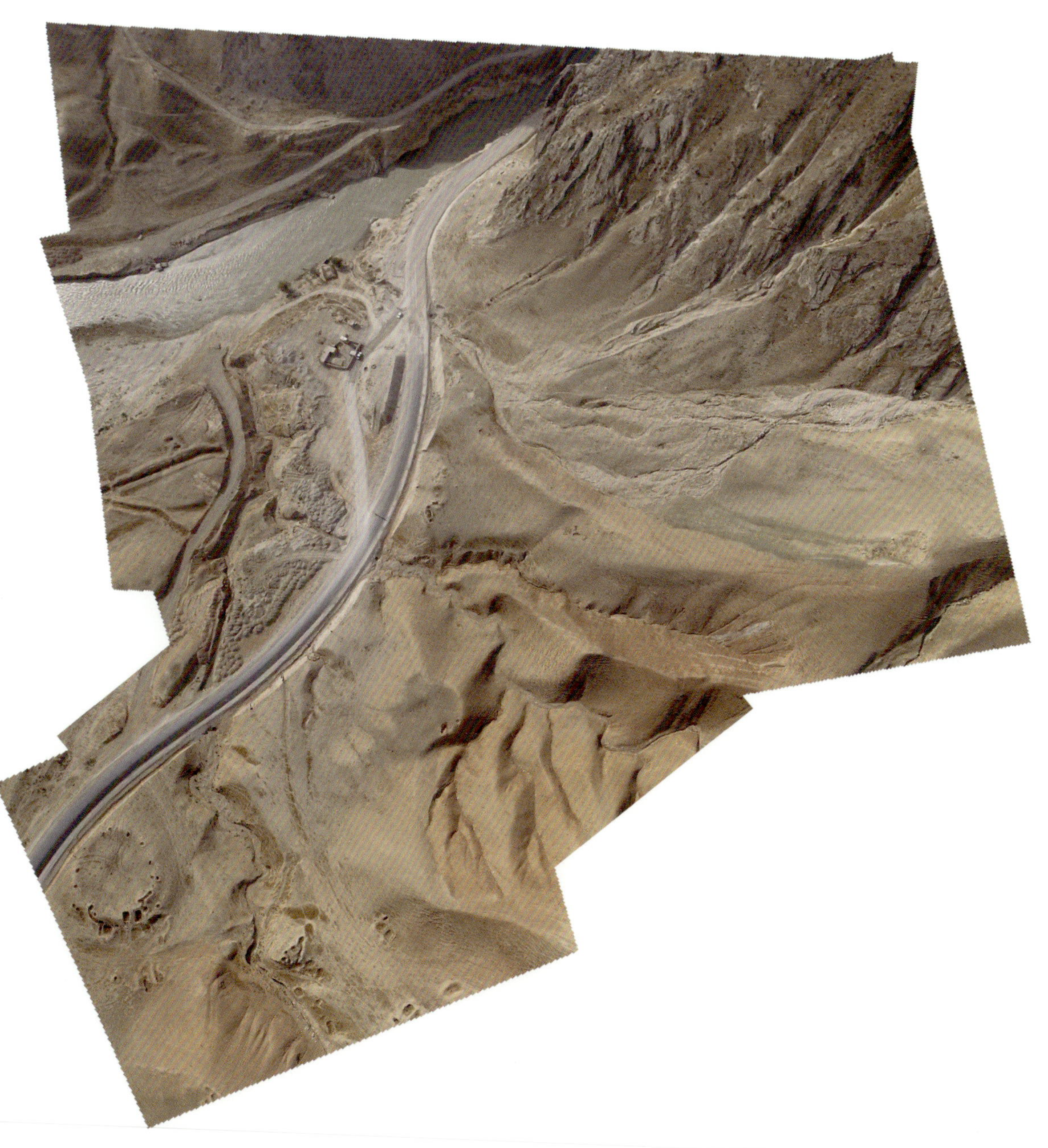

45   RAPHAËL DALLAPORTA

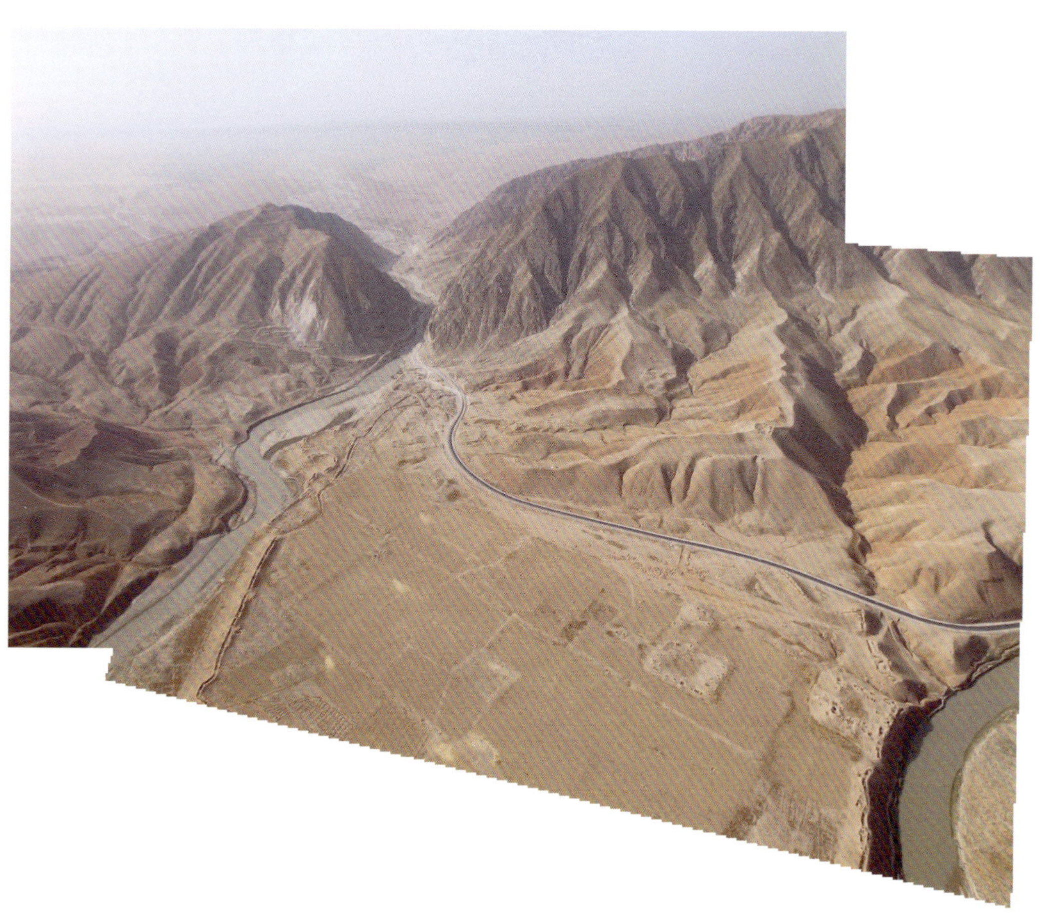

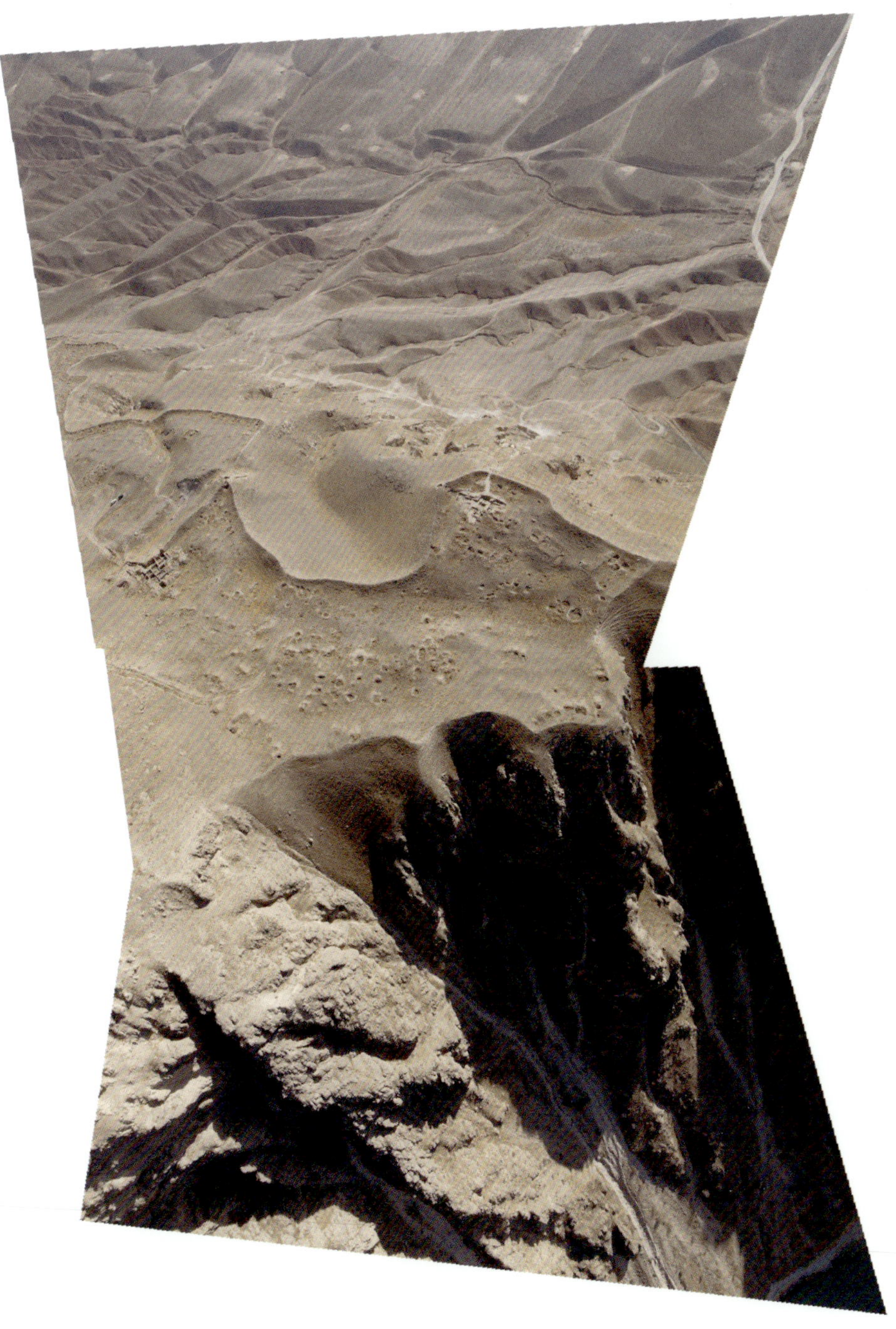

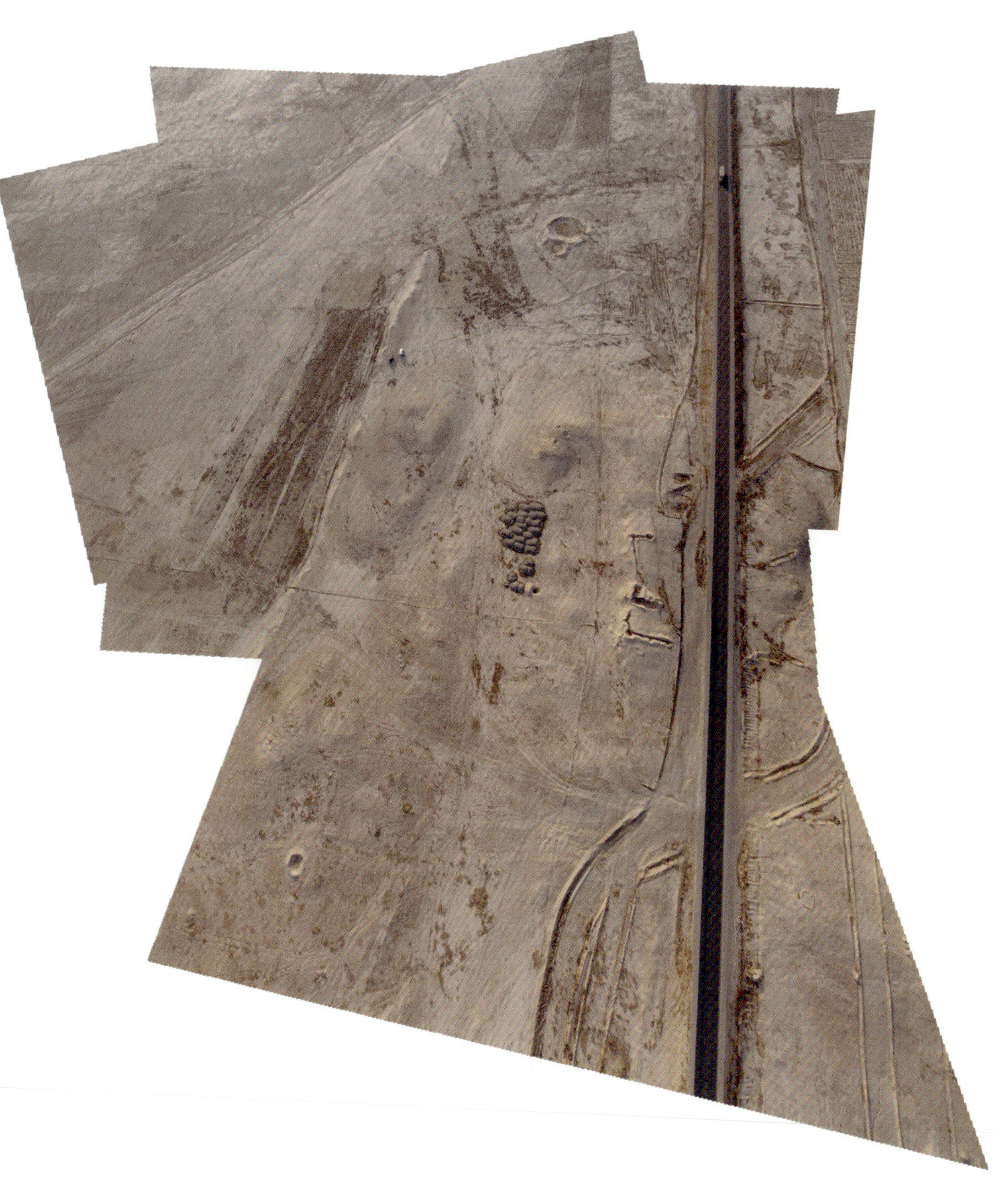

Exhibited Work

***As Yet Untitled*, 1992–95**
Installation: metal, rubber, electronic and mechanical components,
photographs, Plexiglas, archival paperboard box, 157 x 267 x 256 cm.
Gift of Jay Smith, David Fleck, Gilles Ouellette, and Terry Burgoyne, 2007.
Collection: Art Gallery of Ontario.

The destructive nature of technological innovation makes previous forms of technology obsolete and changes existing social relationships; this is the kernel of Max Dean's *As Yet Untitled* (1992–95). A pivoting robotic arm selects and presents the viewer with a family photograph. The viewer can decide to press on the hand-shaped panels in front of the robot, so that the print is saved and placed in an archival box; or do nothing, which causes the print to be shredded, its remains falling onto a conveyor belt to join other destroyed images. The arm then returns to the pile of photographs and repeats the process. The photographic print becomes a disposable item on the quest for a better tomorrow.

Born in 1949 in Leeds, U.K., Max Dean lives and works in Toronto. For over 35 years, his works have been in solo and group exhibitions around the world, including the Art Gallery of Ontario (AGO) in Toronto (2012); the Canadian Cultural Centre in Paris (2004); the National Gallery of Canada (NGC) in Ottawa (2002); ZKM Karlsruhe, Germany (2002); BOZAR, Centre for Fine Art in Brussels (2000); and the Venice Biennale (1999, 2001). His works are in public collections, including the NGC, the AGO, the Ottawa Art Gallery, the Vancouver Art Gallery, and the Winnipeg Art Gallery. He is the recipient of a project grant from the Toronto Friends of the Visual Arts, the Gershorn Isowitz Award, and the Chalmers Award. Dean is represented by Nicholas Metivier Gallery in Toronto.
\ www.metiviergallery.com
\ maxdean.grandportfolio.com

p. 8 \ Detail from an installation view, Art Gallery of Ontario, Toronto, 1997
pp. 51–53 \ Installation views, Art Gallery of Ontario, Toronto, 1997

Courtesy of the artist and the Art Gallery of Ontario

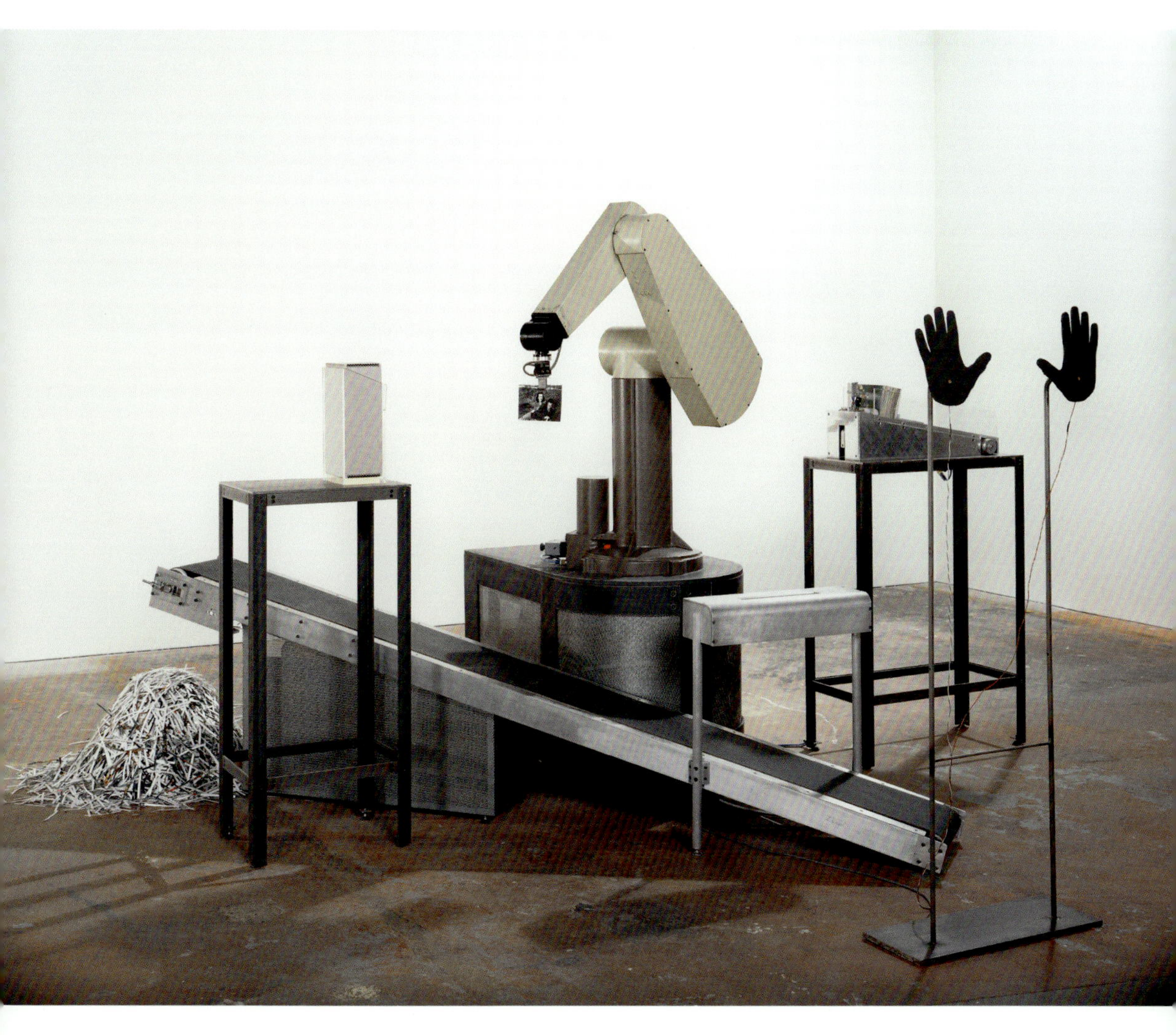

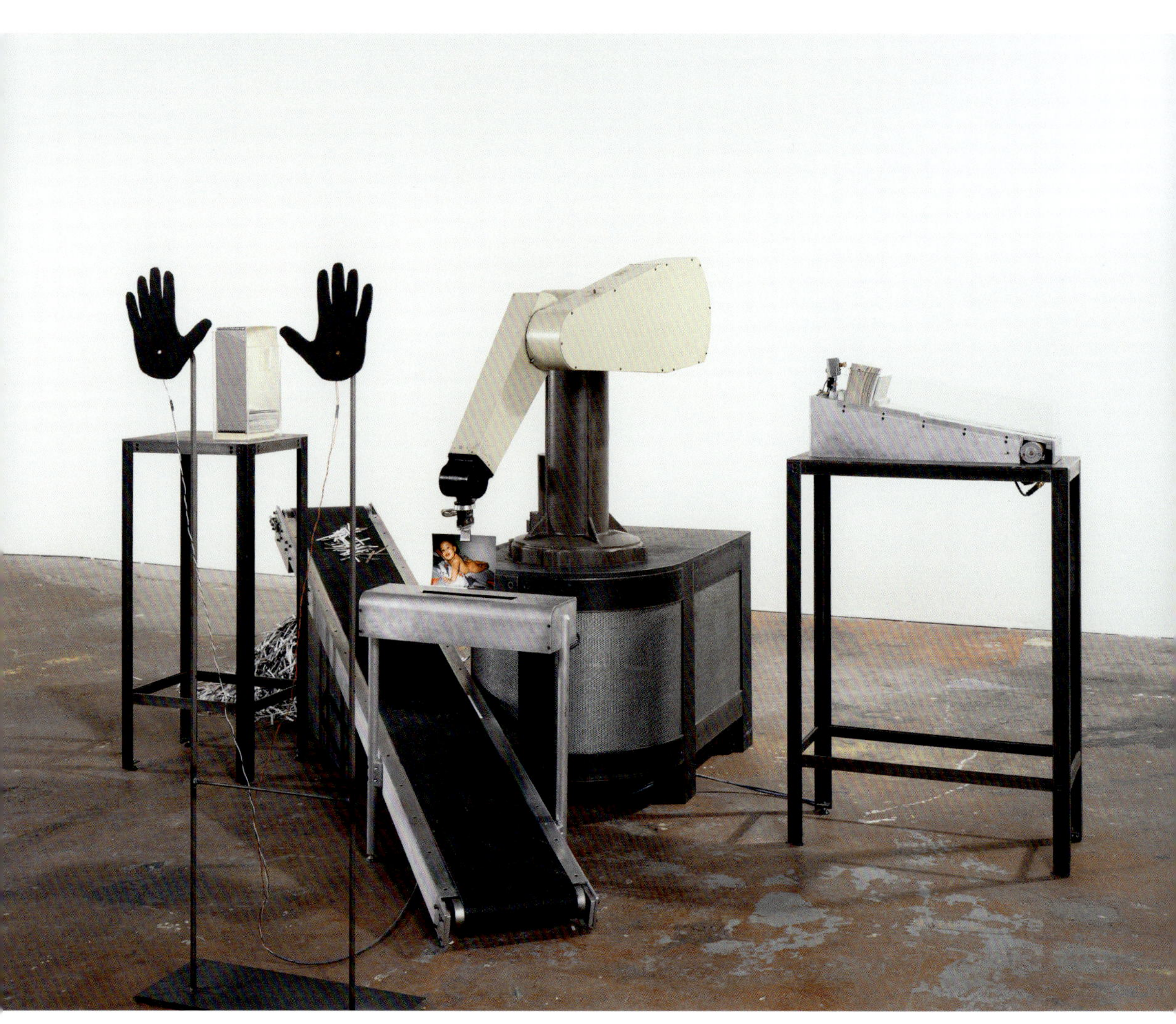

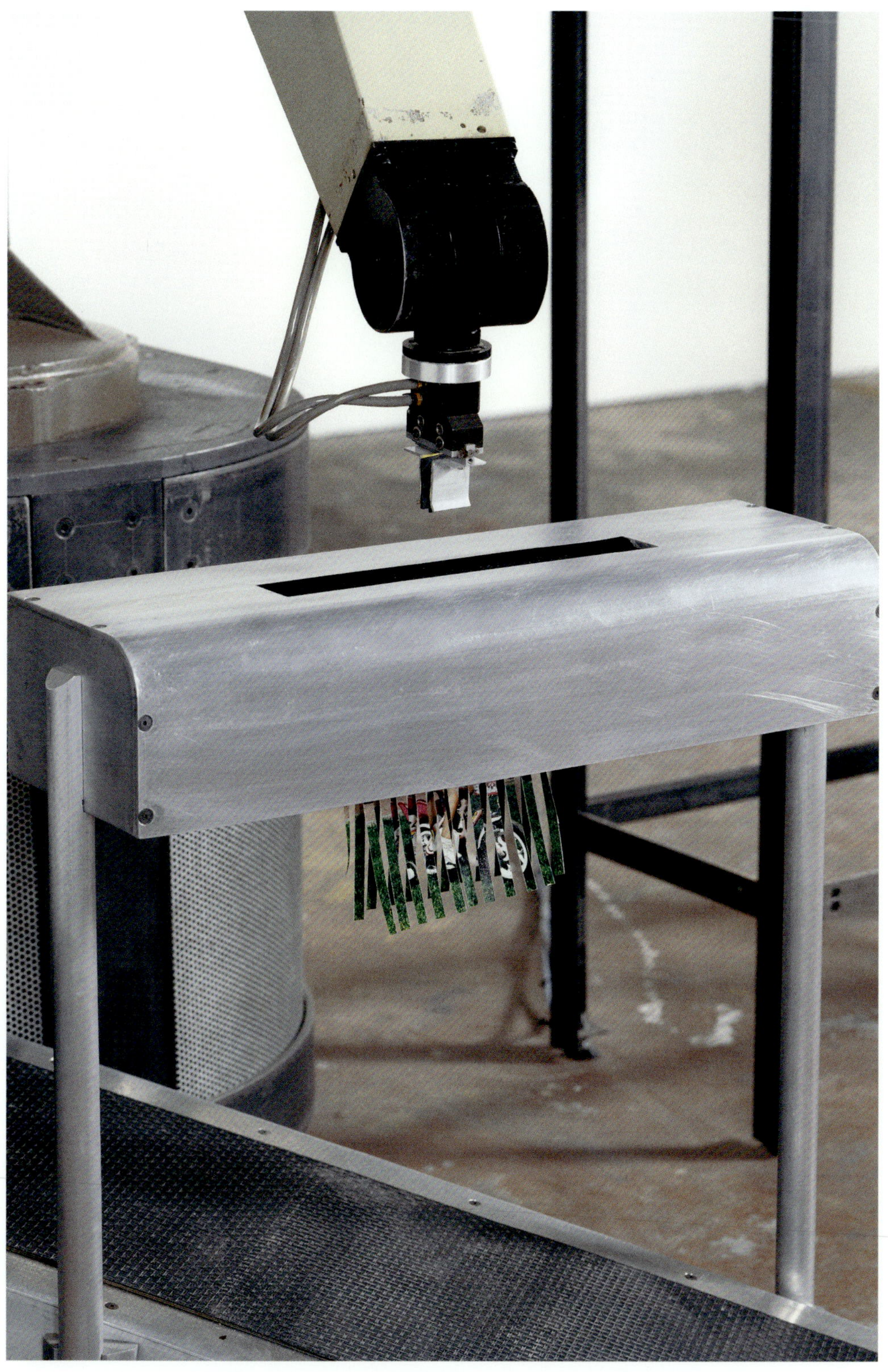

Exhibited Work

Encounters, 2012–13
Slide projections, digital images taken with automatic cameras used for hunting,
variable dimensions.

Can animals take their own pictures? This is what Véronique Ducharme seems to be asking in *Encounters* (2012–13). She works in a similar fashion to Eadweard Muybridge, who used the camera to prove that all four feet of a galloping horse are, for a moment, simultaneously off the ground. Unlike Muybridge, who attached thread to cameras to create each exposure, Ducharme employs a hunting camera to detect movement and heat to trigger the exposure. The resulting images might be called wildlife photographs, in which animals exist beyond human control. Their ghostly images could be from another world, one without humans.

Véronique Ducharme was born in 1983 in Montreal, where she continues to live and work. In 2010, she obtained an MA from the London College of Communication, after receiving a BFA in photography from Concordia University in Montreal in 2007. She was the 2007 recipient of Concordia University's Gabor Szilasi Award. Her works have been presented at A.I.R. Gallery in New York (2013); the Fotografiska Museet in Stockholm (2012); Galerie Les Territoires (2011–12), the McCord Museum (2008), FOFA Gallery (2007), and La Centrale Galerie Powerhouse (2007) in Montreal; and the London College of Communication (2010). In 2006, the Magenta Foundation in Toronto published *Carte Blanche*, which included Ducharme's works.
\ www.veroniqueducharme.com

p. 55 \ *2012/09/27 00:45:37*, 2012
pp. 56–57 \ *2012/08/14 03:46:56*, 2012
p. 58 \ *08/04/12 08:48*, 2012
p. 59 \ *2012/09/30 12:59:17*, 2012

Courtesy of the artist

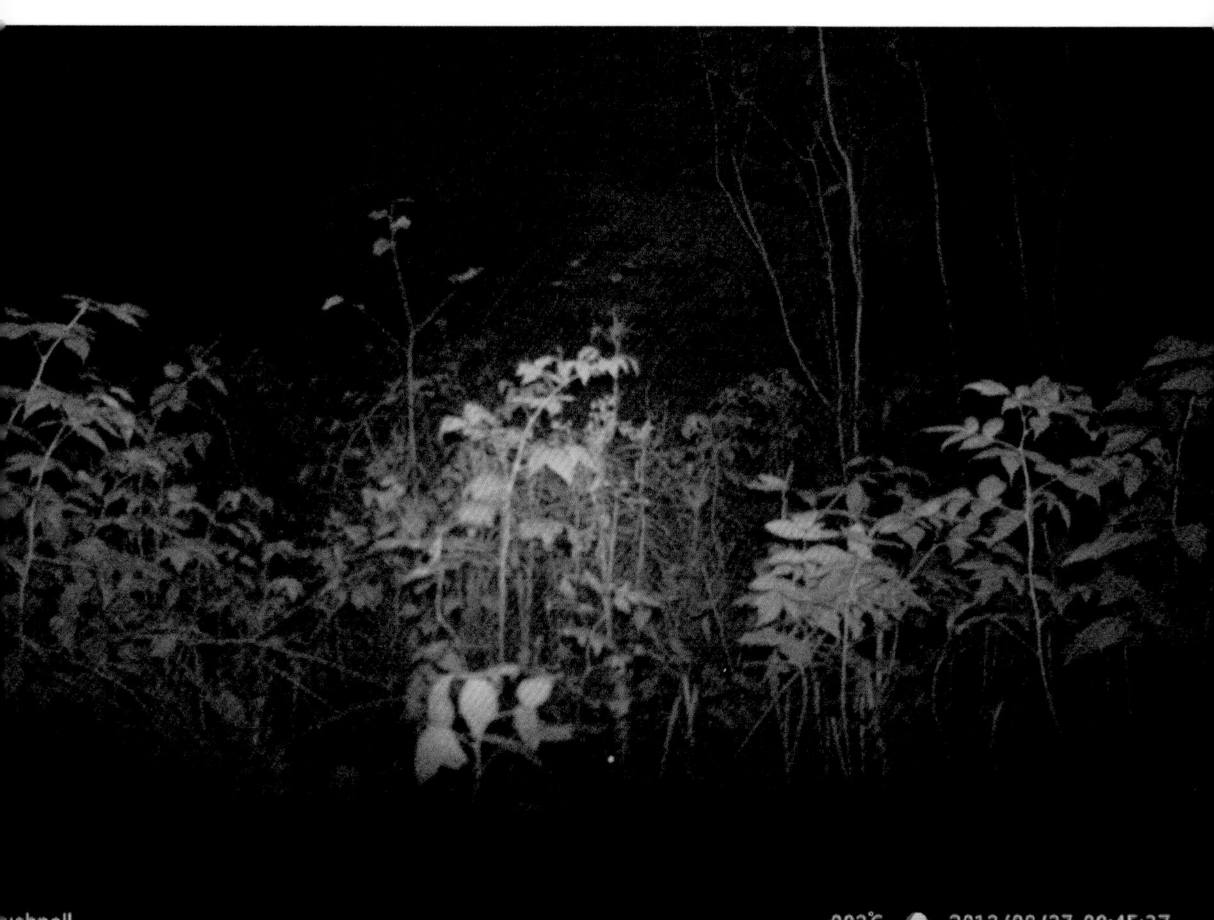
ushnell
002℃   2012/09/27 00:45:37

VÉRONIQUE DUCHARME

011°C   2012/08/14 03:46:56
57   VÉRONIQUE DUCHARME

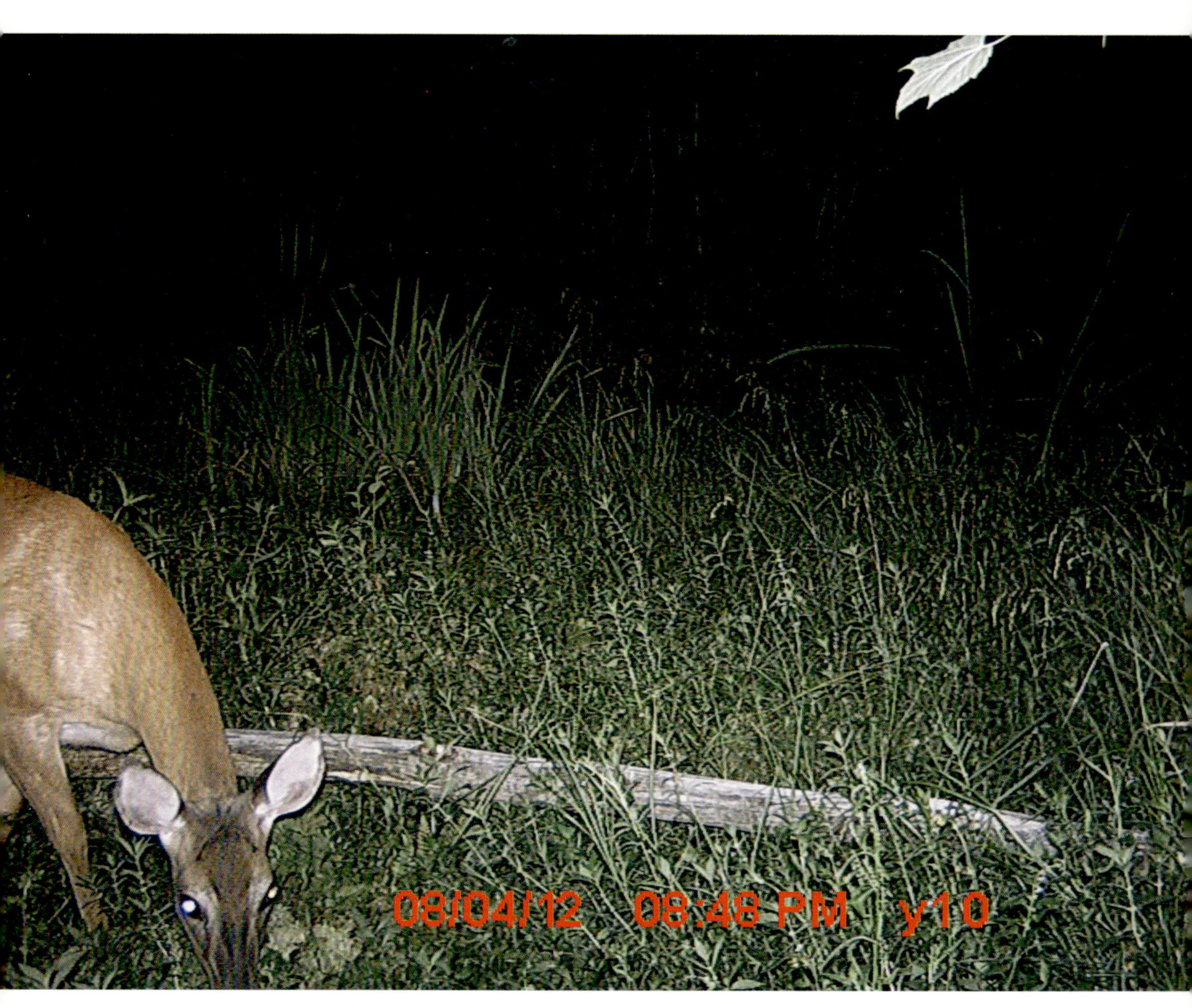
08/04/12   08:48 PM   y10

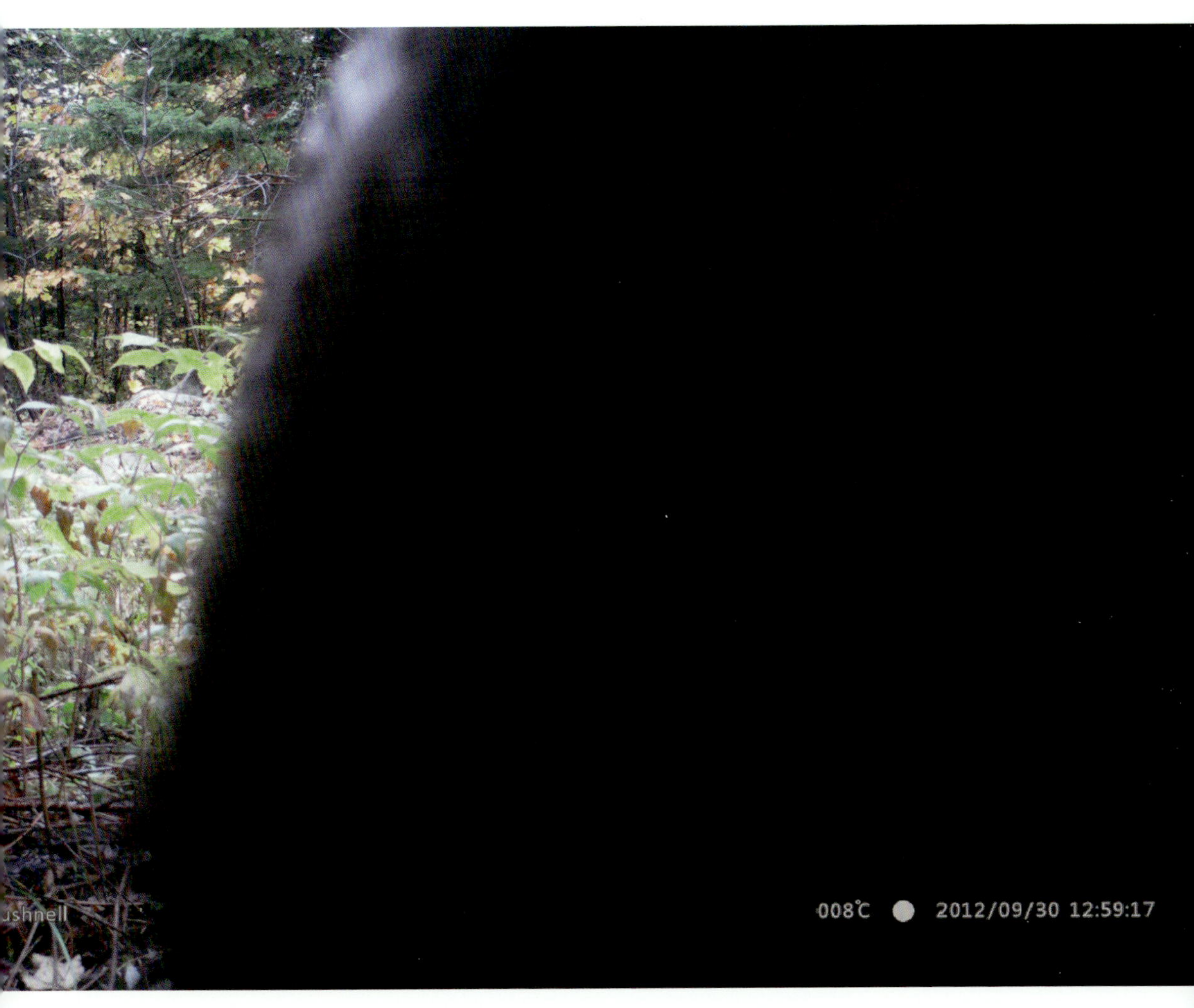

ushnell
008℃   2012/09/30 12:59:17

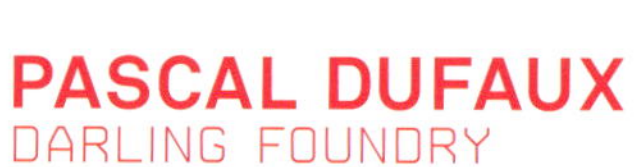

Exhibited Work

The Cosmos in Which We Are, 2009–11

Kinetic video sculpture: machined aluminum, chrome-plated steel, inox mirror,
Plexiglas, 1 CCTV camera, neon tubes, AC motor and control, slip rings, various gears,
183 x 122 x 122 cm.

Looking like some type of space probe that might have landed from another planet, *The Cosmos In Which We Are* (2009–11) was in fact made in Montreal by Pascal Dufaux. Taking his inspiration from the Mars Exploration Rover, Dufaux has made his own vision probe to view life on Earth. A circling video camera is attached by robotic arms to an illuminated mirrored table that is set on a tripod. The camera moves around the perimeter of the table seeking out life and feed back to monitors what it has detected. The result is not a readily recognizable world, but a strange, hallucinatory view of life on Earth.

Born in Marseille in 1963, Pascal Dufaux now lives and works in Montreal. His works have been featured in exhibitions in Canada, Finland, Mexico, France, Switzerland, and Germany. He participated in the first edition of the Biennale Internationale d'Art Numérique/BIAN in Montreal (2012); the Mapping Festival in Geneva (2012); and Lab30 in Augsburg, Germany (2012). His works have been exhibited at the Joyce Yahouda Gallery (2007, 2010) and OBORO (2008, 2012) in Montreal; the Centre en arts actuels Sporobole in Sherbrooke (2010); and the Centre de diffusion de la photographie VU in Quebec City (2007), among others. He has received grants from the Canada Council for the Arts and the Conseil des arts et des lettres du Québec. Dufaux is represented by Galerie Christian Lambert in Montreal. \ www.pascaldufaux.com

p. 61 \ Installation view, Bâtiment d'Art Contemporain, Mapping Festival, Geneva, 2012. Photo: Pascal Dufaux
pp. 62–63 \ Installation view, shooting at night at Centre Daïmon, Gatineau (Quebec), 2009. Photo: Pascal Dufaux
p. 64 \ *SLIPPED IMAGE _ Teenagers*, 2010. Detail from the installation, inkjet print on polyester fabric paper, 127 x 170 cm
p. 65 \ *SLIPPED IMAGE _ Insects*, 2010. Detail from the installation, inkjet print on polyester fabric paper, 127 x 170 cm

Courtesy of the artist

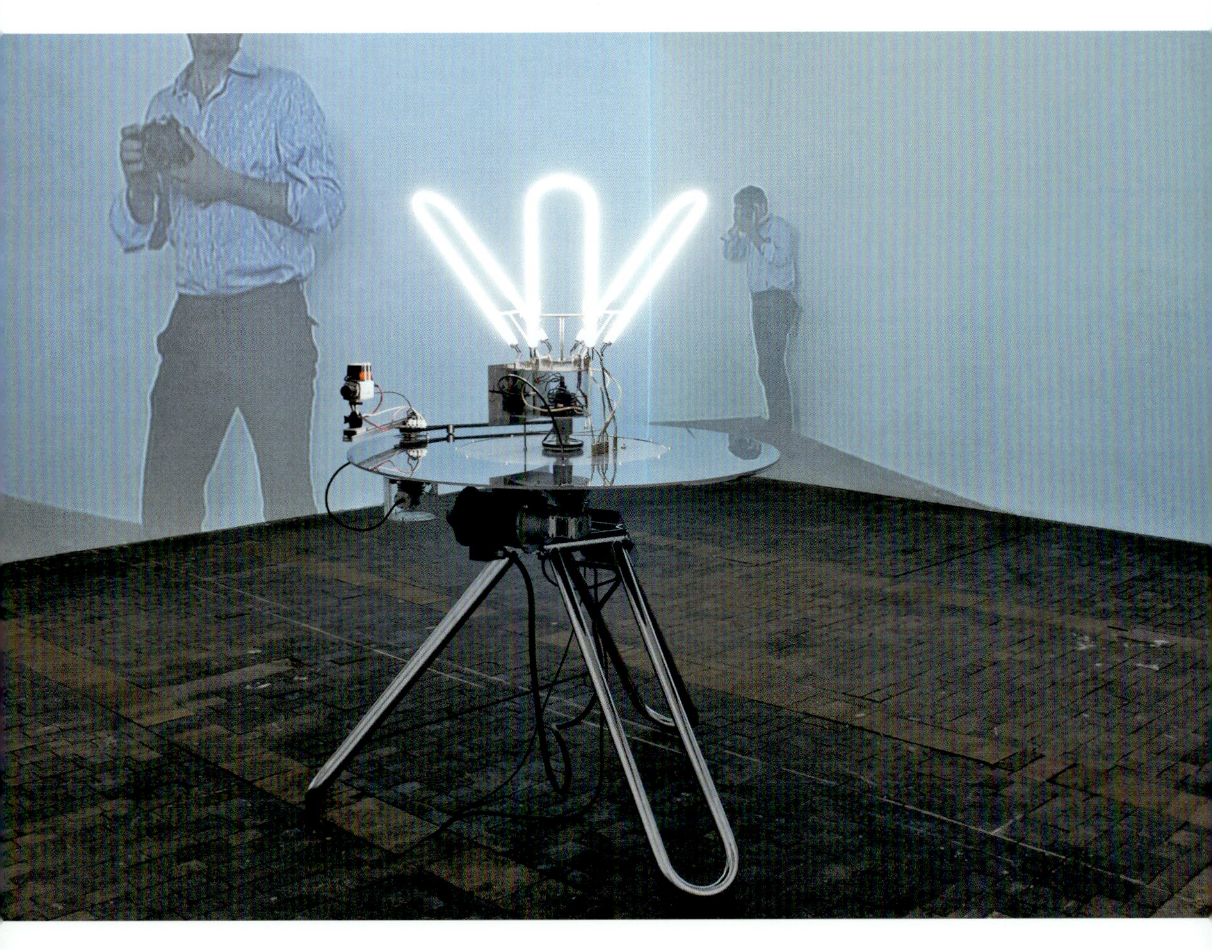

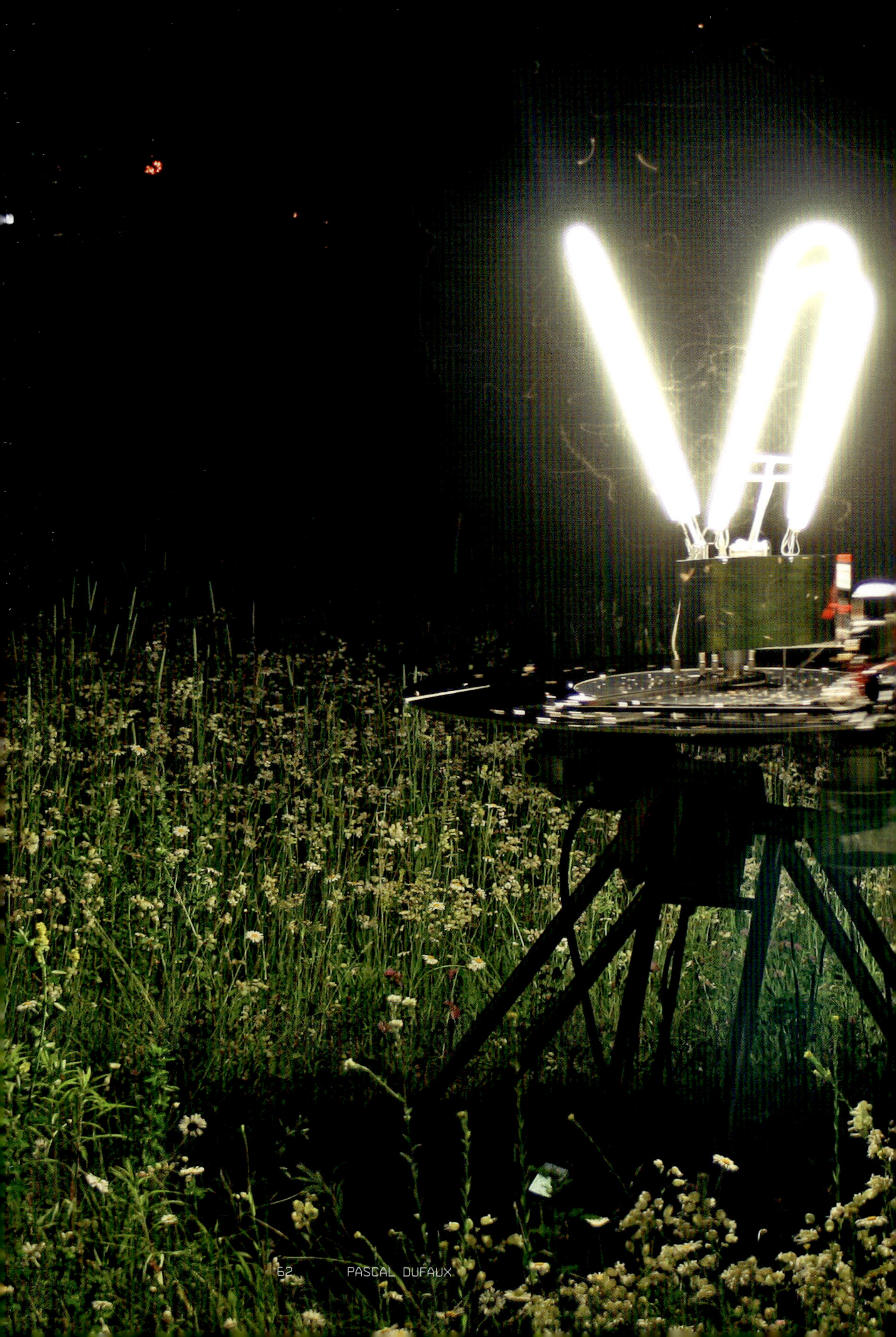

 PASCAL DUFAUX

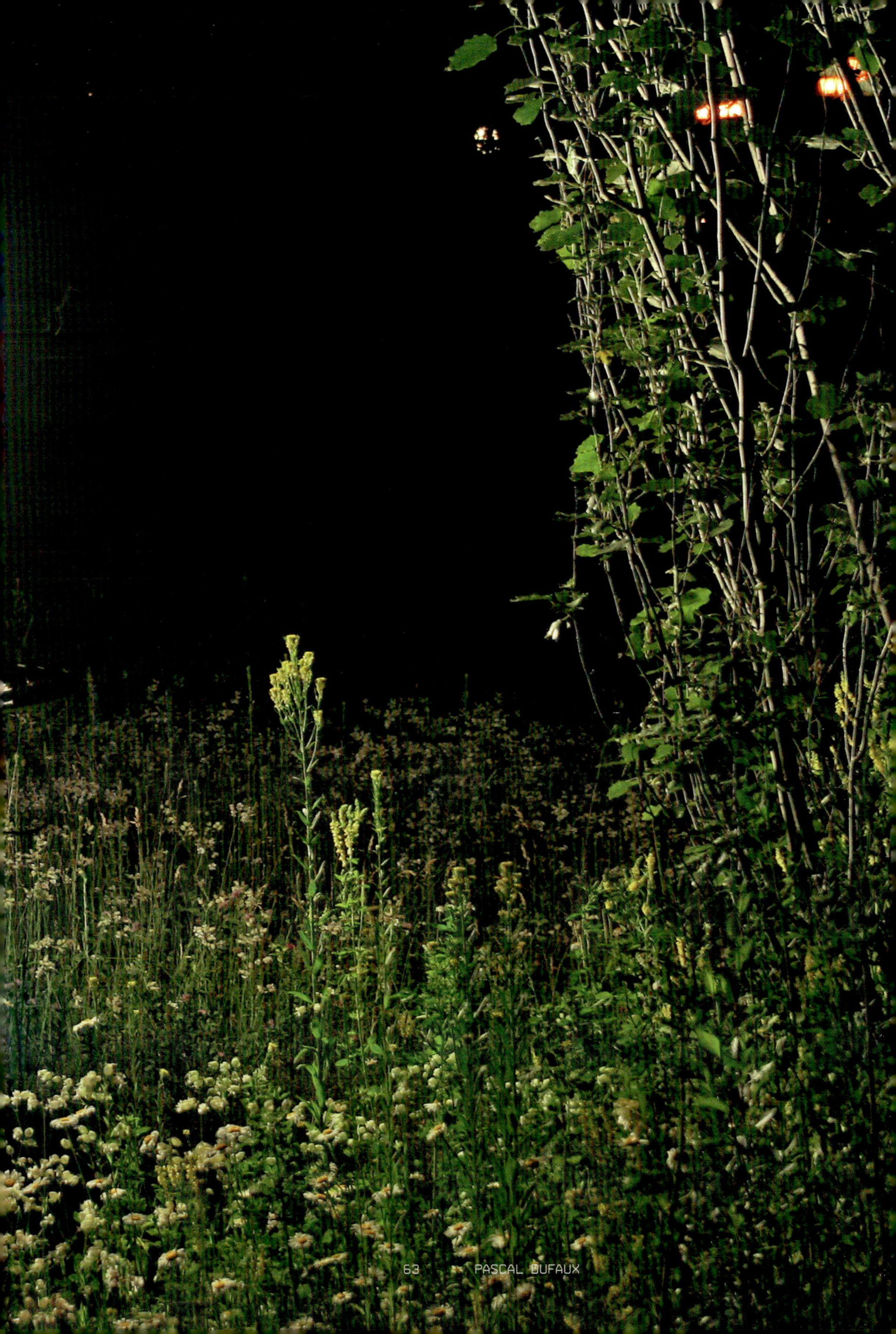

63   PASCAL DUFAUX

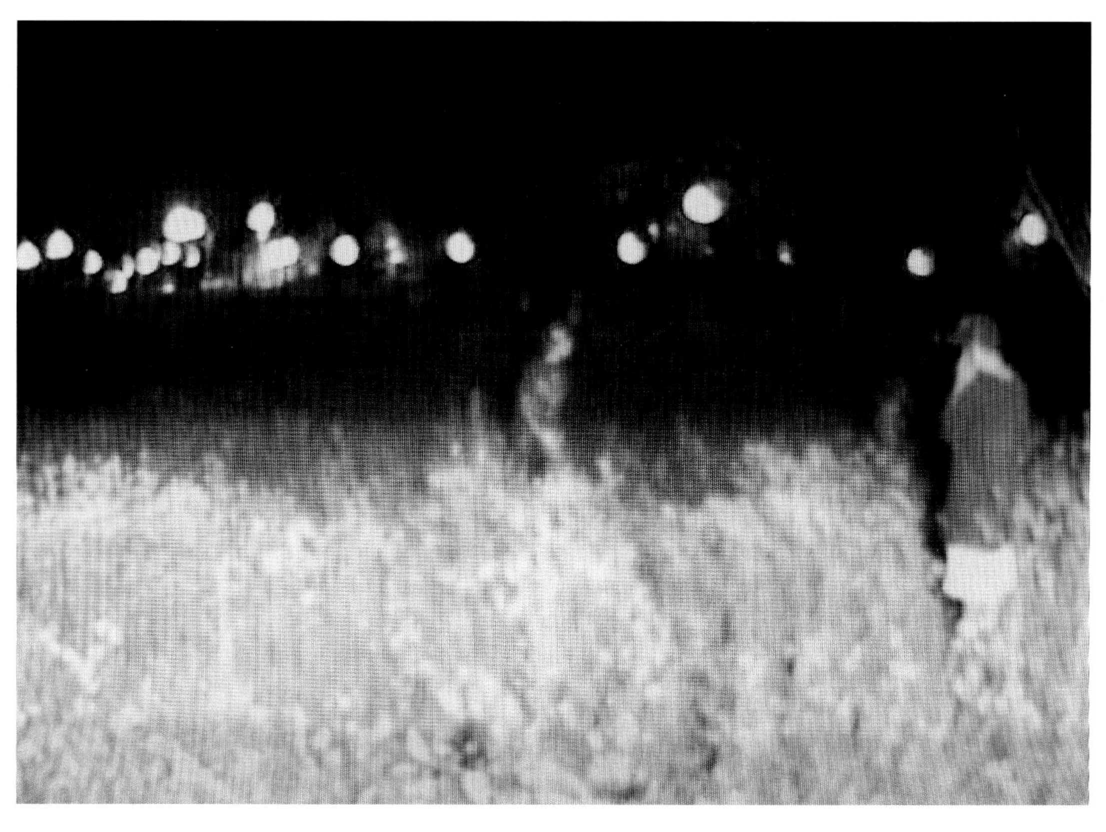

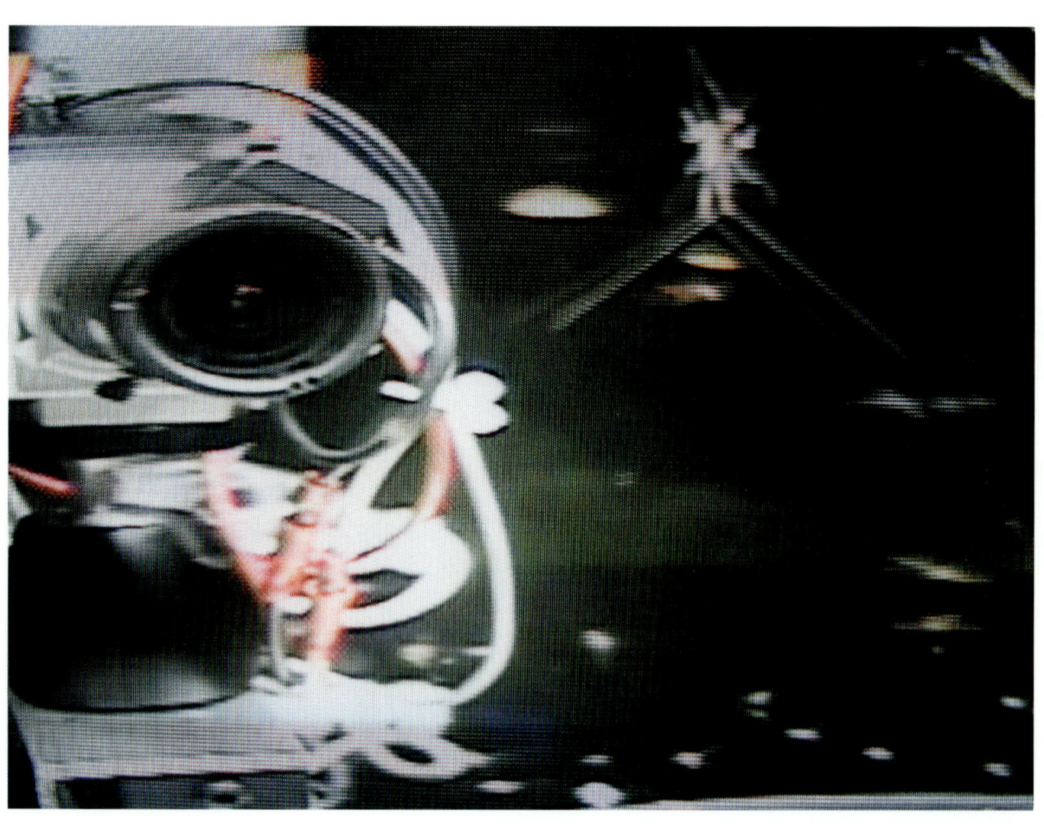

Exhibited Work

Swarm Vision, 2013

Robotics installation, three PTZ cameras mounted on suspended rails, custom software,
two 60" LED screens or two 4300-lumen professional-grade projectors, variable dimensions.
Research development support: Robert W. Deutsch Foundation, National Science Foundation.

Since the 1990s, the discussion about digital photography has centred on the status of the photographic image: its capacity to be easily altered, compressed, and sent around the world in seconds, as well as its capacity to function on different computer-based platforms. However, the camera has come through this transformation in photography's technological nature with little evolution. This is changing. In computational photography, the camera is being fundamentally reconfigured. The ExpVisLab collective (George Legrady, Danny Bazo, and Marco Pinter) is involved in research on developing an intelligent camera. The interactive installation *Swarm Vision* (2013) consists of three cameras that respond to human movement in the gallery. They compare and evaluate each other's results, projecting them onto the gallery wall.

ExpVisLab is a California-based artists' collective formed by George Legrady, Marco Pinter, and Danny Bazo. Born in 1950 in Budapest, George Legrady moved to Montreal in 1956 and to California in 1981. He directs the Experimental Visualization Lab in the Media Arts and Technology (MAT) program at the University of California, Santa Barbara. His interactive media works have been exhibited internationally in the United States, Canada, Finland, France, and China. Marco Pinter holds degrees from Cornell University and the University of California. He has issued patents in the areas of live video technology, robotics, interactivity, and telepresence. Born in 1979 in Lima, Danny Bazo is a doctoral student in the MAT program with a background in visual arts, electrical engineering and computer science. His research is focused on robotics and multimedia signal processing. \ www.georgelegrady.com \ www.marcopinter.com \ www.eastmostpeninsula.net/db.html

pp. 67–68 \ Production photos of the robot, 2012
p. 69 \ Production screen shots, 2012

Courtesy of the artists

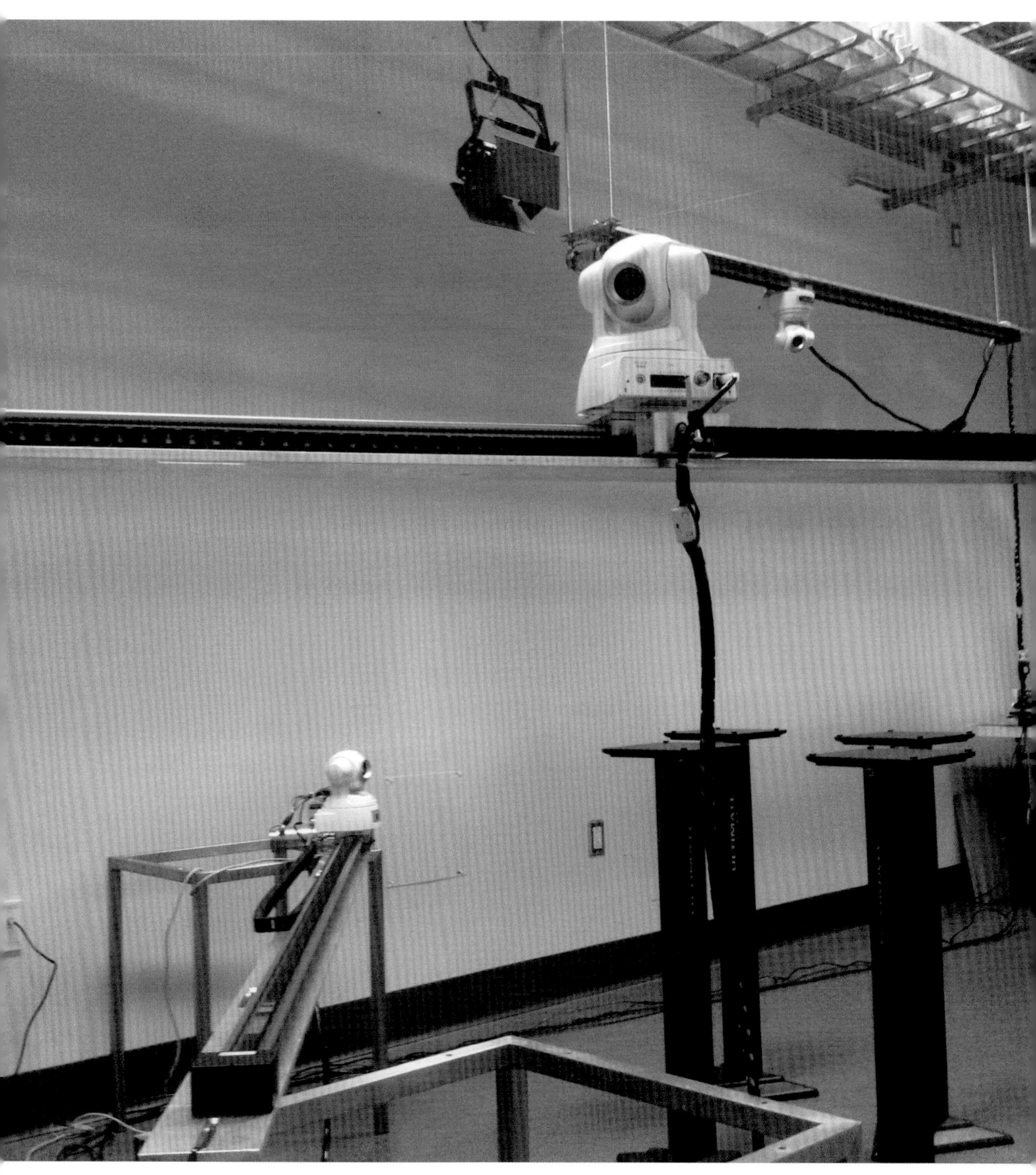

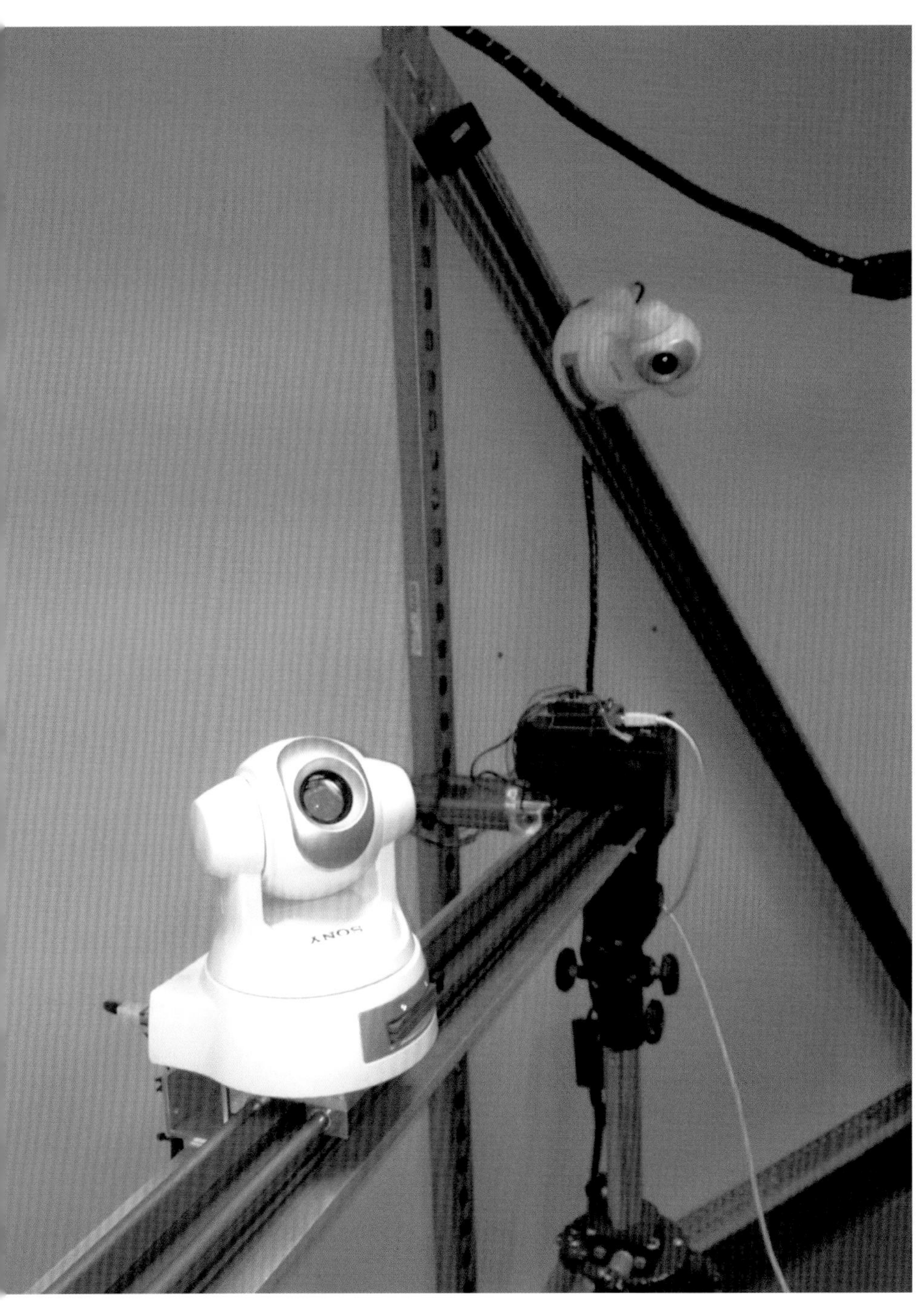

SONY

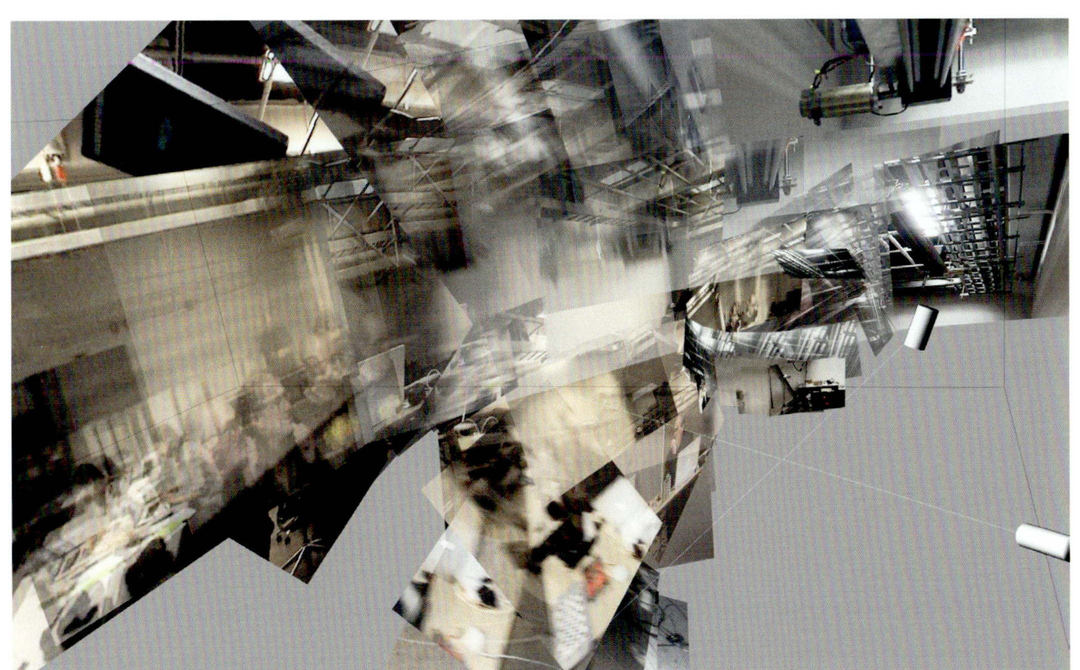

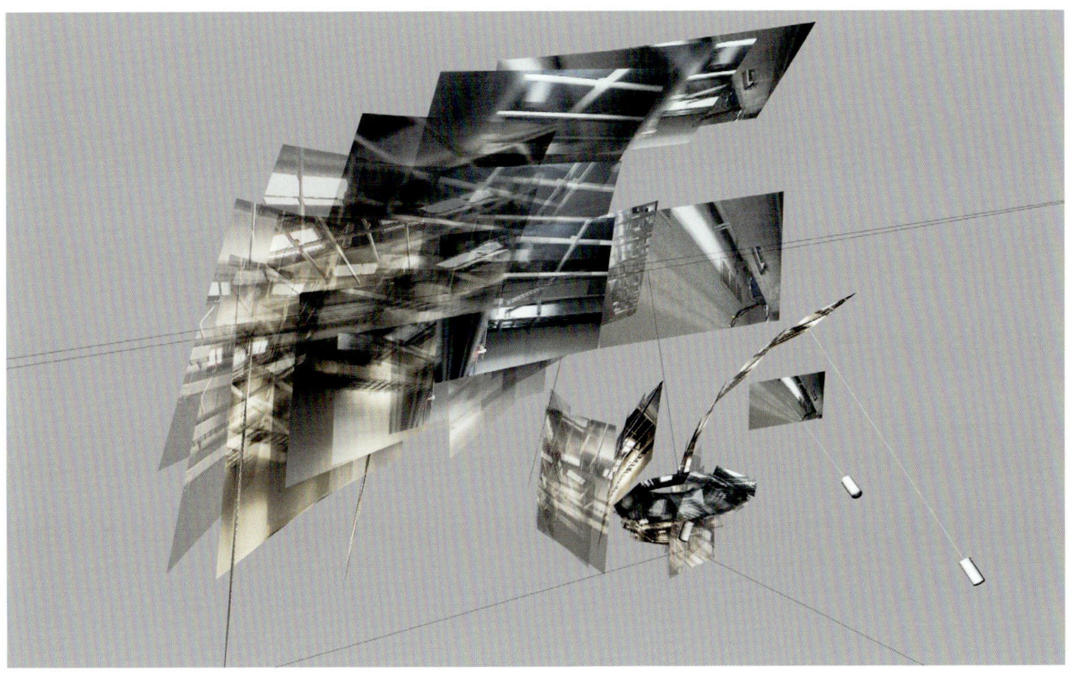

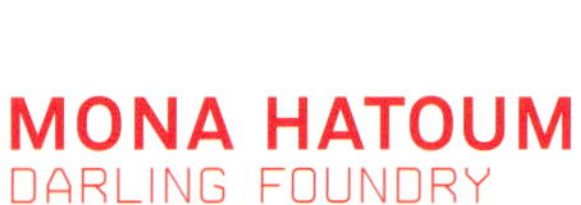

Exhibited Work

Corps étranger, 1994

Video installation with cylindrical wooden structure, video projector, video player, amplifier and 4 speakers, colour video, 30 min, stereo sound, 350 x 300 x 300 cm.

For her video installation *Corps étranger* (1994), Mona Hatoum used endoscopic technology to place a medical camera inside her body. The camera travels to a place that is near but also far away by extending human vision into the interior of the human body. Hatoum has remarked, "The camera is in a sense this alien device introduced from the outside. Also it is about how we are closest to our bodies, and yet it is a foreign territory, which could . . . be consumed by diseases long before we become aware of it."

Born in 1952 to a Palestinian family in Beirut, Mona Hatoum lives and works in London. She has had solo exhibitions at the Joan Miró Foundation in Barcelona (2012); White Cube in London (2011); the Fundación Marcelino Botín in Santander, Spain (2010); the Kunsthalle Wien in Vienna (2009); Galerie Chantal Crousel in Paris (2008, 2010); and the Tate Gallery in London (2000), among others. Her works have been featured in numerous group exhibitions worldwide, including the Seattle Art Museum (2012); the Guggenheim Museum in Bilbao (2012); the Museum of Modern Art in New York (2010); the Venice Biennale (1995, 2005); and documenta XI Kassel (2002). In 2011, Hatoum received the Joan Miró Prize. She is represented by Alexander and Bonin in New York, Galleria Continua in San Gimignano, Beijing, and Le Moulin, Galerie Max Hetzler in Berlin, Galerie Chantal Crousel in Paris, Galerie René Blouin in Montreal, and White Cube in London.
\ www.whitecube.com

p. 71 \ Detail from the installation, Centre Pompidou, Paris, 1994.
Photo: Philippe Migeat

Courtesy of Centre Pompidou, Paris
© Mona Hatoum

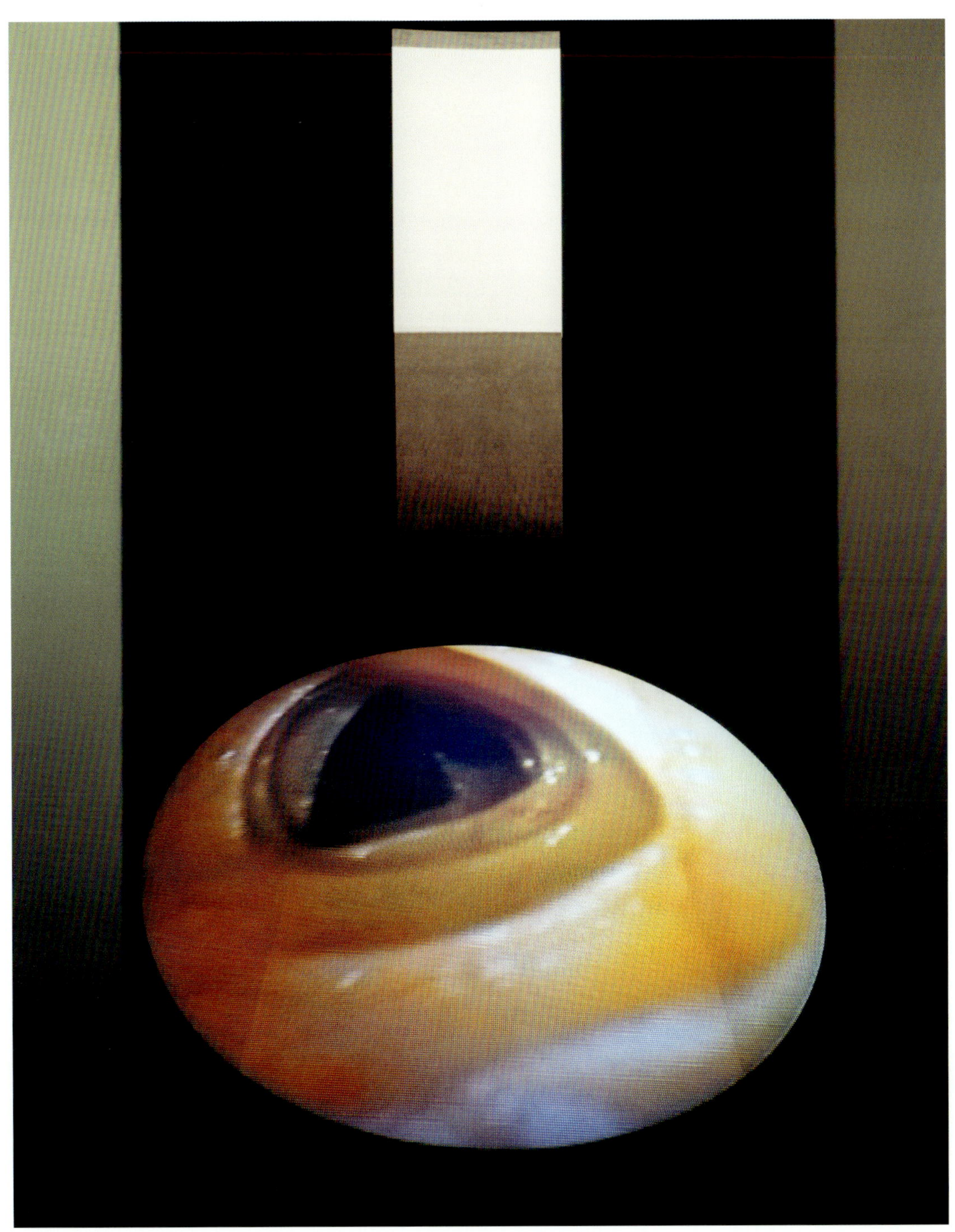

71   MONA HATOUM

PLOTTING FROM ABOVE: MISHKA HENNER + MONTREAL AERIAL SURVEY

MISHKA HENNER

Exhibited Works

Dutch Landscapes, 2011 (McCord Museum)
7 framed archival inkjet prints, 50 x 56 cm each.

Levelland Oil Field, 2013, from the series *The Fields*, 2012–ongoing (Darling Foundry)
Digital print on vinyl, 4 x 7 m.

Mishka Henner belongs to a new generation of artists who have started to use freely available images and data from the Web to make their work. Both *Dutch Landscapes* (2011) and *The Fields* (2012–ongoing) originate from satellite imagery that can either be found on Google Earth or comes from companies that deal with information on mineral exploration and extraction. Henner works in a similar manner, as a kind of Web geologist; he probes deep into the Internet to find important formations of images that he can extract to study and then eventually display in books and on gallery walls.

Born in 1976 in Brussels, Mishka Henner lives and works in Manchester, U.K. He received the ICP Infinity Award for Art in 2013 and the Kleine Hans Award in 2011. Major museums and galleries worldwide have featured his works, including the International Center of Photography in New York (2013); The Photographers' Gallery in London (2013); Centre Pompidou-Metz (2013); the Fotogalerie Wien in Vienna (2012); the FotoMuseum in Antwerp (2012); and Les Rencontres d'Arles (2011). His works are held in public collections at the Centre Pompidou in Paris, the Museum of Fine Arts Houston, the Tate collection, and the Cleveland Museum of Art. He is a member of the ABC Artists' Books Cooperative.
\ www.mishkahenner.com

From the series *Dutch Landscapes*:
p. 6 \ Detail from *Fuel Station Dronrijp, Menaldumadeel*
p. 74 \ *NATO Storage Annex, Coevorden, Drenthe*
p. 75 \ *Unknown Site, Noordwijk Aan Zee, South Holland*
p. 76 \ *Frederikkazerne Army Barracks, The Hague, South Holland*
p. 77 \ *Staphorst Ammunition Depot, Overijssel*

Courtesy of the artist

In collaboration with the McCord Museum

Exhibited Works

Positives on glass from the McCord Museum collection
Thanks to Hélène Samson, Curator, Notman Photographic Archives,
for her valuable collaboration in the development of this project.

In the late 1960s and early 1970s, the City of
Montreal commissioned an aerial photographic
survey of the terrain of the city and outlying
districts. The survey was used to make maps and
to trace changes in land use and major urban
developments. One of its by-products is a group
of black-and-white photographic glass plates,
to be used on a stereo plotting machine, from
which tracing rods would transfer outlines
of roads and buildings onto a drawing table.
These glass plates are displayed in the exhibition
Montreal Aerial Survey. Showing the same area
at slightly different heights and angles and
using geodetic coordinates, the plates were
used by cartographers in the production of
maps. The process is called aerotriangulation.

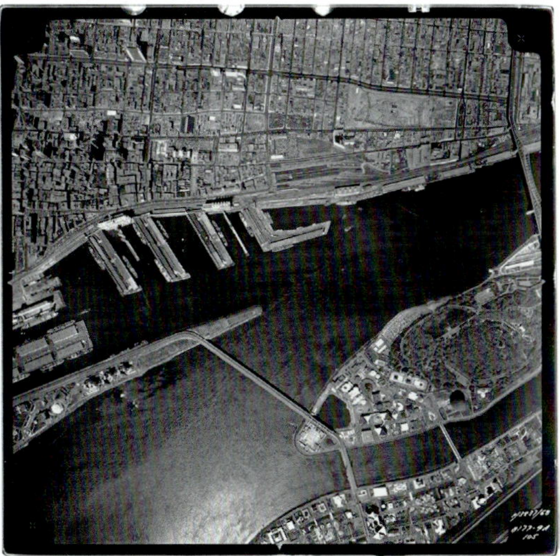

Above \ St. Helen's Island and the port of Montreal, aerial view, 1968.
Positive on glass, 24 x 24 cm. © McCord Museum, M2006.100.1.336.P1
pp. 78–79 \ Original envelope and positive on glass. The Bonaventure Expressway and
University Street, Montreal, aerial view, 1968. © McCord Museum, M2006.100.1.337.P2
Ville de Montréal, Public Works, Technical and Surveying Division.

Courtesy of the McCord Museum

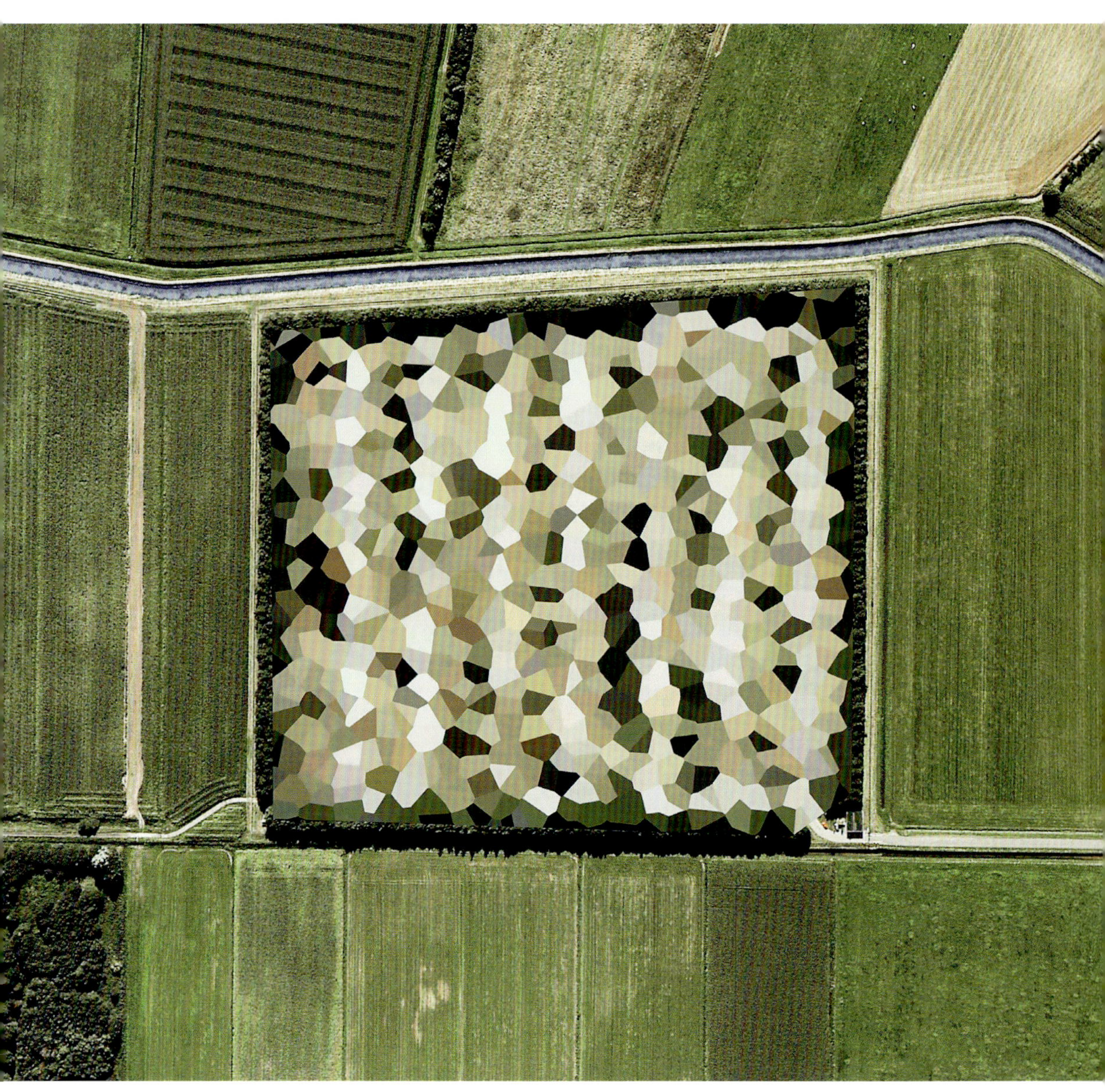

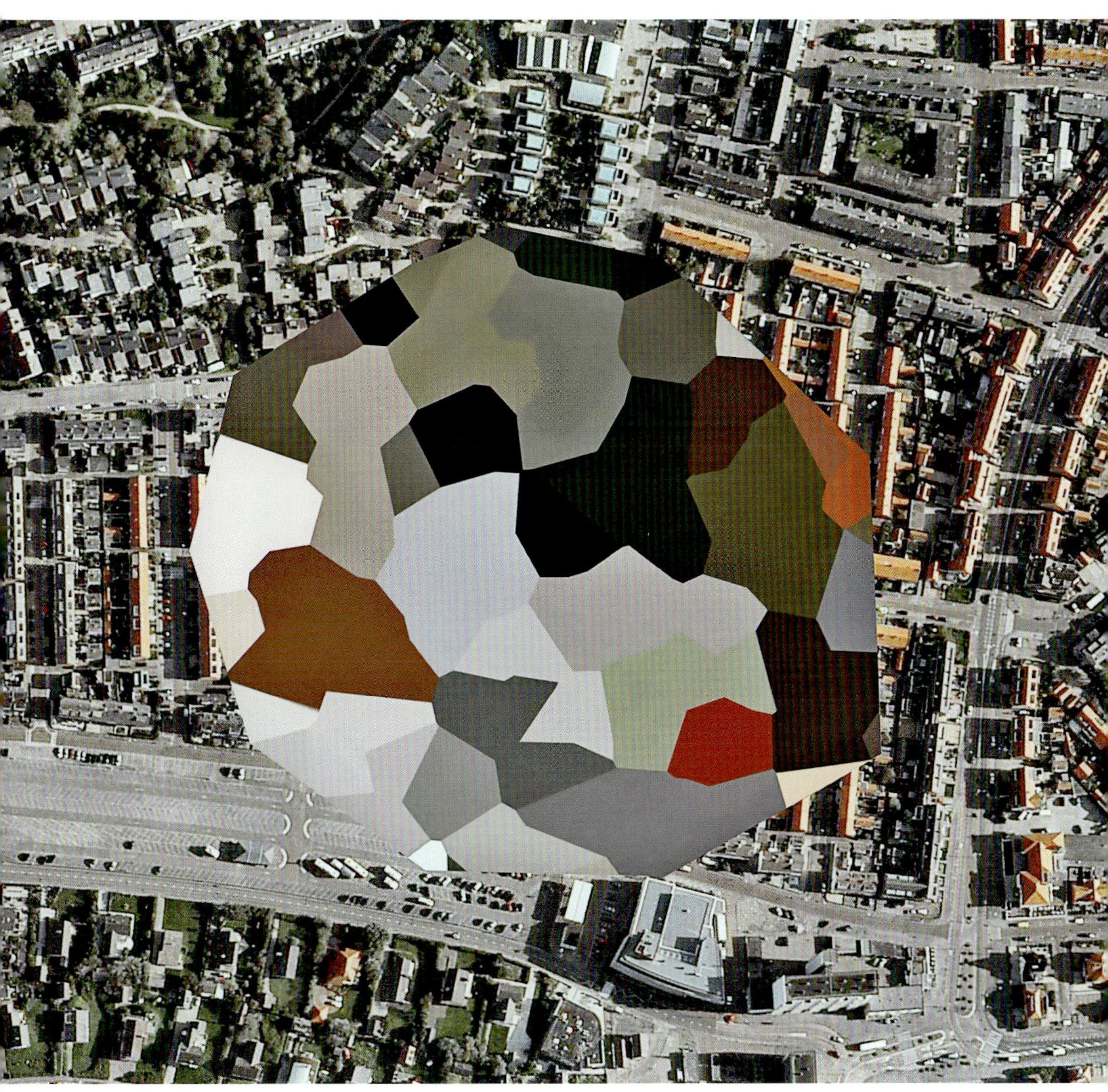

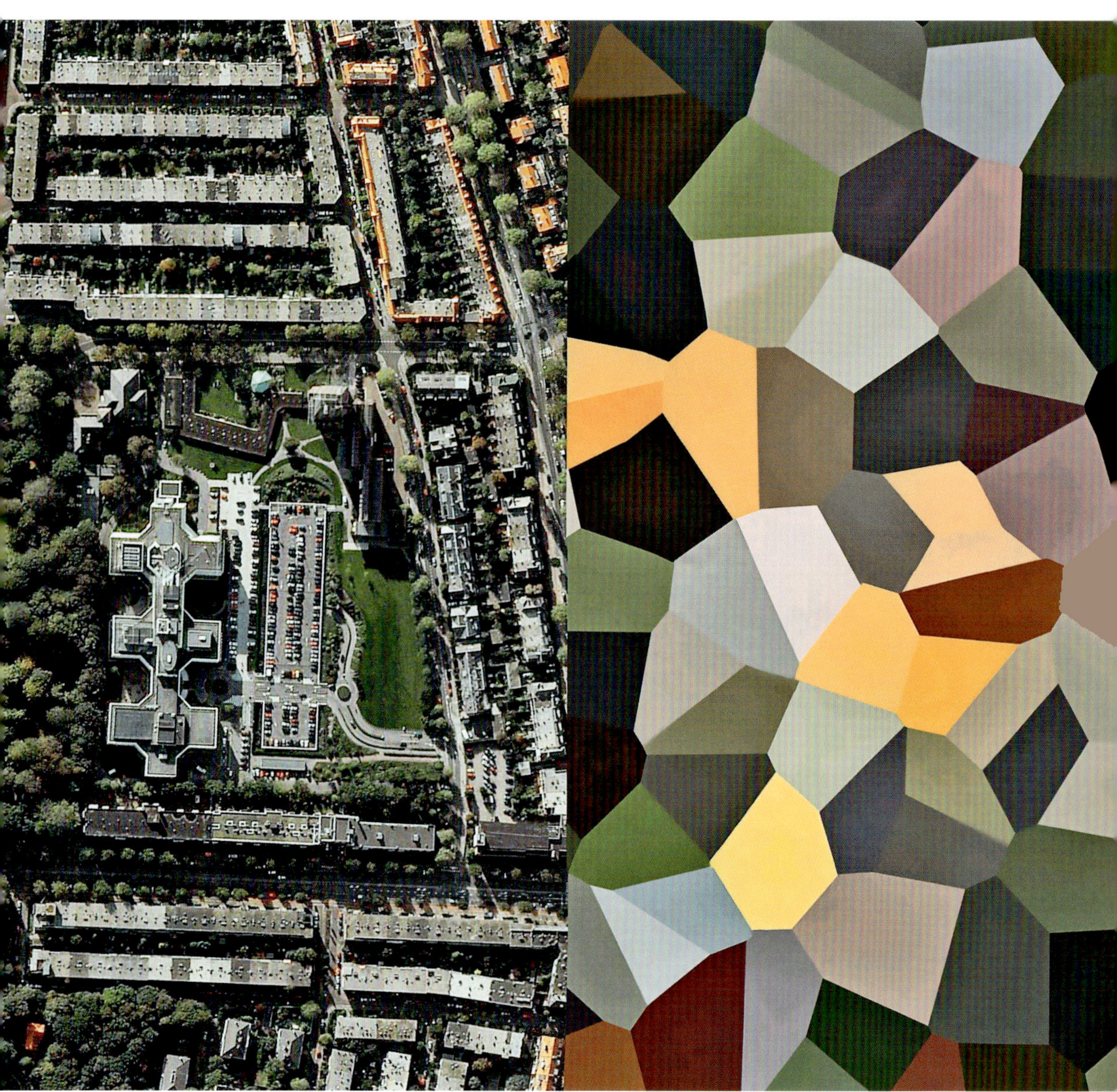

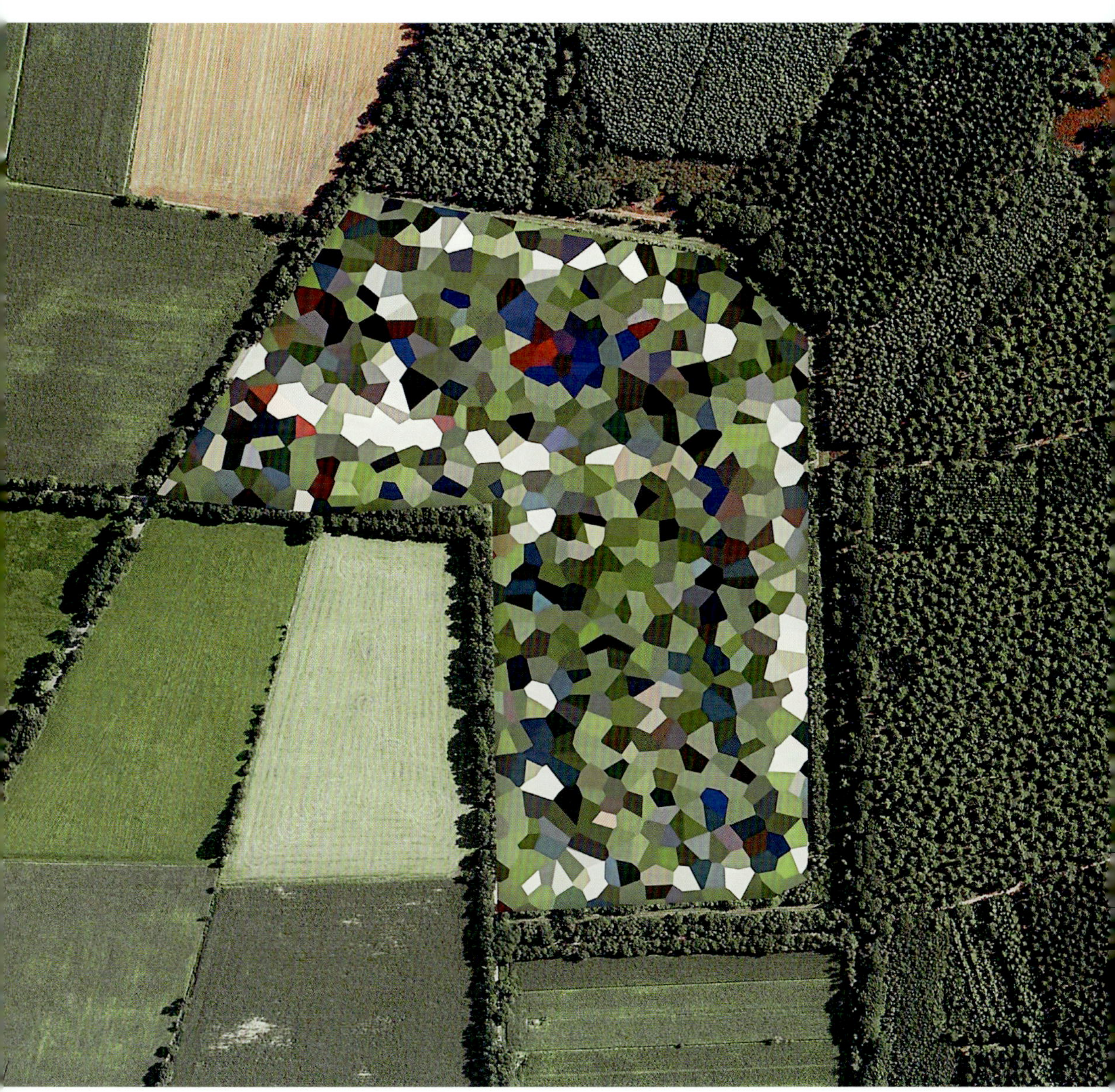

DOSSIER No.: _______________

M 2006.100.1.328

CONTRAT No.: _______P/3237_______

DATE DE PRISE DE VUE: _______1968_______

ÉCHELLE DE PHOTO: _____1000' = 1 po_____

RÉGION PHOTOGRAPHIÉE: Bonaventure +
                       Rue Université

PHOTO No.: _____106_____

LIGNE DE VOL No: _____94_____

ROULEAU No: _____8177_____

FOCALE: _____152.55_____

FEUILLET No: _______________

REMARQUES: _______________
           ____
           ____
           ____
           ____

DOCUMENT PLANIMÉTRIQUE		OP.	DATE
PUG	HAUT		
	CENTRE		
	BAS		
INTERPRÉTATION			
RESTITUTION			

VILLE DE MONTRÉAL

TRAVAUX PUBLICS   DIVISION TECHNIQUE
                              ARPENTAGE

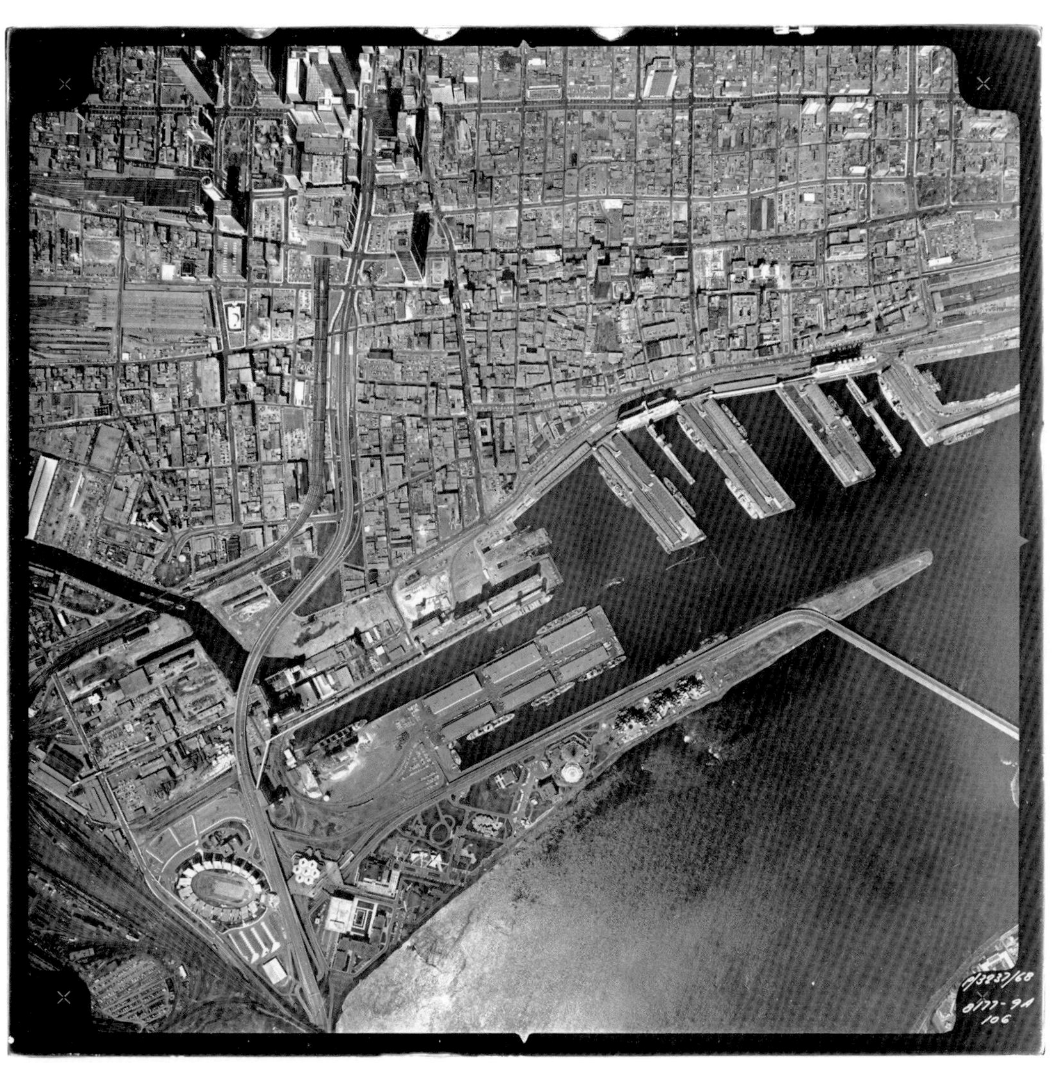

79   MONTREAL AERIAL SURVEY

Exhibited Work

Black Box, 2002–13

Installation: ceiling tile, metal studs, fluorescent lights, carpet, Sony AIBO ERS-7M3 robot, inkjet prints, 99 x 259 x 107 cm.

In 1999 Sony introduced a new gadget, the AIBO pet dog. This robot was able to learn, adapt to its home environment, and respond to its owner's functional and emotional needs. It could emit friendly sounds and take its own photographs. Three years later, in his work *Black Box* (2002–13), Craig Kalpakjian placed a Sony AIBO robot dog inside a sealed wooden box, not unlike a larger version of a Skinner box used by researchers to study the behaviour of animals in a controlled environment. It is not possible to see into the box, but each day the robot dog takes a photograph of the interior. These photographs are then displayed outside the box on the gallery wall.

Born in 1961 in Huntington, New York, Craig Kalpakjian lives and works in New York. He has a BA in art history from the University of Pennsylvania. His works are included in the collections of the Metropolitan Museum of Art (MET) and the Whitney Museum of American Art in New York, the San Francisco Museum of Modern Art, and the Centre Pompidou in Paris. Major exhibitions featuring his works include *After Photoshop: Manipulated Photography in the Digital Age* (2012) and *Reality Check* (2008) at the MET. He has exhibited extensively, including at the Greene Naftali Gallery (1998, 2011), David Zwirner (2010), the Andrea Rosen Gallery (2002, 2004), and the New Museum (2002) in New York, as well as at the Wexner Center for the Arts in Columbus (2005). \ www.kalpakjian.com

p. 81 \ Exhibition view, Andrea Rosen Gallery, New York, 2002
pp. 82–83 \ Images taken by Sony AIBO robot, inkjet prints, 2002

Courtesy of the artist

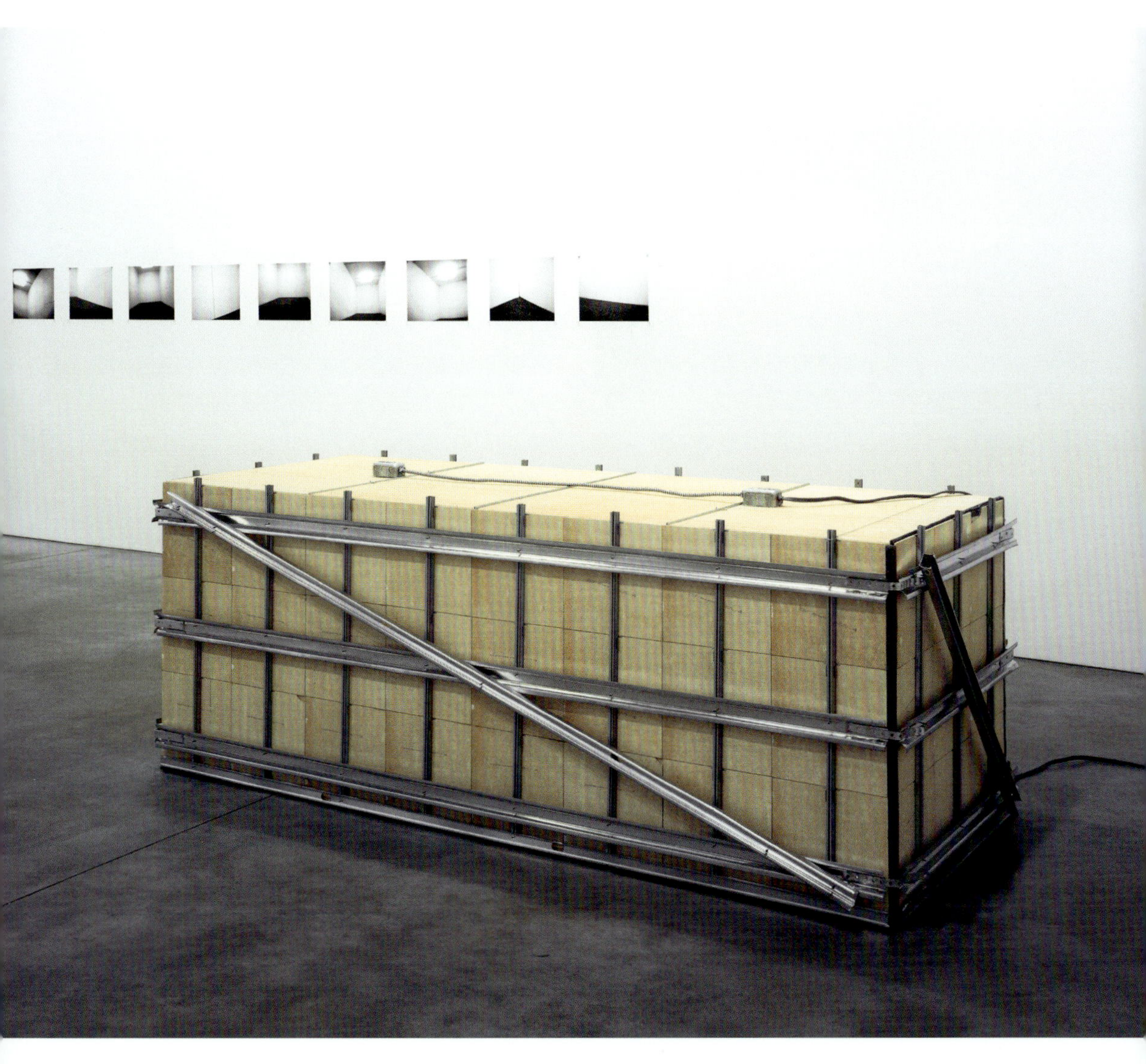

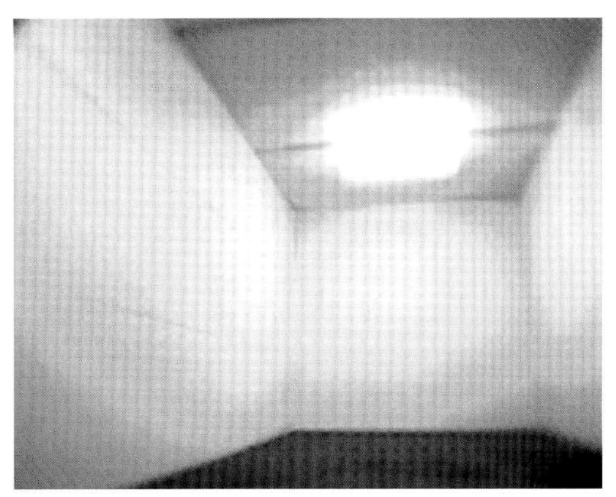 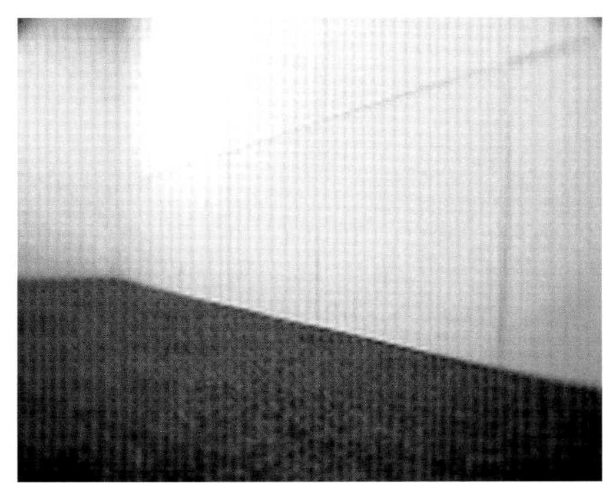

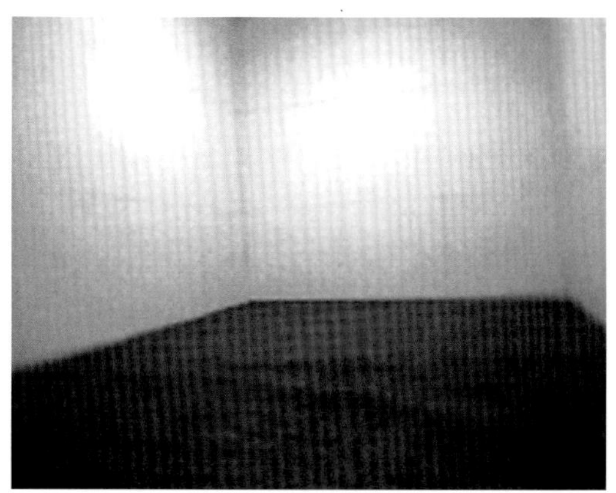 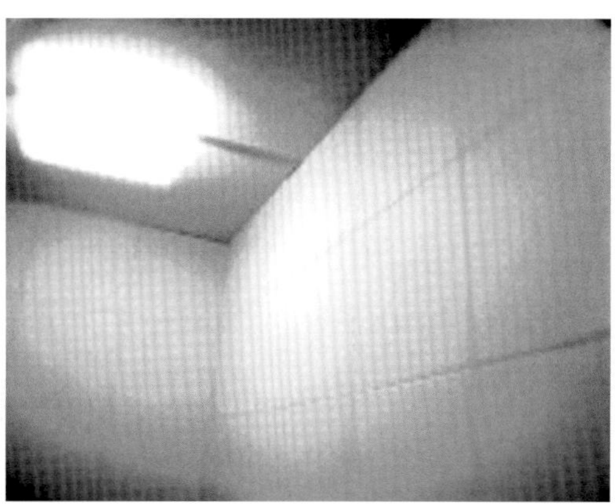

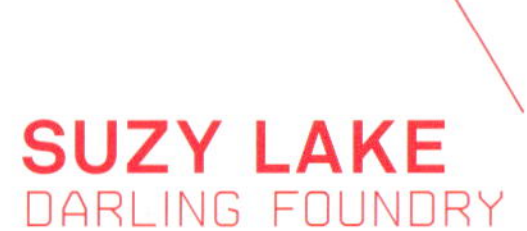

SUZY LAKE
DARLING FOUNDRY

Exhibited Work

Reduced Performing (2008–09)
Lightjet print mounted on Dibond, 206.0 x 83.5 cm each. Edition 1 of 3.

"How far I can reduce the photographic activity's narrative while still retaining a body-reading that reveals itself in time?" This was the proposition set out by Suzy Lake that resulted in *Reduced Performing* (2008–09). Made on a flatbed scanner, these self-portraits took seven minutes as the scanner traced her body. During this expanded "exposure" she was breathing, blinking, and sometimes crying. Lake chose these involuntary movements because they are generally overlooked and taken for granted. The result produces a strangely still form that is a cross between a stylized catalogue image and a saintly figure descended from heaven.

Born in 1947 in Detroit, Suzy Lake moved to Canada in 1968 and is now based in Toronto. Her work has been included in numerous major exhibitions, including *WACK! Art and the Feminist Revolution 1965–1980* at the Los Angeles Museum of Contemporary Art (2007), and travelling to the National Museum of Women in the Arts in Washington, D.C., P.S.1 Contemporary Art Center in New York, and the Vancouver Art Gallery; and *Traffic: Conceptual Art in Canada, 1965–1980* at the Art Gallery of Alberta (2012), the University of Toronto (2012), the Vancouver Art Gallery (2012), and the Badischer Kunstverein in Karlsruhe, Germany (2013). In 2014 the Art Gallery of Ontario in Toronto will present her major touring retrospective exhibition *Introducing Suzy Lake*. Lake is represented by Galerie Donald Browne in Montreal and Georgia Scherman Projects in Toronto. \ www.suzylake.ca

p. 85 \ *Reduced Performing: Breathing #5*, 2009 \ *Reduced Performing: Crying #1*, 2009
p. 86 \ *Reduced Performing: Blinking and Breathing #1*, 2008 \ *Reduced Performing: Blinking and Breathing #2*, 2008
p. 87 \ *Reduced Performing: Breathing #1*, 2008 \ *Reduced Performing: Breathing #6*, 2009

Courtesy of the artist and Donald Browne Gallery, Montreal

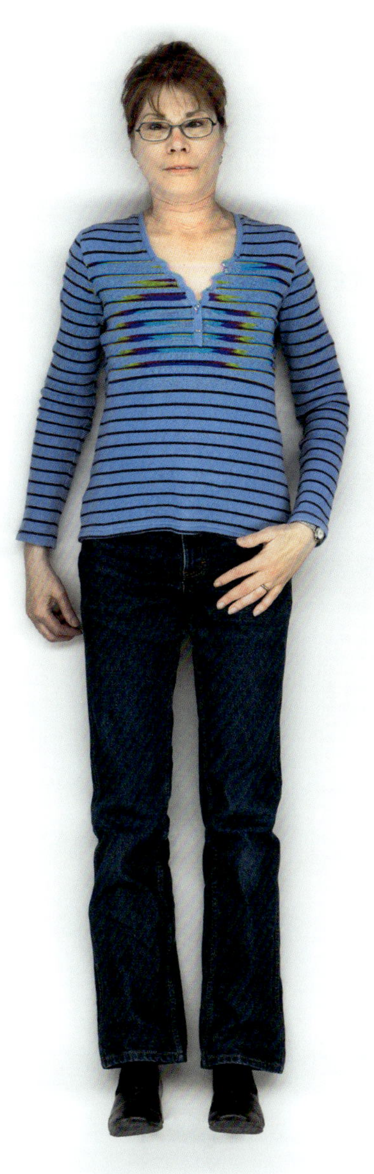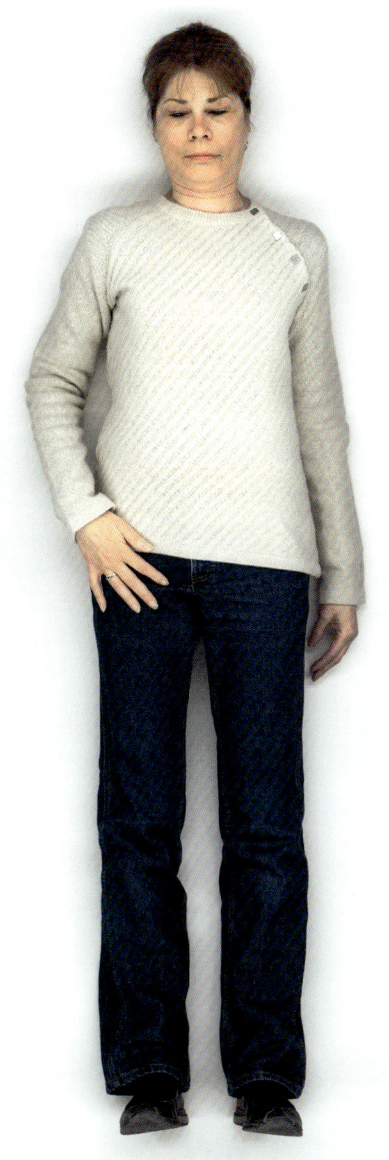

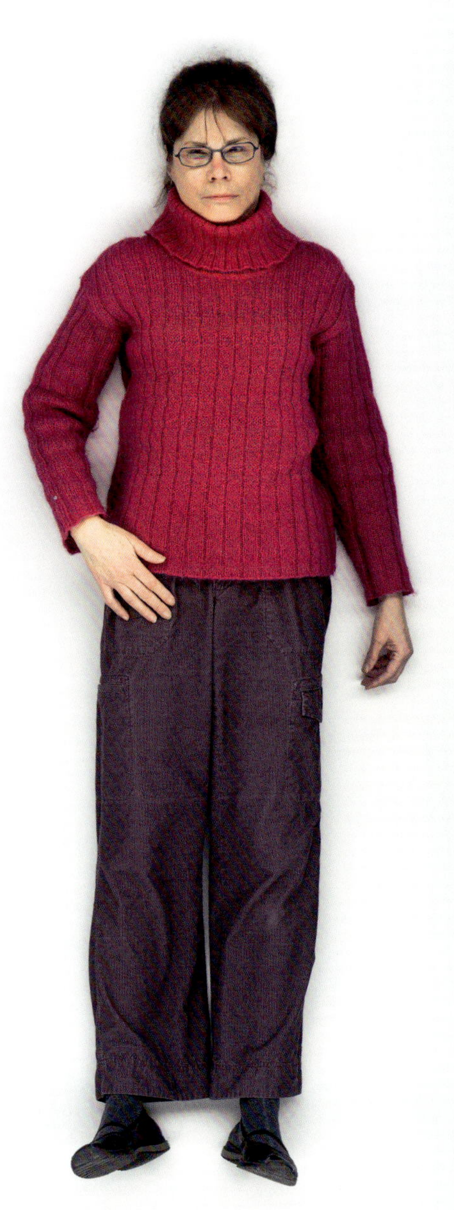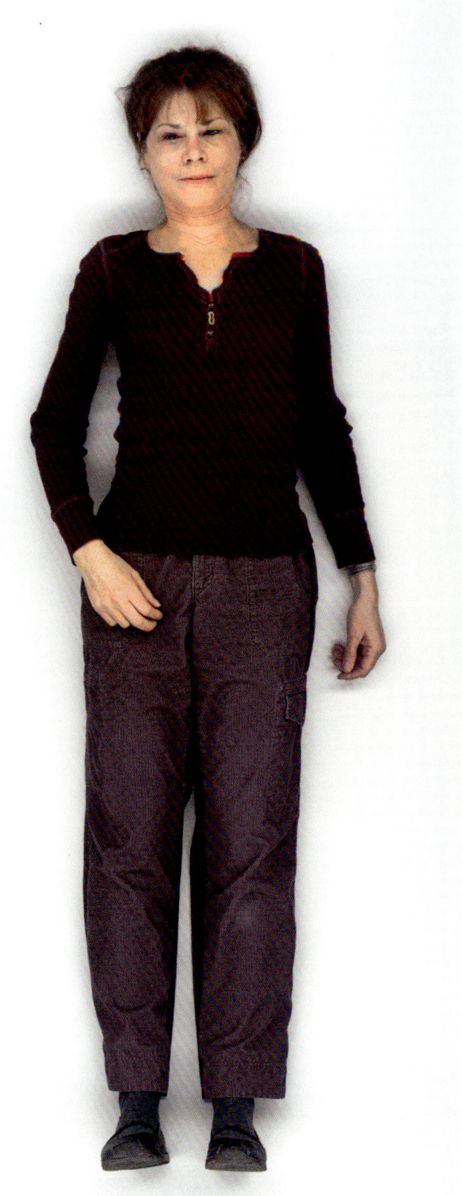

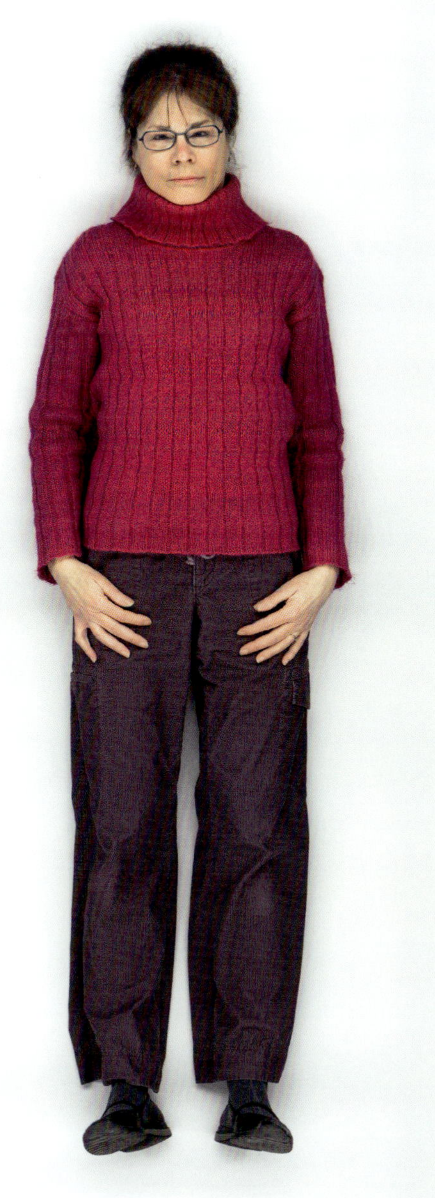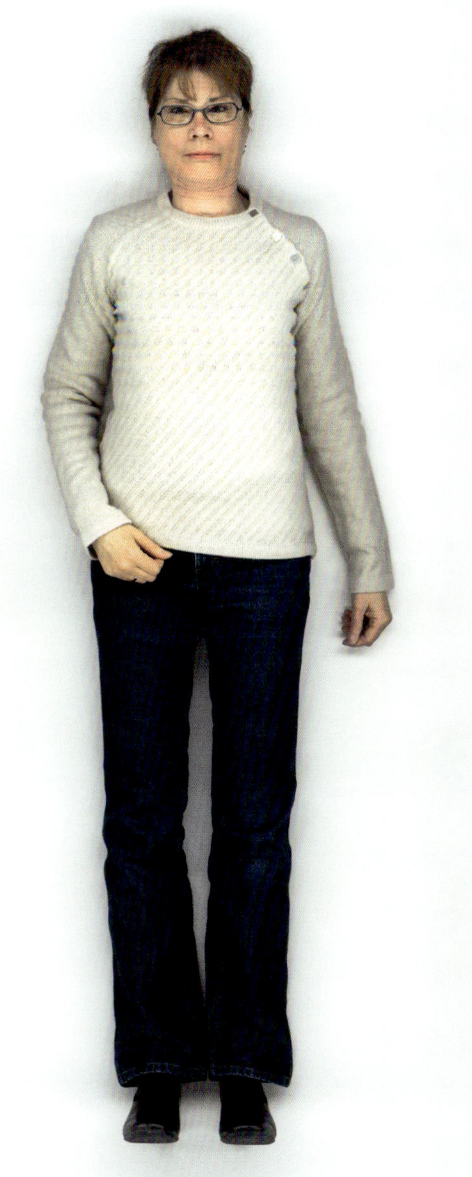

TREVOR PAGLEN

Exhibited Works

Chromogenic prints, variable dimensions, 2006–11

***Drone Vision*, 2010**
Video, 5 min, colour, sound, loop.

Trevor Paglen is known for his extensive research on the clandestine activities of the United States military. His work deliberately blurs the boundaries between science, art, and journalism. In his photographic works, Paglen investigated the use of drones and how the American landscape has been invaded by military technology, thus redefining the aesthetics of the sublime. "For me, seeing the drone in the twenty-first century is a little bit like Turner seeing the train in the nineteenth century."

Born in 1974 in Maryland, Trevor Paglen lives and works in New York. He holds an MFA from the Art Institute of Chicago and a PhD in geography from the University of California, Berkeley. Paglen is the recipient of a Smithsonian Artist Research Fellowship (2011), the SECA Award from the San Francisco Museum of Modern Art (SFMOMA) (2008), and the Aperture West Prize (2008). He has had solo and group exhibitions at the Walker Arts Center in Minneapolis (2010, 2011); Kunsthall Oslo (2010); the New Museum in New York (2010); the Tate Modern in London (2010); SFMOMA (2009, 2010); and the Berkeley Art Museum (2008), among others. Paglen is represented by Metro Pictures in New York, Altman Siegel in San Francisco, and Galerie Thomas Zander in Cologne. \ www.paglen.com

p. 89 \ *Reaper Drone: Indian Springs, NV; Distance – 2 miles*, 2010, 76.20 x 91.44 cm
p. 90 \ *Control Tower (Area 52); Tonopah Test Range, NV; Distance – 20 miles; 11:55 am*, 2006, 76.20 x 91.44 cm
p. 91 \ *Untitled (Reaper Drone)*, 2010, 121.92 x 152.40 cm

Courtesy of the artist; Metro Pictures, New York; Altman Siegel, San Francisco; and Galerie Thomas Zander, Cologne

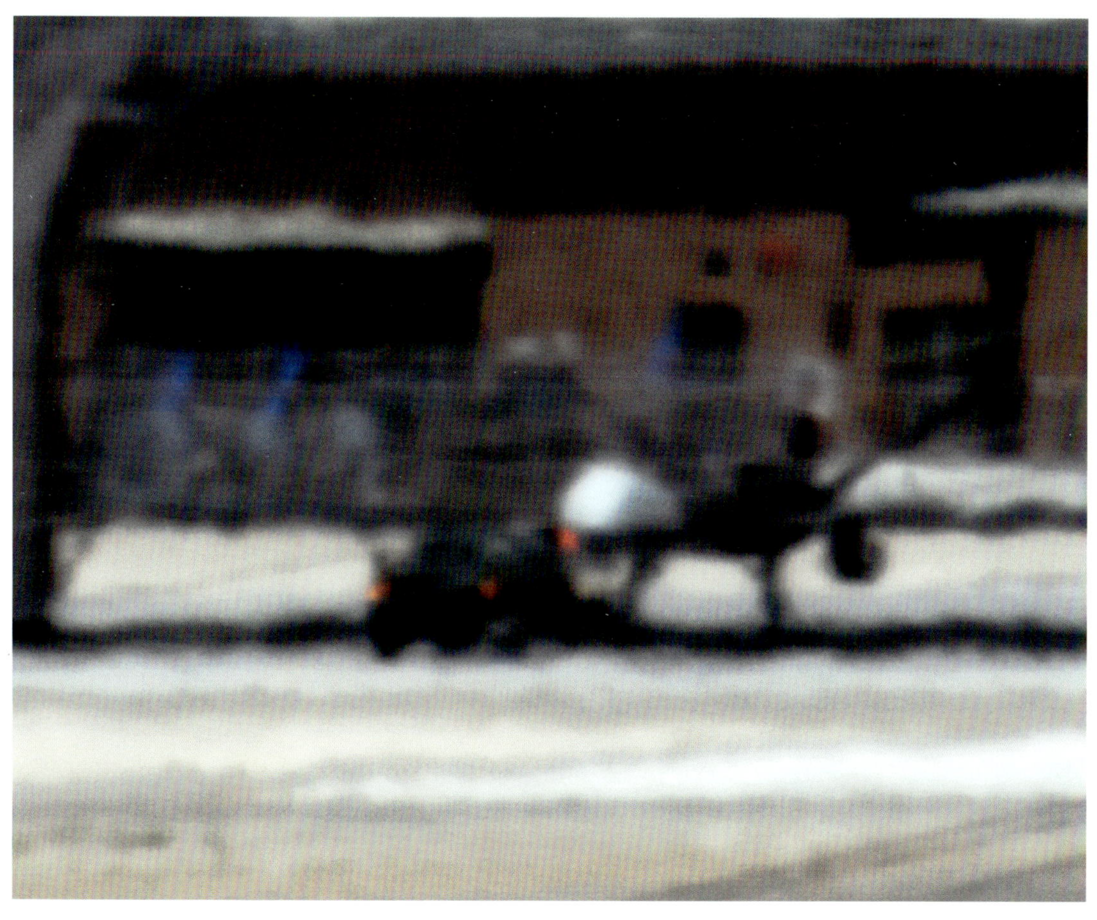

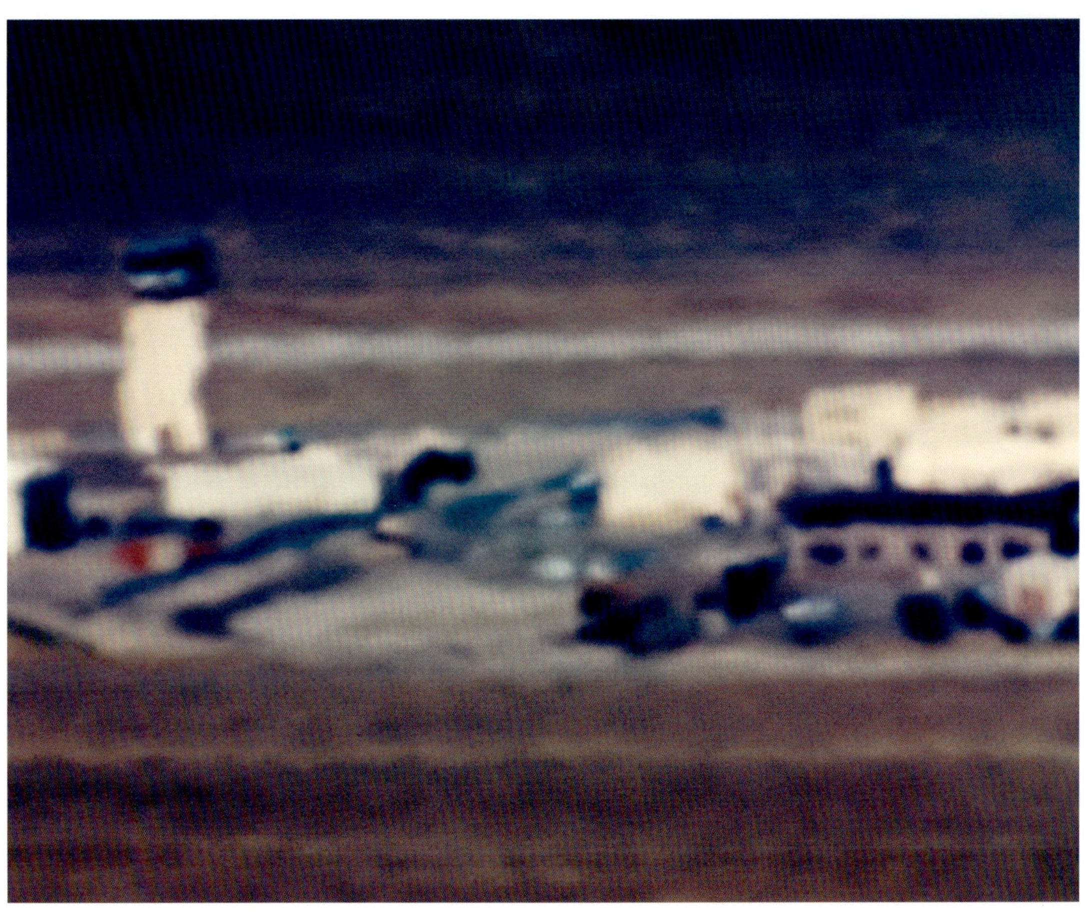

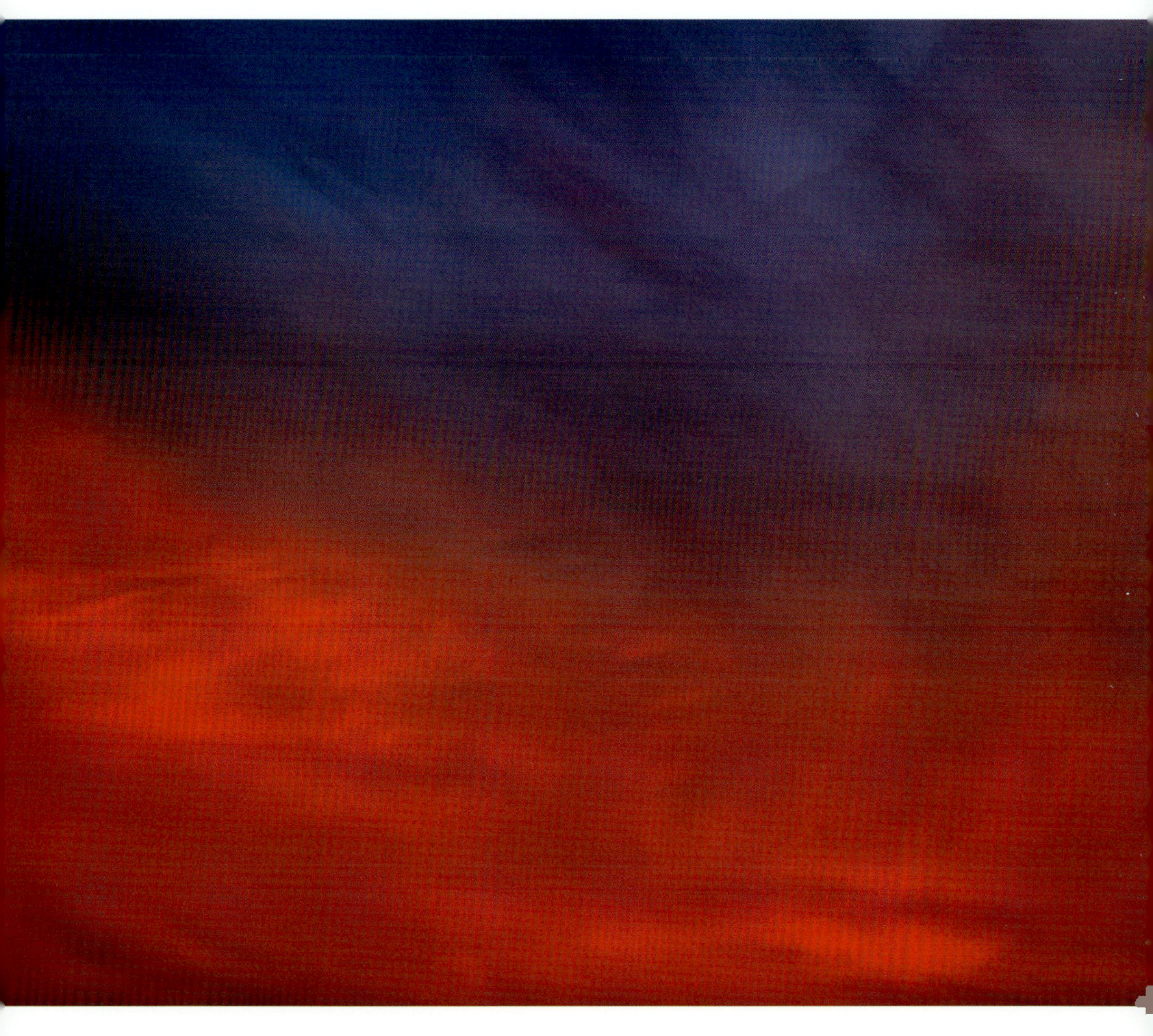

Exhibited Work

Exposure #55: Munich, Waisenhausstrasse 65, 01.17.08, 1:55 p.m., 2008
Ultrachrome ink on cotton paper. 12 parts, 75 x 112 cm each.

By using multiple cameras placed in different locations, and with exposures simultaneously triggered by a radio-controlled release, Barbara Probst dissects the photographic moment. The *mise en scène* of *Exposure #55: Munich, Waisenhausstrasse 65, 01.17.08, 1:55 p.m.* (2008) is a sparsely furnished apartment. Twelve cameras, disposed at various angles and distances, peer through keyholes and doorways and around furniture, framing figures in ambiguous arrangements. Cameras take photographs of cameras taking photographs of cameras. The viewer enters a labyrinth of vision with no easy route out.

Born in 1964 in Munich, Barbara Probst divides her time between New York and Munich. She has received the Philip Morris Award in Dresden in 2002, and the Photography Award of the Arts Council in Munich in 1994. She has had solo exhibitions at the National Museum of Photography in Copenhagen (2013), the Kunstverein Oldenburg (2009), the Madison Museum of Contemporary Art (2008), and the Museum of Contemporary Photography in Chicago (2007); and been in group exhibitions at major museums worldwide, including the Saint Louis Art Museum (2012), the Tate Modern in London (2010), the Centre Pompidou in Paris (2010), and the Museum of Modern Art in New York (2006, 2010). Probst is represented by Murray Guy Gallery in New York, Kuckei + Kuckei Gallery in Berlin, Monica de Cardenas Gallery in Milan, and Galleri Lars Bohman in Stockholm. \ www.barbaraprobst.net

pp. 93–95 \ Four images from the work

Courtesy of the artist and Murray Guy, New York
© VG Bild-Kunst, Barbara Probst / SODRAC (2013)

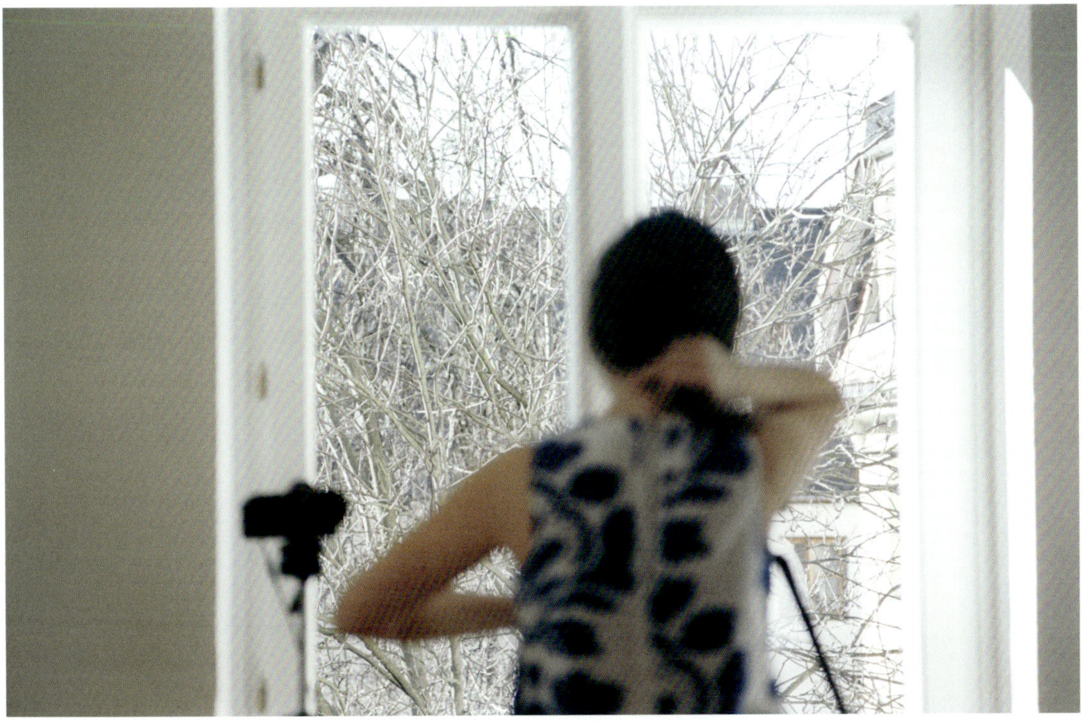

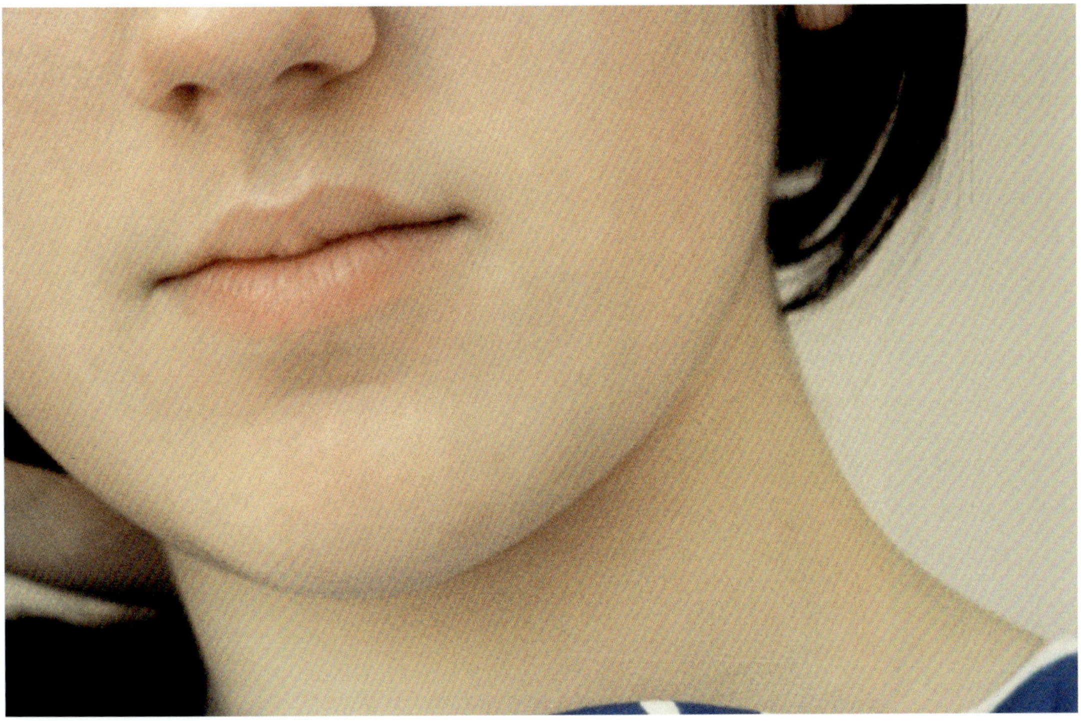

    BARBARA PROBST

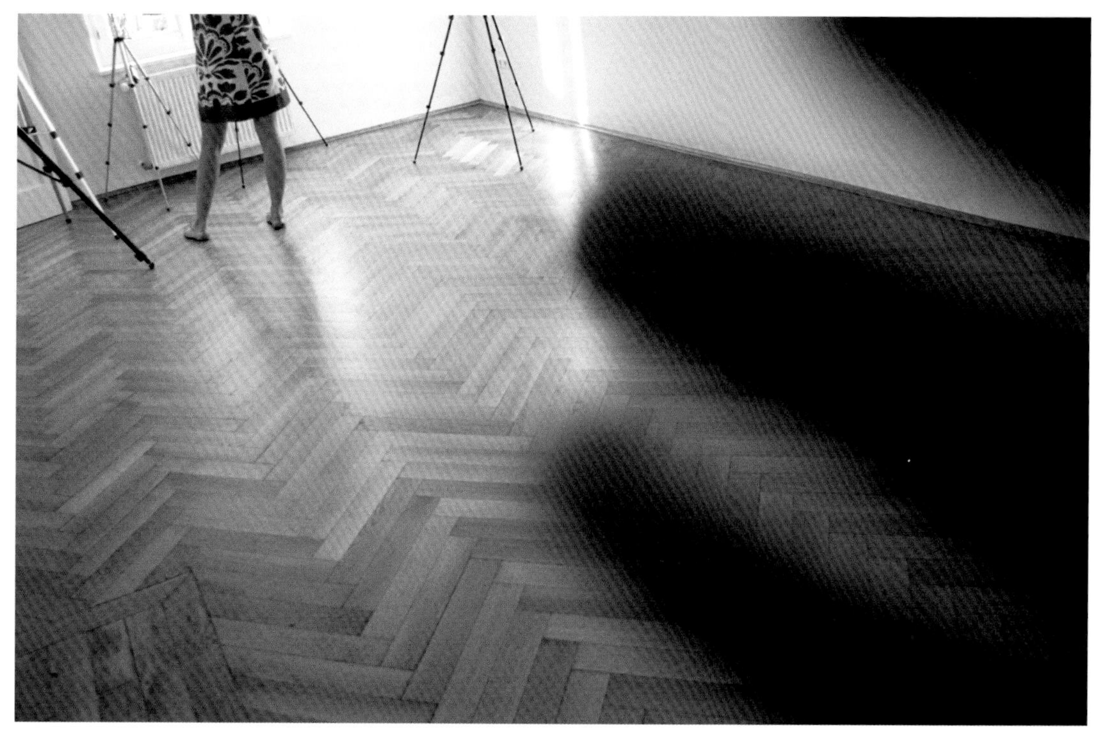

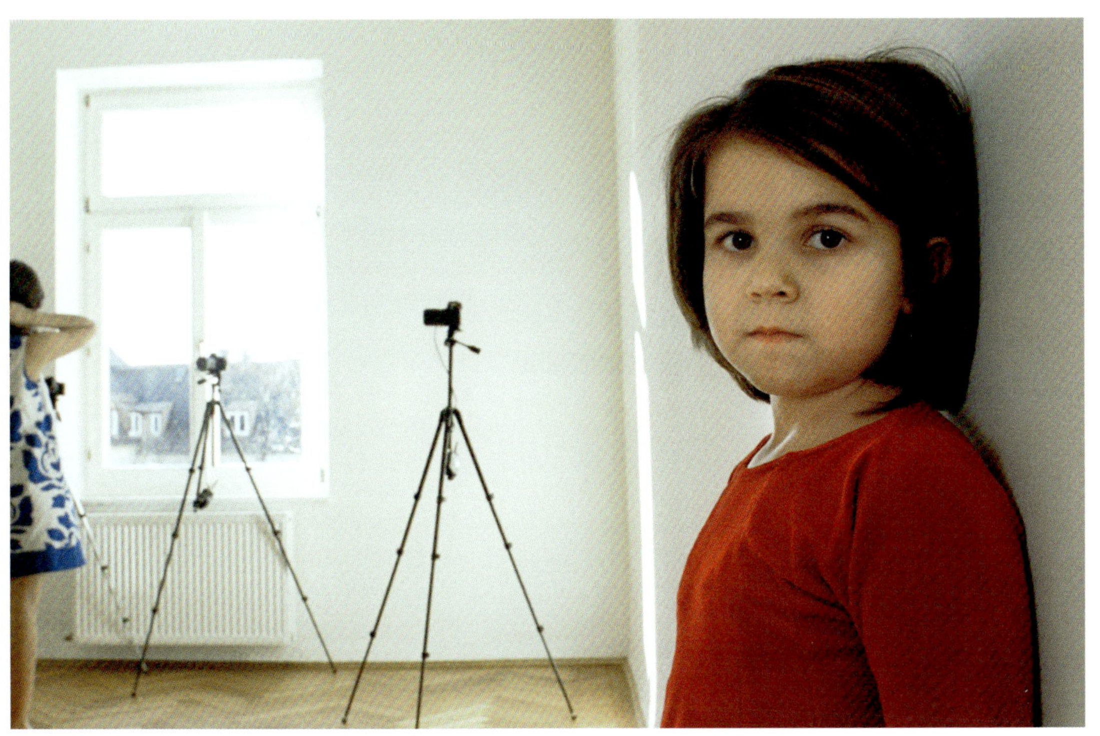

95   BARBARA PROBST

JON RAFMAN
MAISON DE LA CULTURE MARIE-UGUAY
MAKE ART PUBLIC

Exhibited Works

The Nine Eyes of Google Street View, 2008–ongoing
Hanhnemuehle Matte Photo Rag 308g mounted on Dibond in a thin white frame,
101.6 x 162.6 cm each.

You, the World and I, 2011
HD video, 6 min 10 s, colour, sound.
http://youtheworldandi.com

Jon Rafman belongs to a small group of artists who base their work on the large Google Street View archive and image repository. The title of his series, *The Nine Eyes of Google Street View* (2008–ongoing), makes direct reference to the nine cameras mounted on each hybrid electric car sent by Google Maps to chart the world. Rafman selects images of weird events captured by the seemingly impartial automatic camera while on the road. The results thus generated are bewildering photographs that question any rational understanding of the world. The everyday becomes mysterious, disorienting, and very strange.

Jon Rafman was born in 1981 in Montreal, where he continues to live and to work as a filmmaker and artist. After receiving a BA in philosophy and literature at McGill University in 2004, he obtained an MFA at the School of the Art Institute of Chicago in 2008. His works have been featured in exhibitions worldwide, including at the Contact Photo Festival and the Museum of Contemporary Canadian Art in Toronto (2012); Les Rencontres d'Arles (2011); the New Museum in New York (2010); the Museum of Contemporary Art of Rome (2010); and the Ars Electronica Festival in Linz (2010). Rafman is represented by the Zach Feuer Gallery in New York, Galerie Antoine Ertaskiran in Montreal, Seventeen Gallery in London, and M+B Gallery in Los Angeles. \ www.jonrafman.com

From the series *The Nine Eyes of Google Street View*:
p. 97 \ *Zanddijk, North Holland, Netherlands*, 2013
p. 98 \ *Unknown Road, Võru County, Estonia*, 2013
p. 99 \ *Kraków, Lesser Poland Voivodeship, Poland*, 2013
p. 100 \ *Lakeside Drive, Coffeyville, Kansas*, 2013
p. 101 \ *Arroio do Só, Rio Grande do Sul, Brazil*, 2012

Courtesy of the artist; Galerie Antoine Ertaskiran, Montreal;
Zach Feuer Gallery, New York; and Seventeen Gallery, London

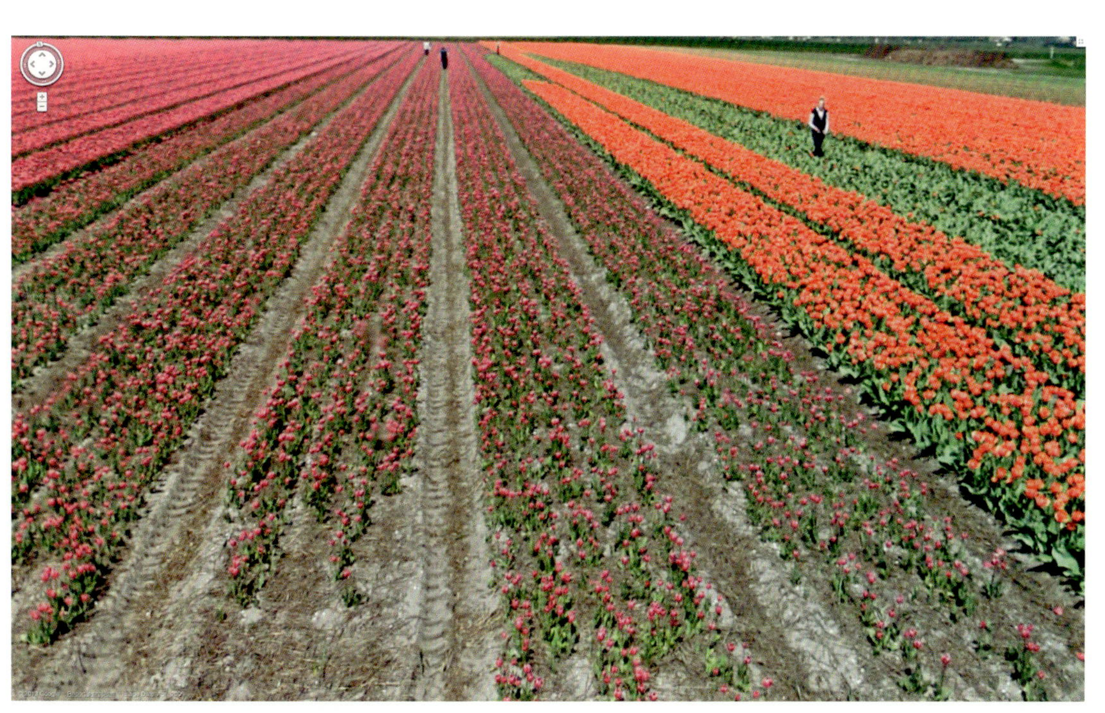

97   JON RAFMAN

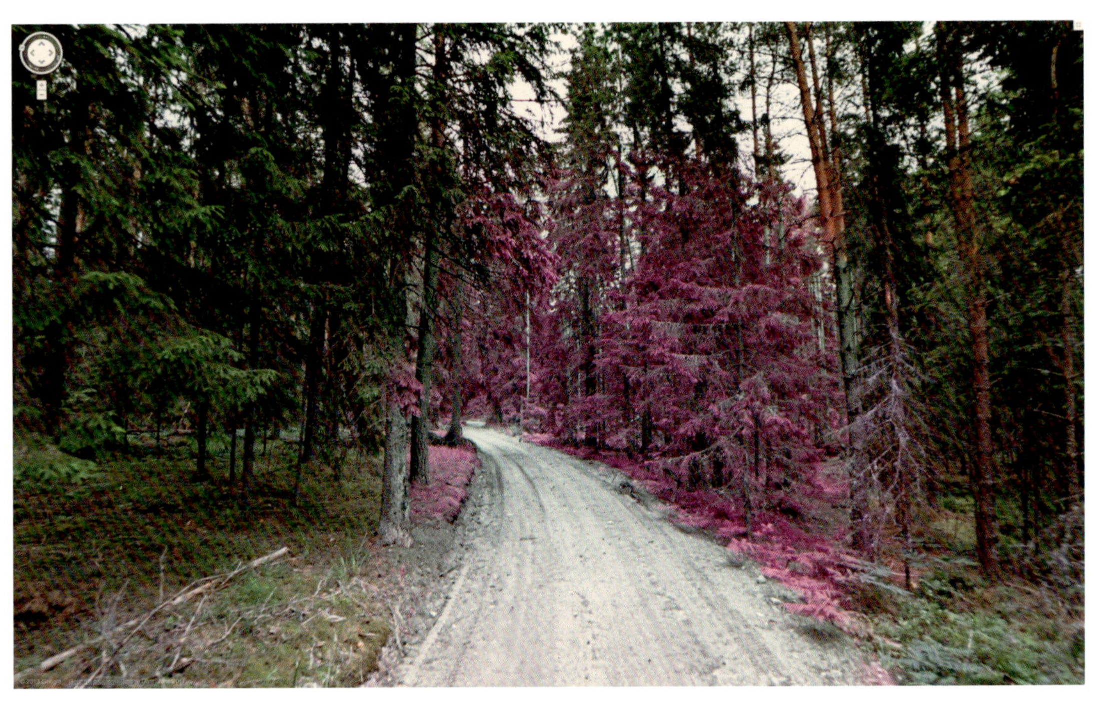

   JON RAFMAN

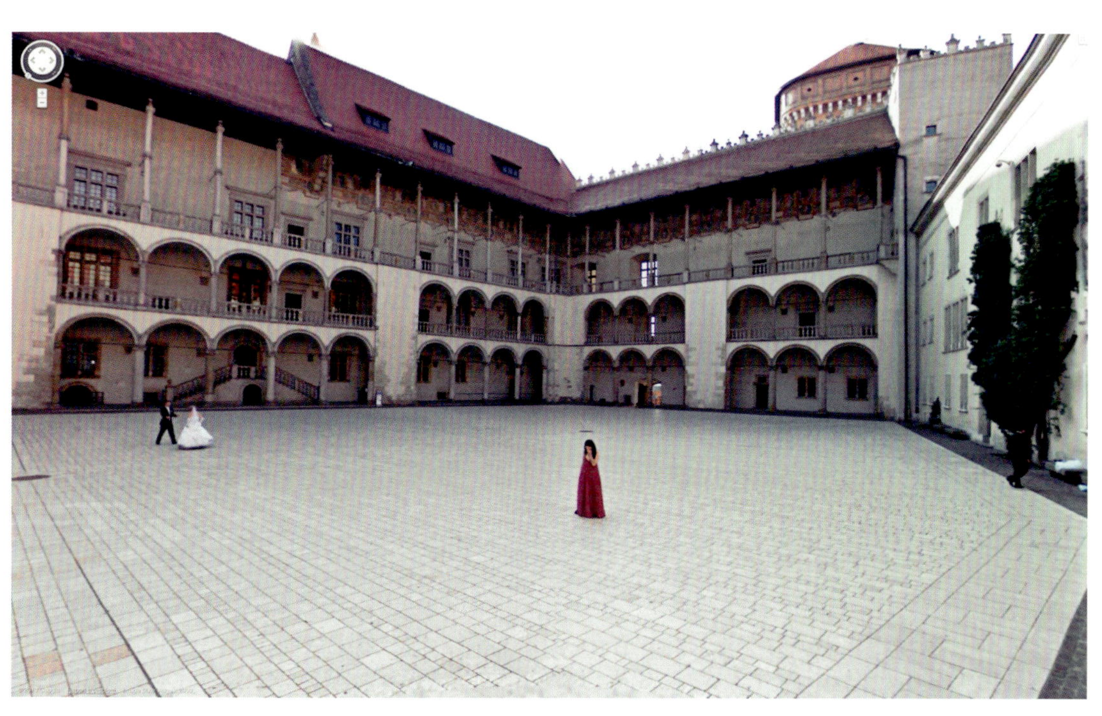

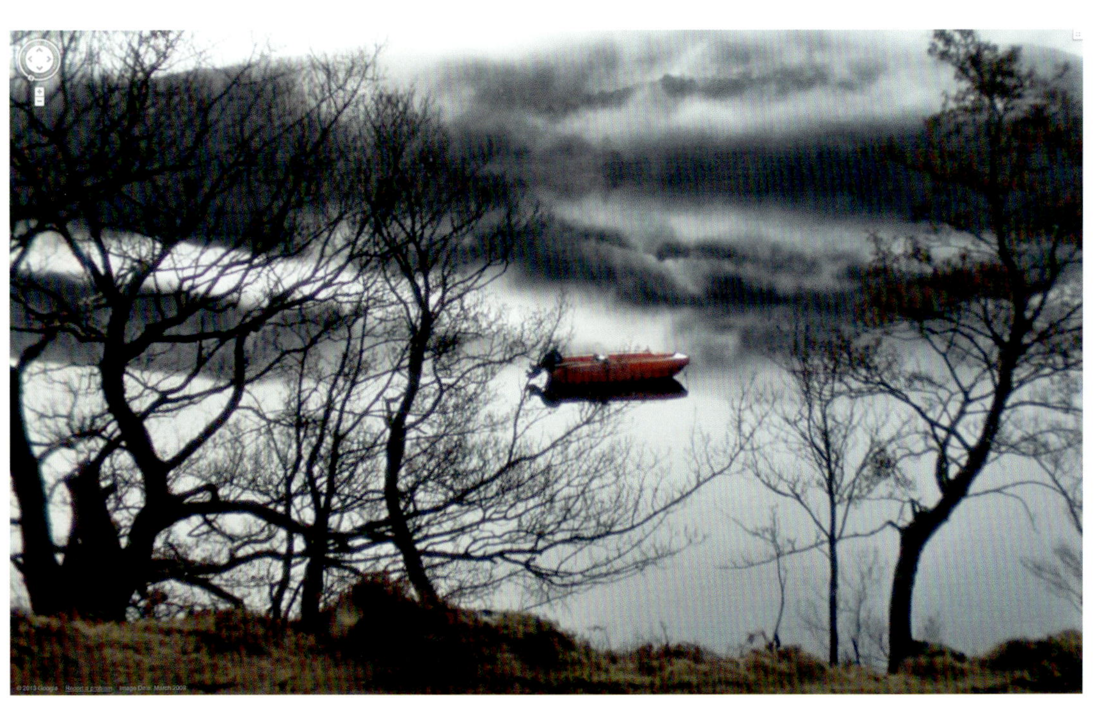

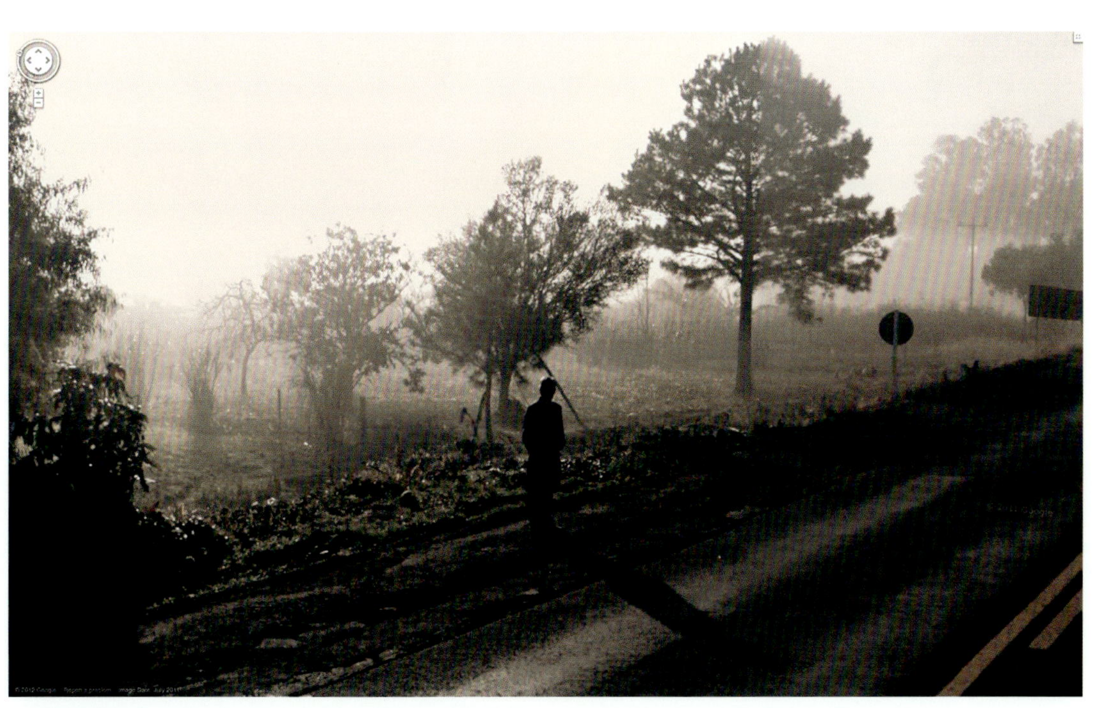

DAVID K. ROSS
MAISON DE LA CULTURE DU PLATEAU-MONT-ROYAL

Exhibited Work

Le Phare, 2012
16 mm film transfer to 2K, 13 min 20 s, colour, sound Dolby 5.1, loop.

The famous light beacon located on the roof of Place Ville Marie in Montreal starts its rotating performance every day at sunset. David K. Ross's film *Le Phare* (2012) is a portrait of this fully automated beacon with its four beams.
The film was made by attaching the camera to the revolving unit to follow the trajectory of bright rays illuminating the Montreal sky. Ross provides an opportunity to view the light in detail and to observe what it "sees."

Born in 1966 in Weston, Ontario, David K. Ross lives and works in Montreal and Chicago. He received an MA in architecture from the University of Toronto and a BA from the University of Waterloo. Recently, his works have been in solo and group exhibitions at the Musée d'art contemporain de Montréal (MACM) (2008, 2010, 2012–16); the National Gallery of Canada in Ottawa (NGC) (2012); and the Musée des beaux-arts de Sherbrooke (2012). His works are included in the collections of the NGC, the Musée National des Beaux-Arts du Québec, the MACM and the Canadian Centre for Architecture. Ross has received numerous grants and fellowships, among them from the Canada Council for the Arts (2009, 2012), the National Film Board of Canada (2010, 2011, 2012), and Arts Council England (2005). \ www.inferstructure.net

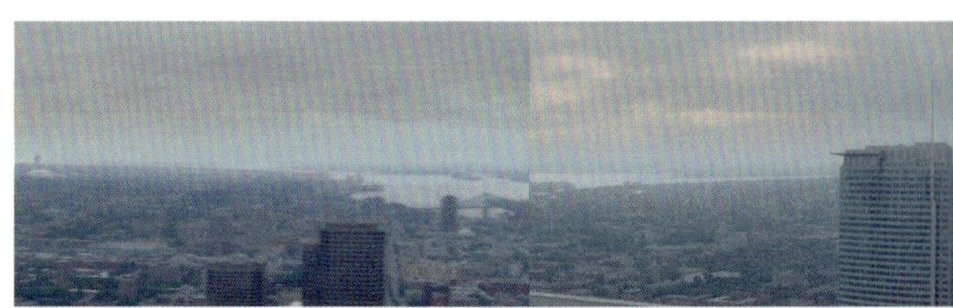

p. 7 \ Detail from a location research photo
for *Le Phare*, 2011. Photo: David K. Ross
p. 103 \ **Upper row:** Location research photos, 2011.
Photos: David K. Ross \
Bottom row: Film stills, 2012
pp. 104–05 \ Location research photo, 2011.
Photo: David K. Ross
pp. 106–07 \ **Upper row:** Film production photos, 2011.
Photos: David K. Ross and Michael Doerksen \
Bottom row: Film stills, 2012

Courtesy of the artist

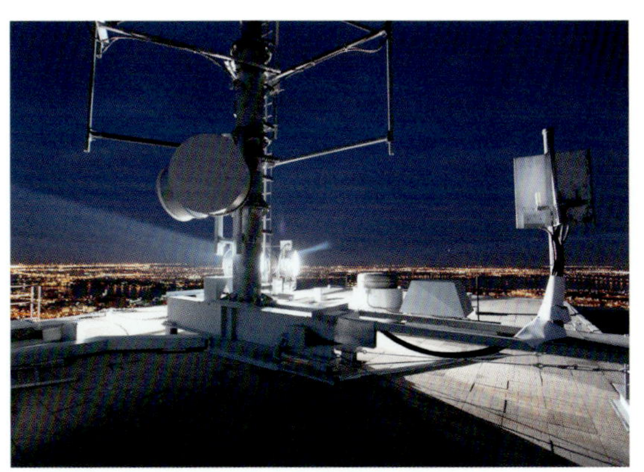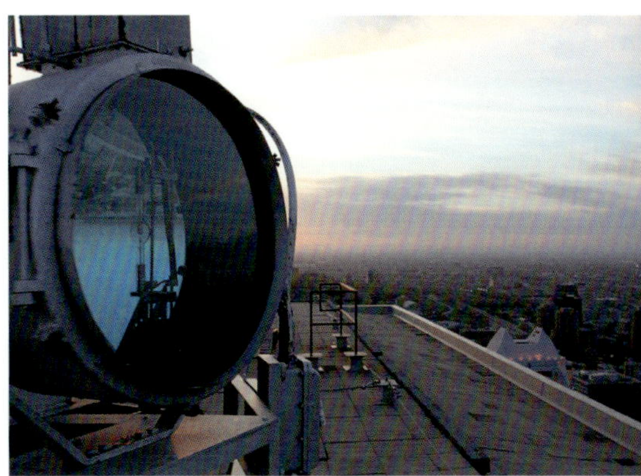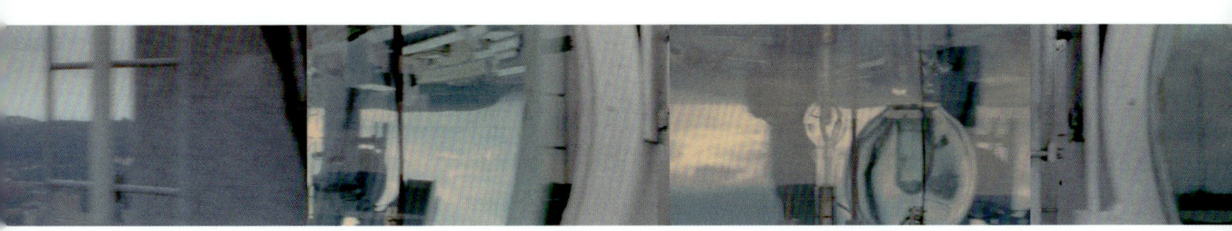

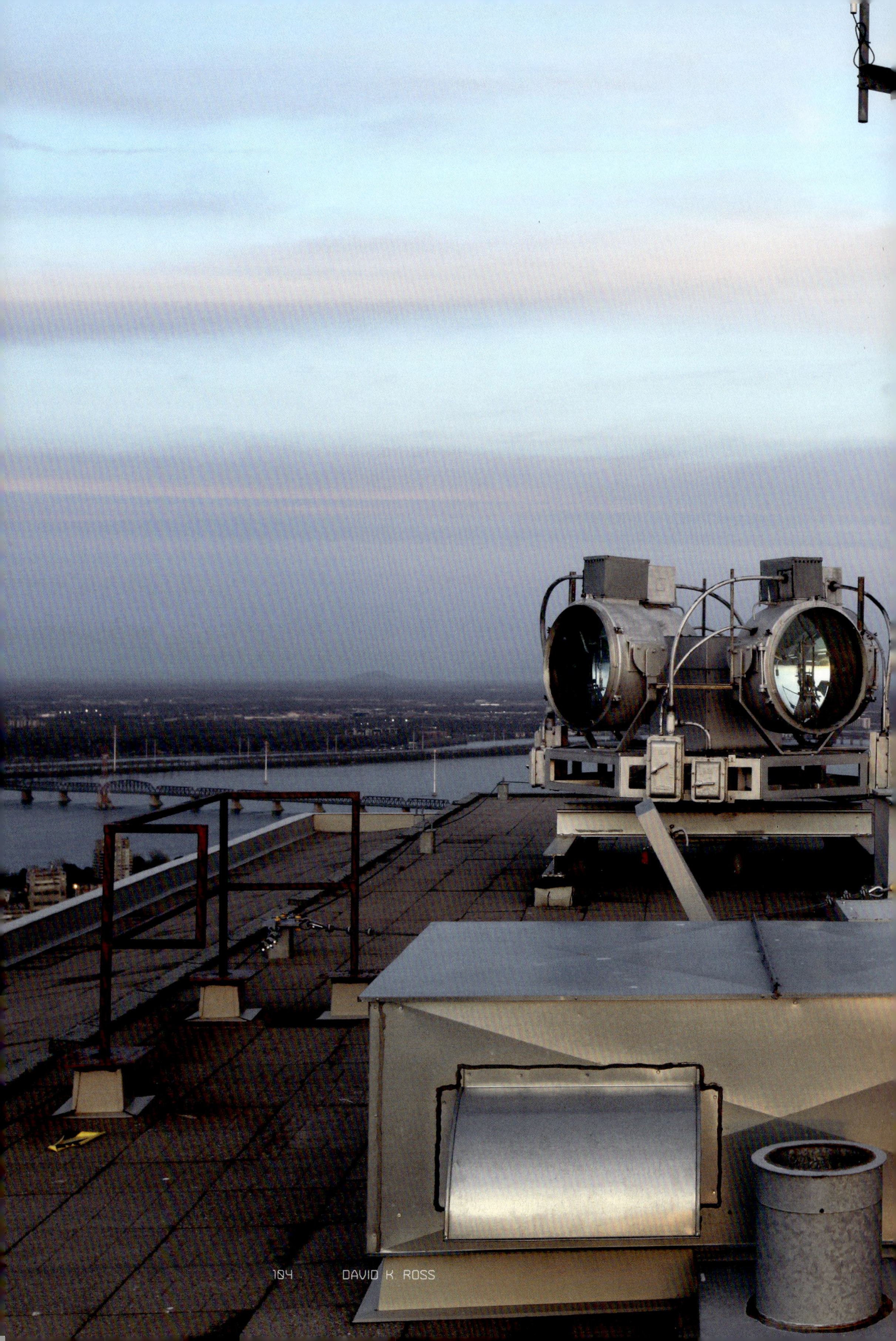

 DAVID K. ROSS

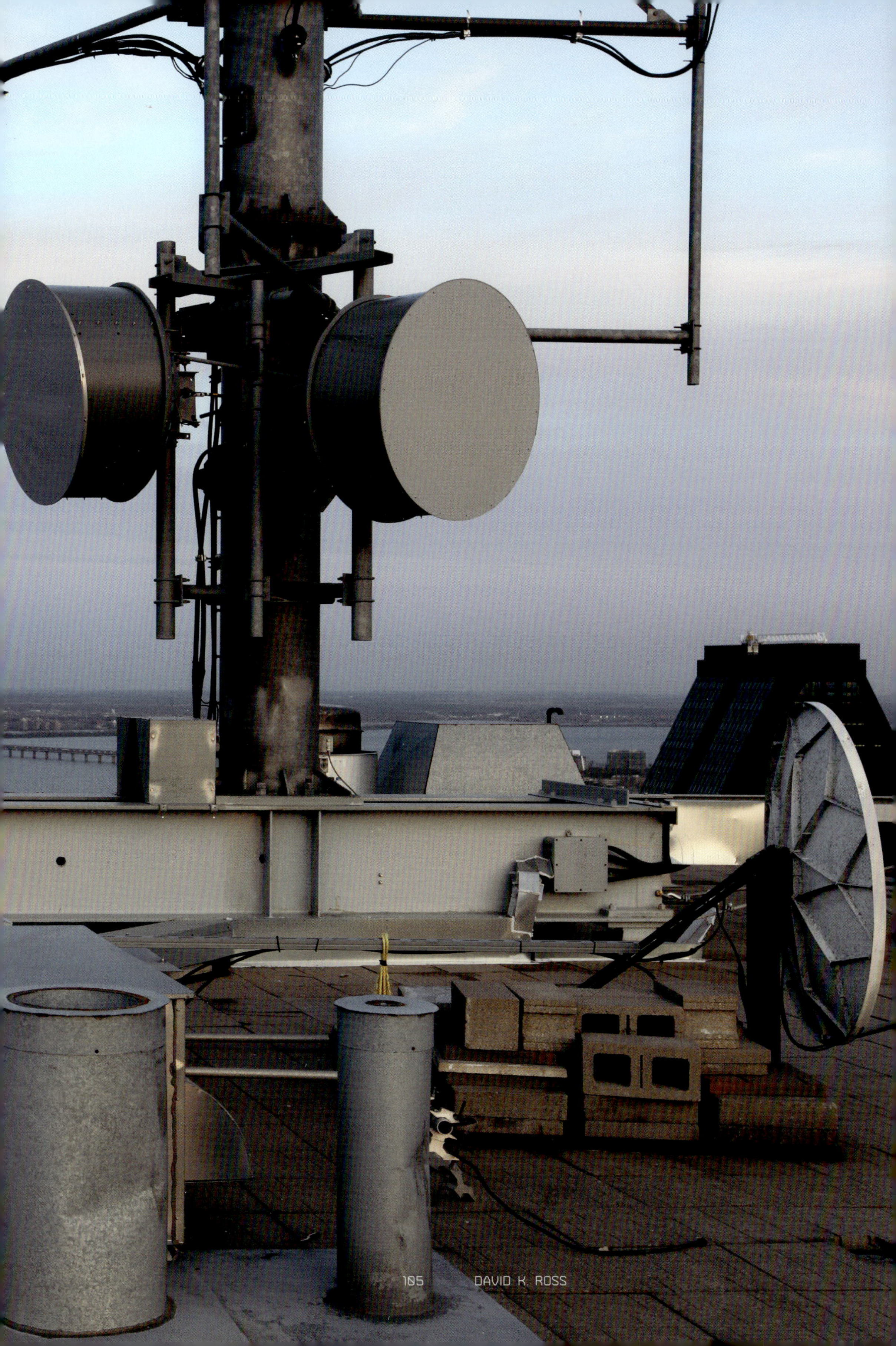

 DAVID K. ROSS

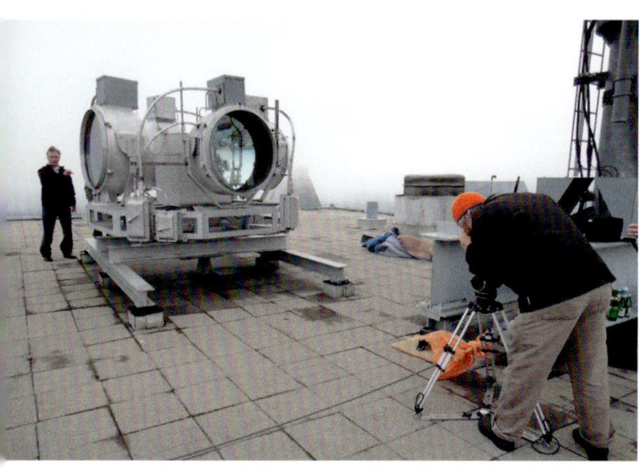 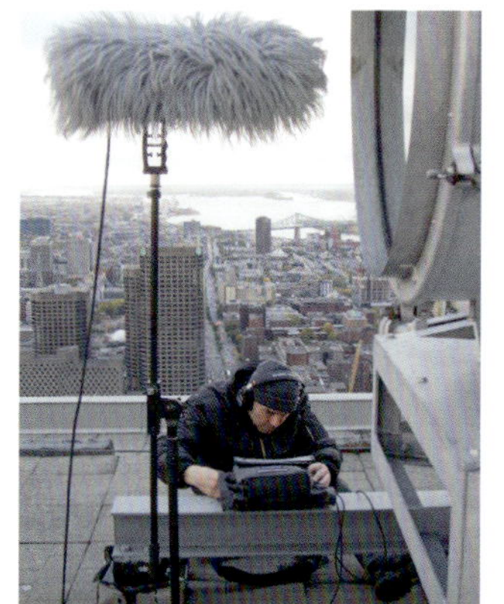 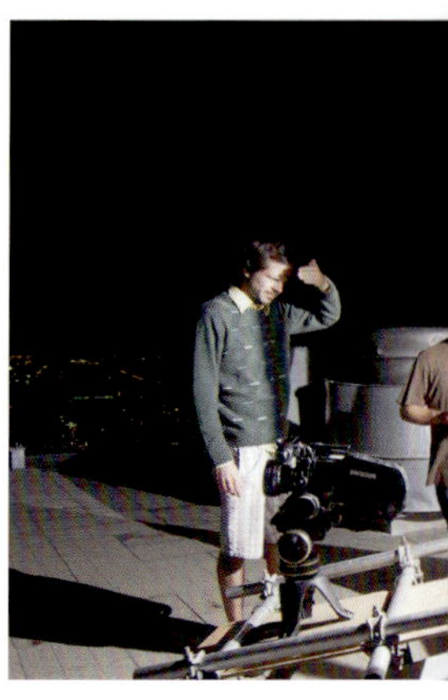

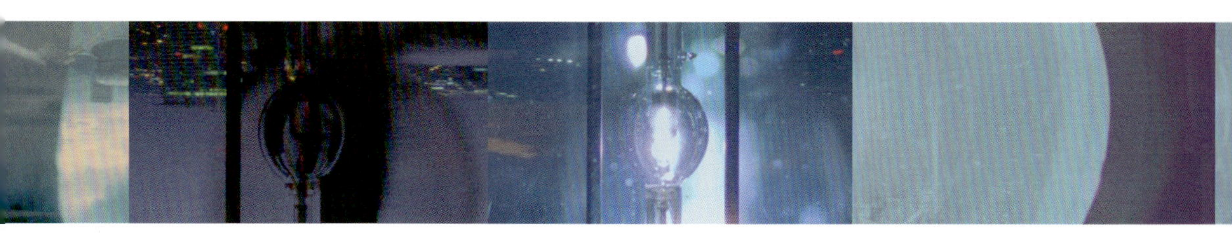

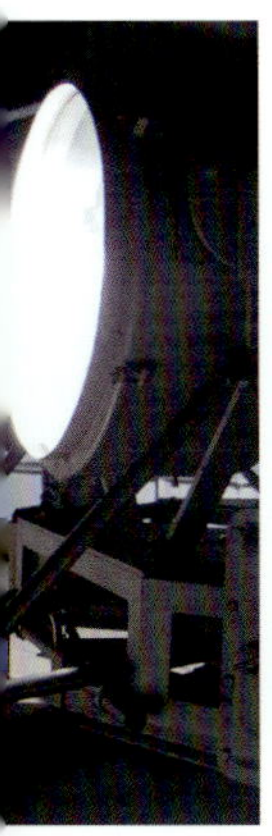
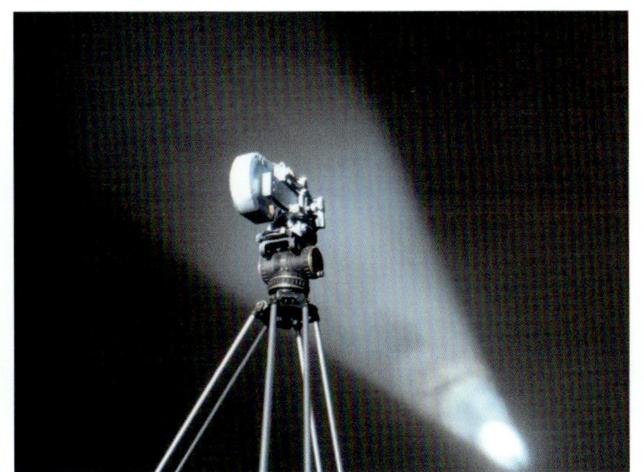
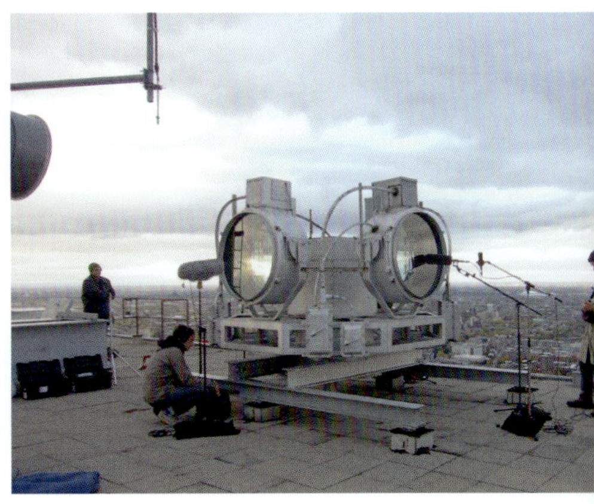
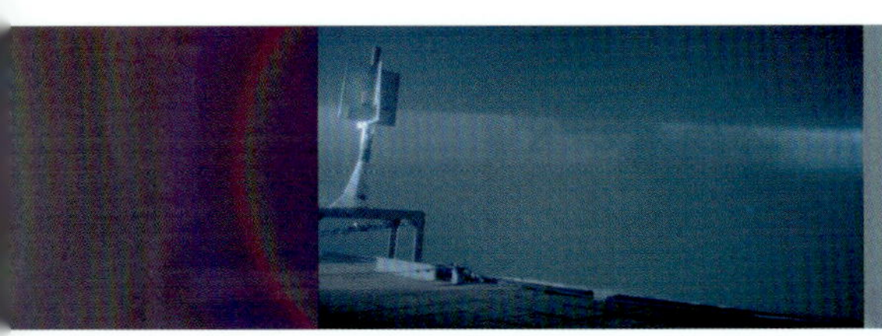
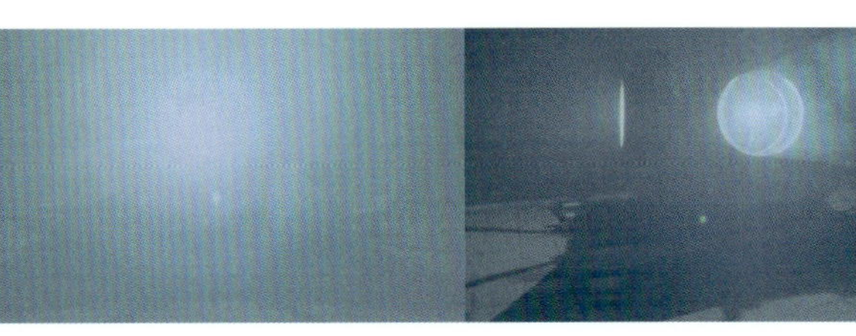

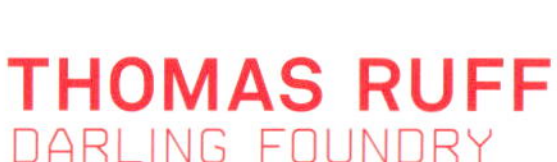

Exhibited Work

ma.r.s., 2010–ongoing
Chromogenic prints, 255 x 185 cm each.

Thomas Ruff's long-term interest in astronomy is evident in many of his works throughout his career. His most recent series, *ma.r.s* (2010–ongoing), continues his fascination with space exploration. This series is produced from images sent back from the Mars Reconnaissance Orbiter. Ruff has reconfigured these images by adding colour and changing the perspective to suggest that the camera is hovering over the planet. This gives the impression that the planet is in a constant state of flux, while the surface appears to be liquid. Maybe Ruff has found life on Mars.

Born in 1958 in Zell am Harmersbach, Germany, Thomas Ruff lives and works in Düsseldorf. He is the recipient of the PHotoEspaña 2011 Award and the 2006 ICP Infinity Award. Major museums worldwide have presented his works, including the Museum of Contemporary Art Chicago (2011); Kunsthalle Wien in Vienna (2009); and the Moderna Museet in Stockholm (2007). His retrospective exhibition *Thomas Ruff: Photographs 1979 to Present* travelled to nine museums between 2001 and 2004. His works are in the collections of the Art Institute of Chicago, the Dallas Museum of Art, the Hamburger Bahnhof-Museum, the Hirshhorn Museum and Sculpture Garden in Washington, D.C., as well as the Metropolitan Museum of Art and the Guggenheim Museum in New York. Ruff is represented by David Zwirner in New York, the Gagosian Gallery in London, Johnen Galerie in Berlin, and Galerie Wilma Tolksdorf in Frankfurt.

p. **109** \ *ma.r.s.01_III*, 2011
p. **110** \ *ma.r.s.24*, 2011
p. **111** \ *ma.r.s.04_I*, 2011

Courtesy of the artist
© Thomas Ruff / SODRAC (2013)
NASA / JPL / University of Arizona

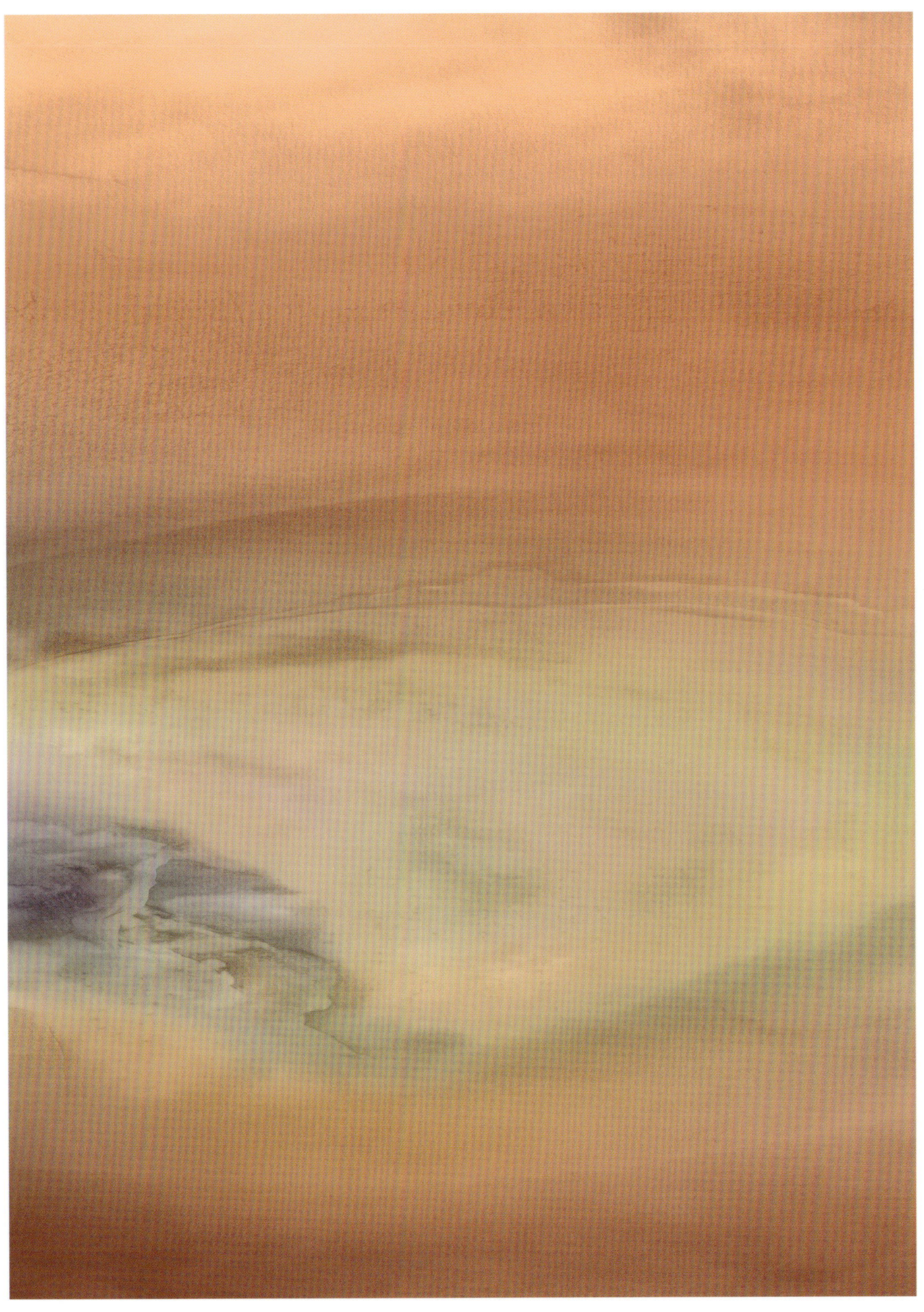

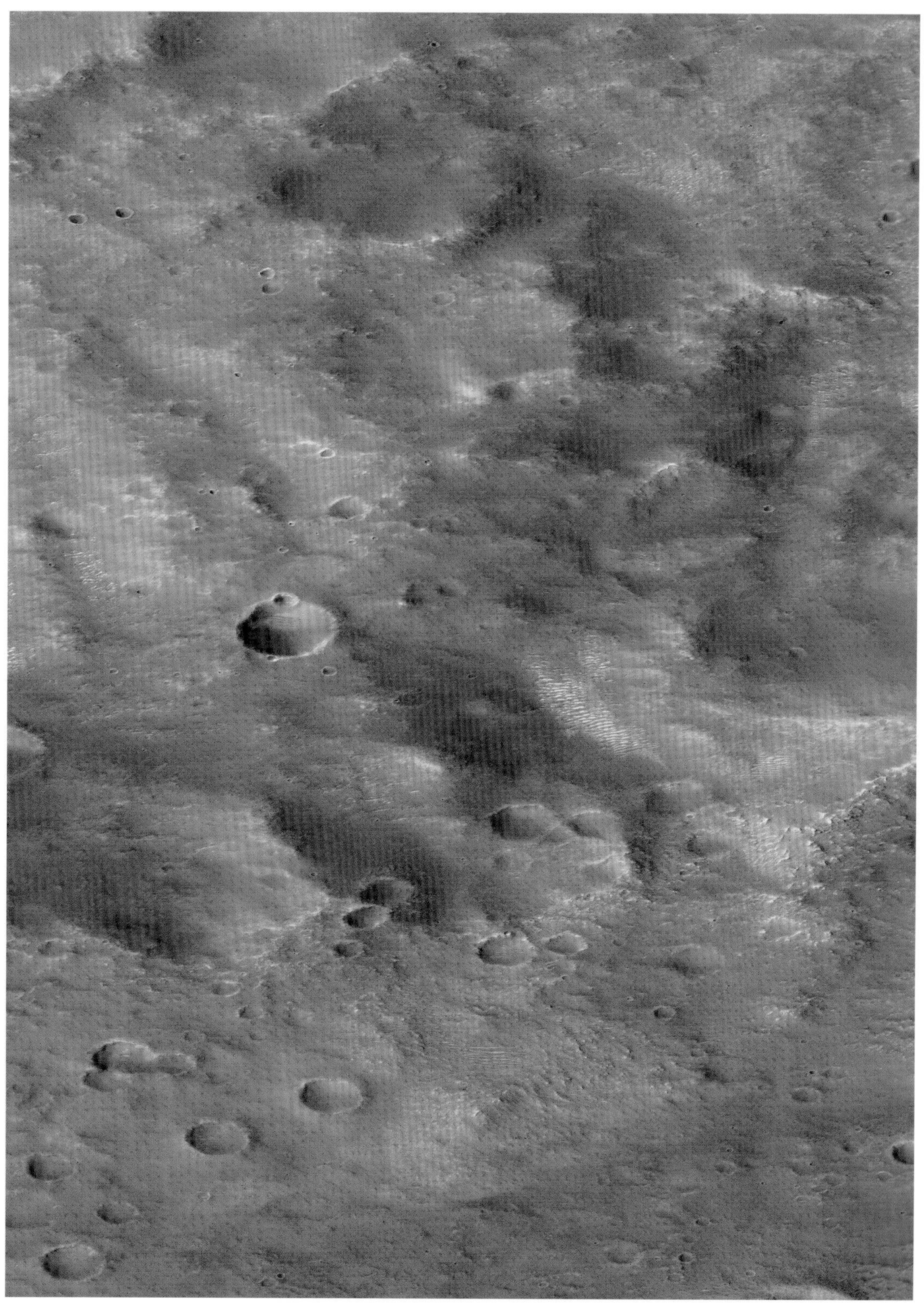

    THOMAS RUFF

    THOMAS RUFF

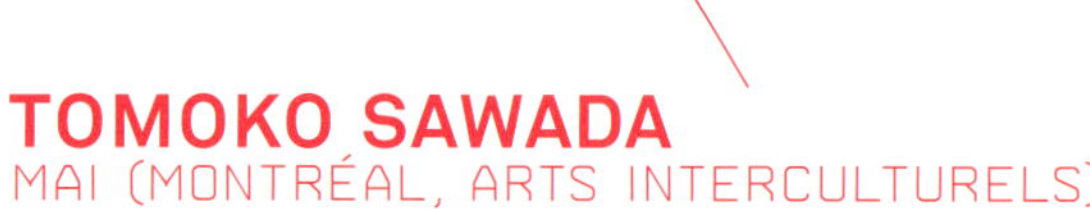

TOMOKO SAWADA
MAI (MONTRÉAL, ARTS INTERCULTURELS)

Exhibited Works

ID400, 1998
4 frames, 100 gelatin silver prints each, frame: 124.5 x 99.5 cm,
each sheet: 10.3 x 8.8 cm. Edition of 15.

SKINHEAD, 1998
4 gelatin silver prints, 114 x 89 cm each. Edition of 15.

Tomoko Sawada's *ID400* (1998) was produced while she was a student in Kobe. "The photo machine, a small vending machine-like contraption, can be found in numerous locations around the city." Sawada spent weeks changing her physical appearance with make-up, clothing, and hairstyles, creating 400 different identities using a machine whose sole purpose is to produce stable images for official documents. The facial characteristics are so varied that the photographic project becomes a compelling study of physiognomy.

Born in 1977 in Kobe, Japan, Tomoko Sawada lives and works in Kobe and New York. She is the recipient of the Higashikawa Prize in 2008, photo-eye's Best Books of 2006, the Bleue Mer Award in 2006, and the ICP Infinity Award in 2004. She has exhibited extensively, including at the Andy Warhol Museum in Pittsburgh (2012); the Joan Miró Foundation in Barcelona (2008); and the Museum of Modern Art (MoMA) in New York (2005). Her works are in major public collections, including the National Museum of Modern Art in Kyoto, the Maison Européenne de la Photographie in Paris, MoMA, and the International Center of Photography in New York. Sawada is represented by MEM Gallery in Tokyo. \ www.e-sawa.com

p. 113 \ Frame from the series *ID400*
p. 114 \ *SKINHEAD*
p. 115 \ Details from the series *ID400*

Courtesy of the artist and MEM, Tokyo
© Tomoko Sawada

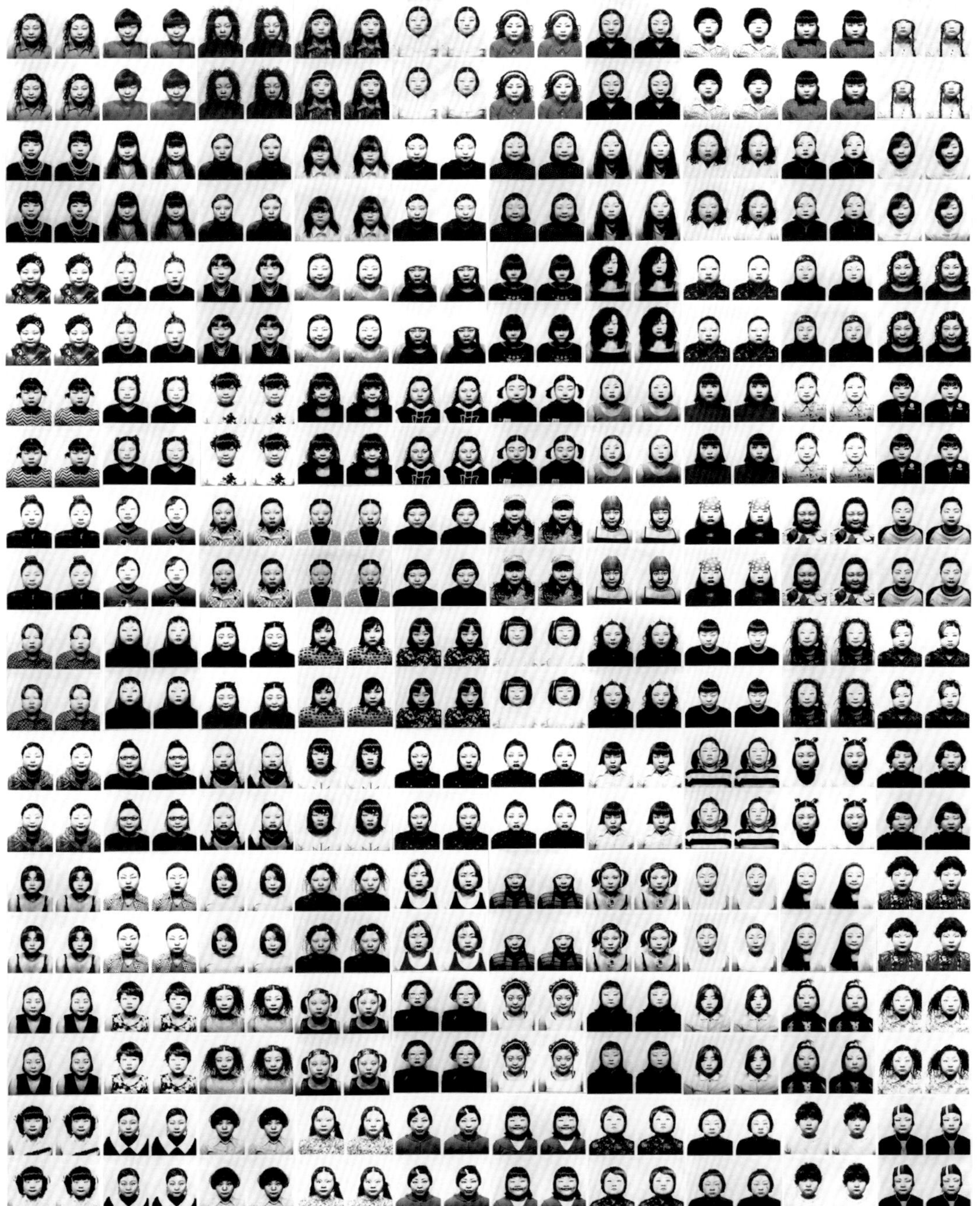

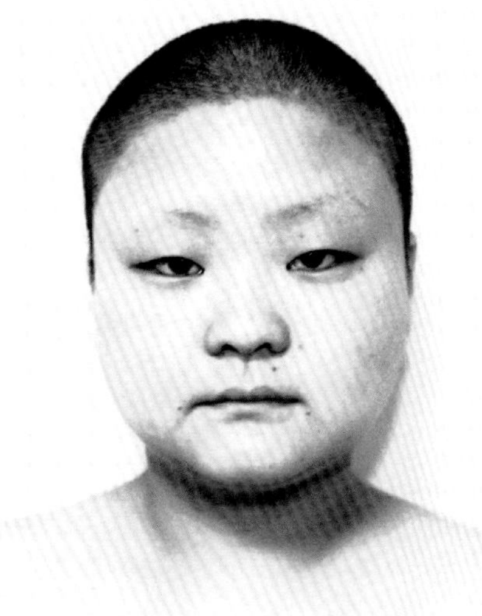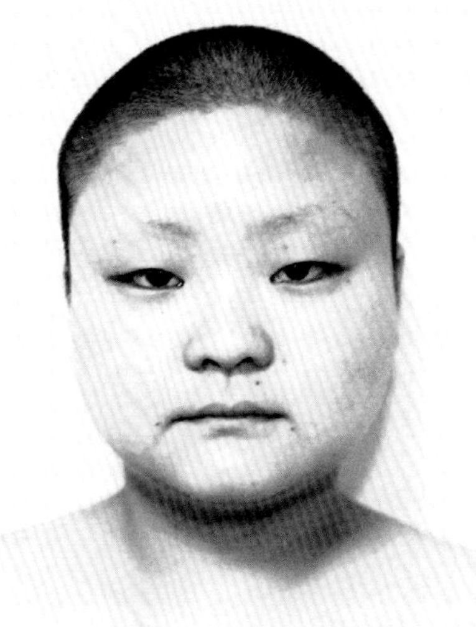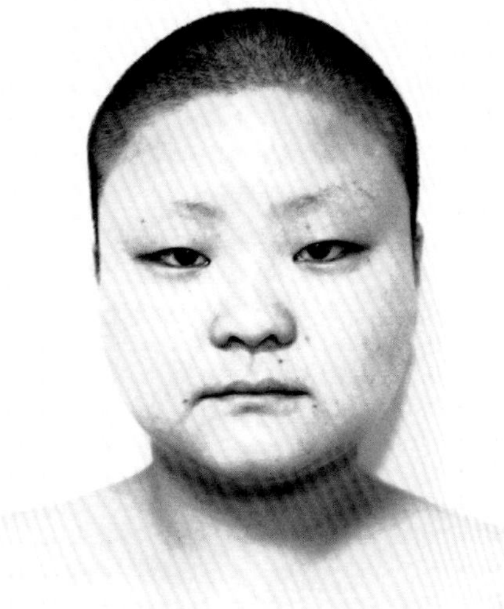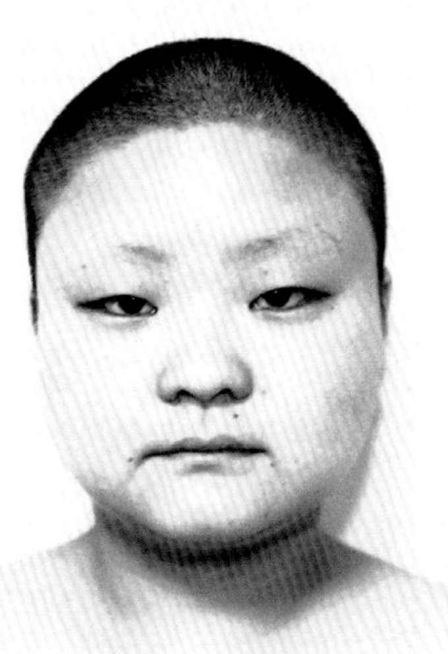

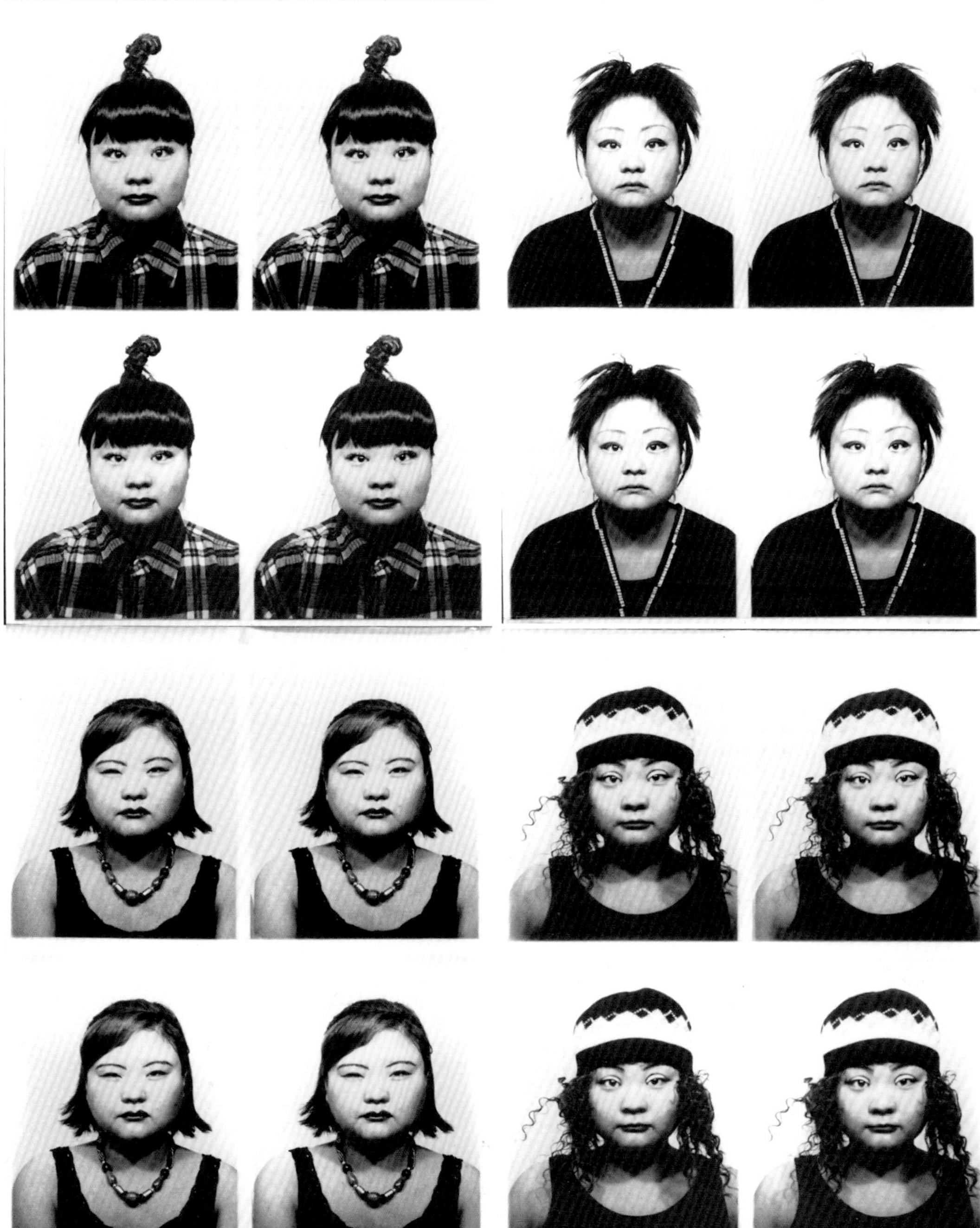

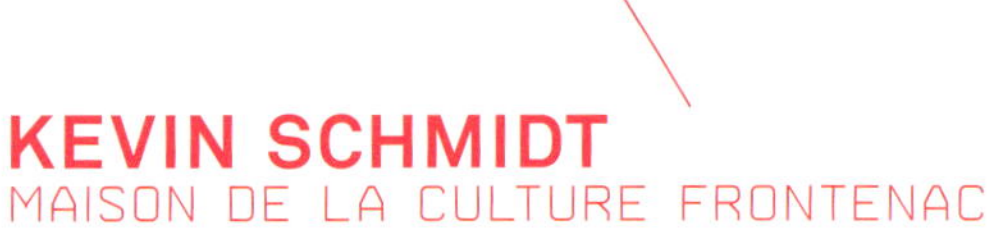

KEVIN SCHMIDT
MAISON DE LA CULTURE FRONTENAC

Exhibited Work

High Altitude Balloon Harmless Amateur Radio Equipment, 2013
Projection of a 4" x 5" transparency.

For his work *High Altitude Balloon Harmless Amateur Radio Equipment* (2013), Kevin Schmidt launched a large camera 35,000 metres above Earth by attaching it to a weather balloon. The timing and right conditions to release the shutter are carefully calculated so that the camera points away from the sun toward the horizon. The resulting 4" x 5" transparency photograph of the stratosphere is presented as a large projection in the gallery. The viewer standing between the projector and the image becomes part of the aerial scene as a silhouette. Playing with themes of modernity, landscape, and technology, this work suggests a new form of the sublime – one not indebted to the romantic idea of experiencing nature first-hand, but based on extending the human vision by technical means.

Born in 1972 in Ottawa, Kevin Schmidt lives and works in Vancouver. In 2008, he received the VIVA Award from the Jack and Doris Shadbolt Foundation for the Visual Arts in Vancouver. He has had solo exhibitions at the Justina M. Barnicke Gallery and the Power Plant Contemporary Art Gallery in Toronto (2011); the Musée d'art contemporain de Montréal (2011); the Catriona Jeffries Gallery in Vancouver (2010); Galerie van der Mieden in Antwerp (2009); and Galerie Barbara Thumm in Berlin (2009). His works have been in group exhibitions at the Anchorage Museum (2012); the Leonard & Bina Ellen Art Gallery in Montreal (2010); and the Vancouver Art Gallery (2009), among others. Schmidt is represented by Catriona Jeffries Gallery in Vancouver. \ www.catrionajeffries.com

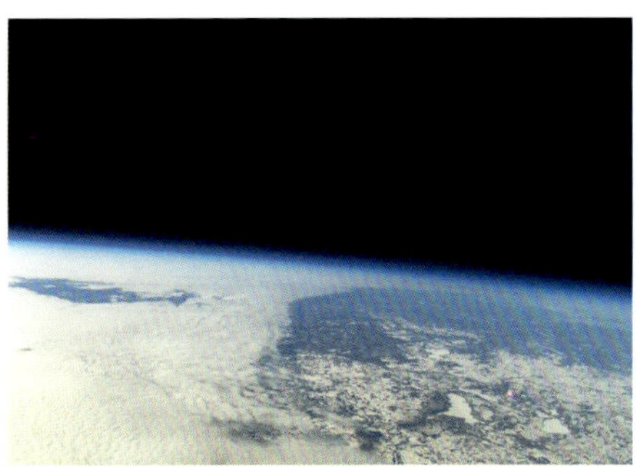

p. 5 \ Detail from a production photo for *High Altitude Balloon Harmless Amateur Radio Equipment*, 2012.
Photo: Barry Sloan
Right \ Video still taken at the same moment as the 4" x 5" shutter tripping during first attempt, 2012.
Photo: Kevin Schmidt
p. 117 \ Production photo, 2012. Photo: Barry Sloan
p. 118 \ 4" x 5" camera for high-altitude balloon, 2012.
Photo: Kevin Schmidt
p. 118 \ Production photo, 2012. Photo: Kevin Schmidt

Courtesy the artist and Catriona Jeffries Gallery, Vancouver

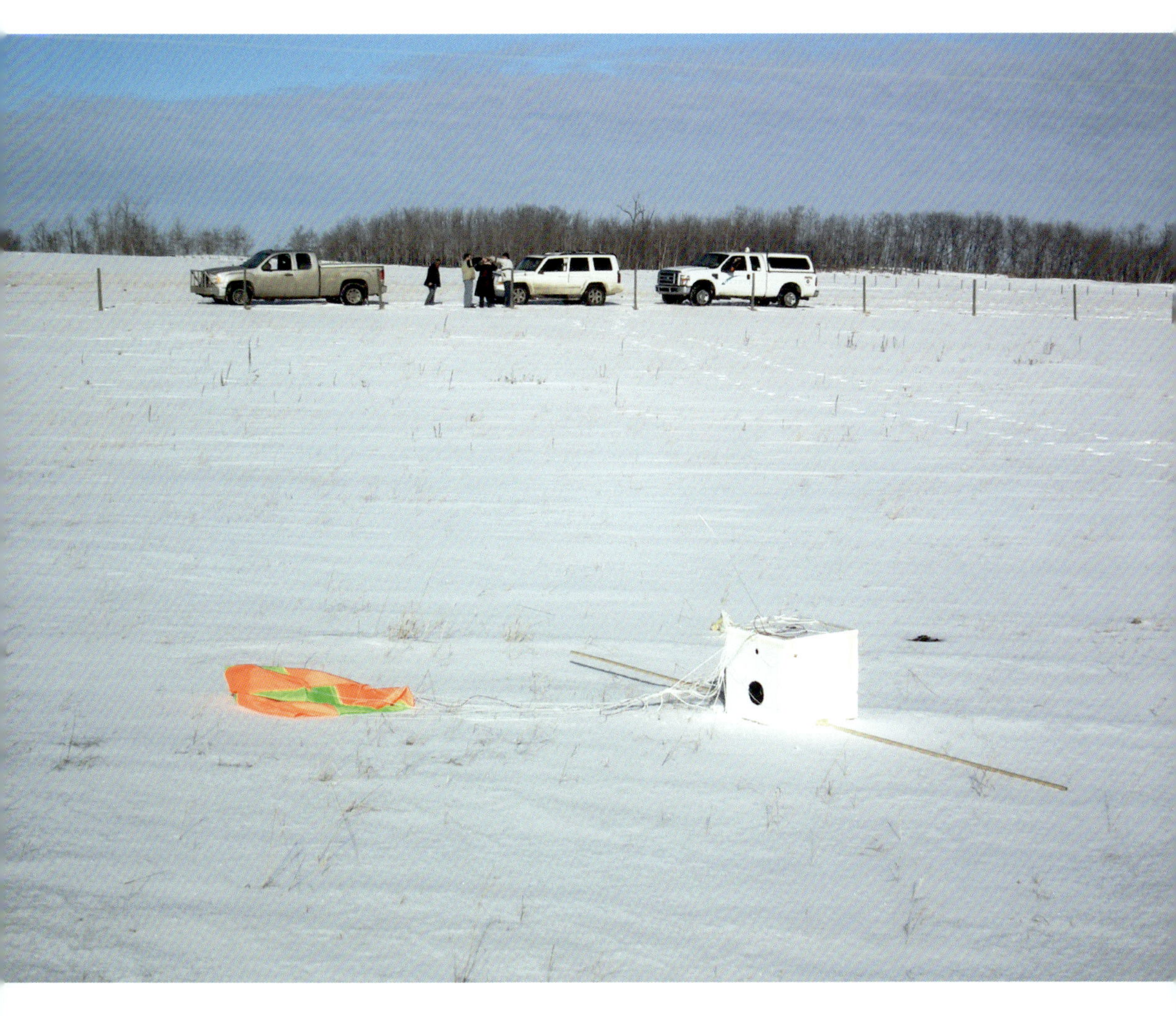

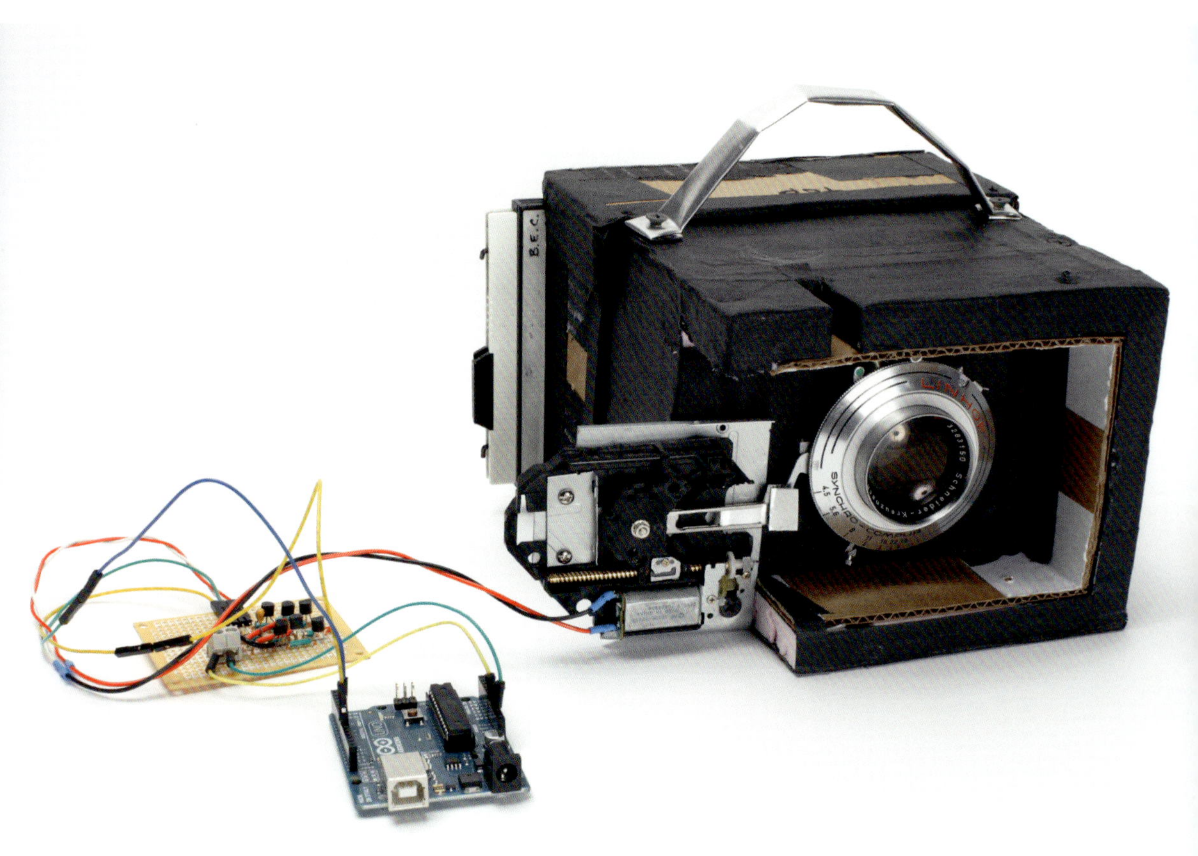

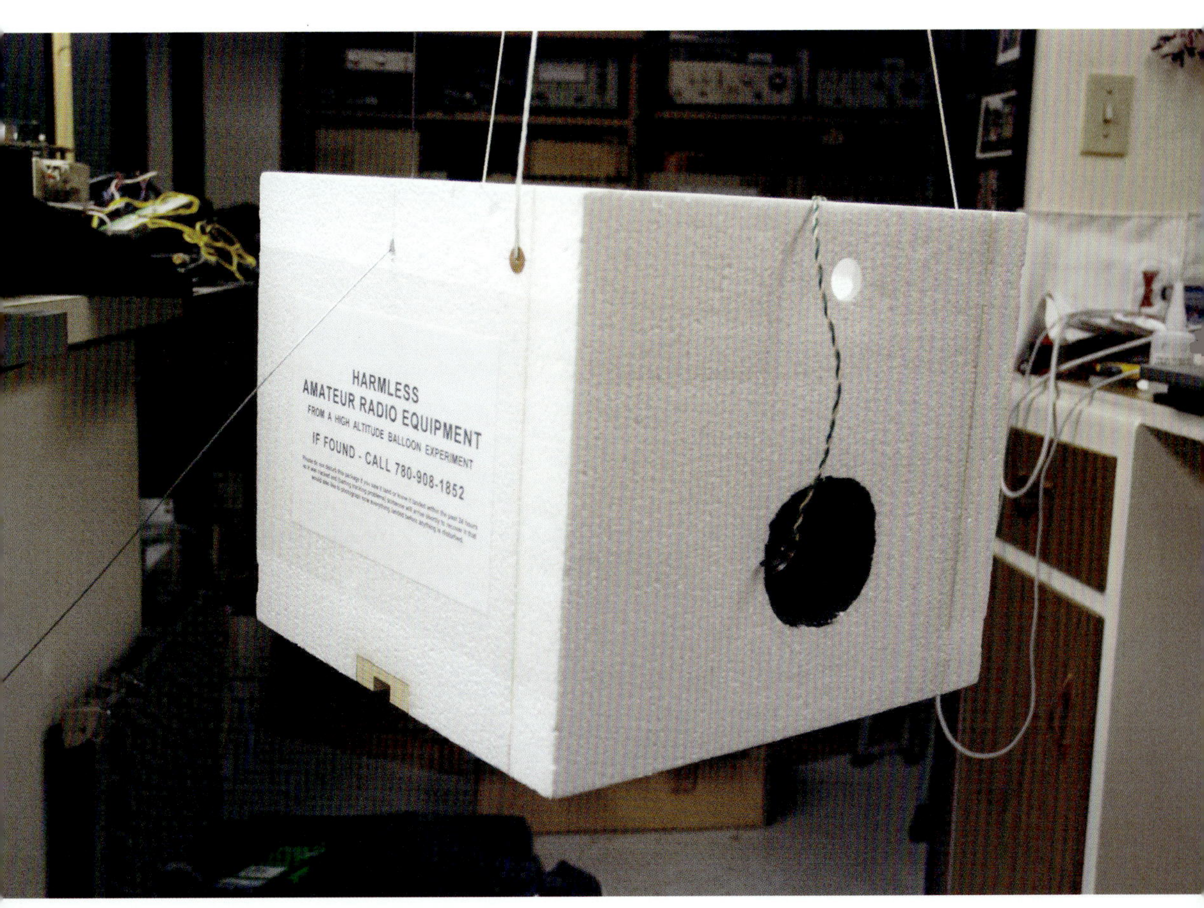
HARMLESS
AMATEUR RADIO EQUIPMENT
FROM A HIGH ALTITUDE BALLOON EXPERIMENT
IF FOUND - CALL 780-908-1852

CHERYL SOURKES
GALERIE B-312

Exhibited Works

Everybody's Autobiography, 2012
Interactive projection, variable dimensions.

Facebook Albums, 2010
iPad presentation, colour digital images, variable dimensions.

BRB, 2010
Video projection of an ebook, variable dimensions.

Webcams and social media sites have now become ubiquitous, integrated into our daily life; we have forgotten that they are silently watching the human condition. Images are shared and exchanged with little consideration for the content depicted. The once-private space of the home, previously witnessed only by its inhabitants, is now available online for all to view. For some years, Cheryl Sourkes has been excavating webcams and social media sites, seeking suitable material to make works such as *Everybody's Autobiography* (2012), *Facebook Albums* (2010), and *BRB* (2010). In these artworks she raises questions about the relationship between voyeurism and surveillance and the boundaries between public and private.

Born in 1945 in Montreal, Cheryl Sourkes lives and works in Toronto. She studied psychology and biology at McGill University in Montreal before attending Simon Fraser University in Vancouver. In 2007, the National Gallery of Canada (NGC) in Ottawa presented her travelling exhibition *Public Camera*, also shown at the Tom Thomson Art Gallery in Owen Sound, the Southern Alberta Art Gallery in Lethbridge, and Peak Gallery in Toronto. In 2012, her works were featured in the *Desire* exhibition hosted by the Bergen Kunsthall in Norway. Her works are in both private and public collections, including the Canadian Museum of Contemporary Photography and the NGC in Ottawa, Museum London, the Seattle Art Museum, the Vancouver Art Gallery, and the Winnipeg Art Gallery. \ www.cherylsourkes.com

p. 121 \ Details from *Facebook Albums*. Photos: Cheryl Sourkes
p. 122 \ Details from *BRB*. Photos: Karen Asher
p. 123 \ Details from *Everybody's Autobiography*. Photos: Cheryl Sourkes

Courtesy of the artist

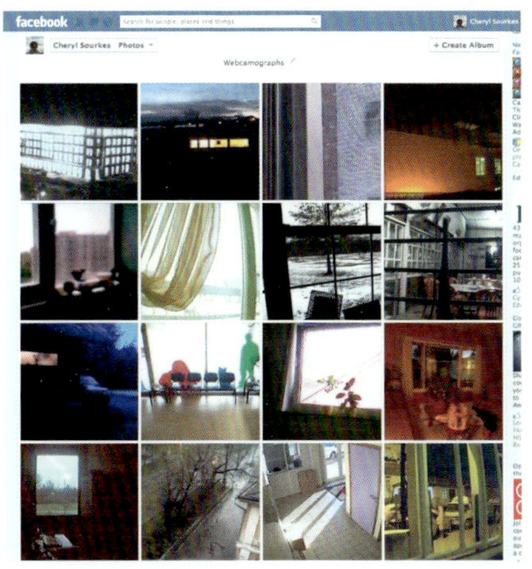

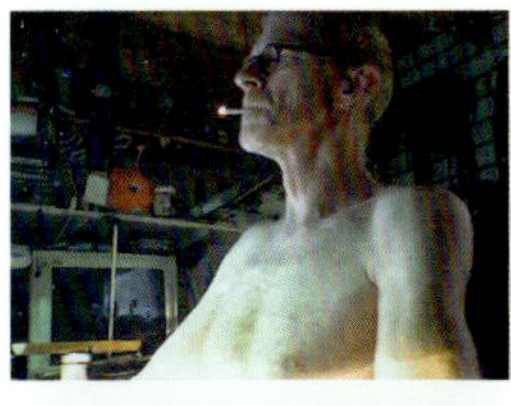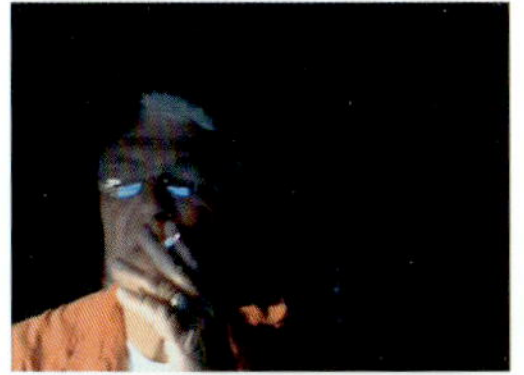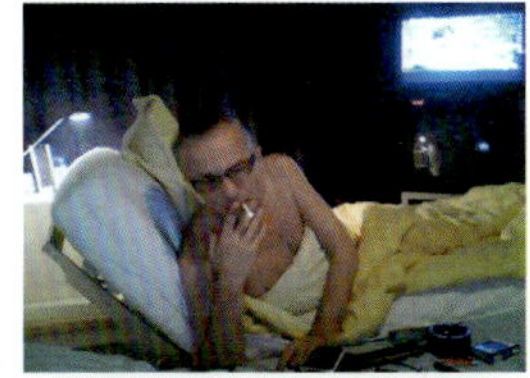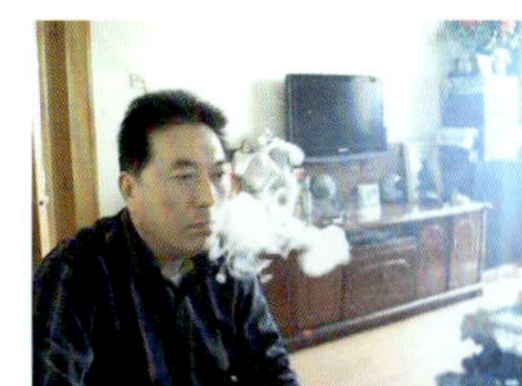

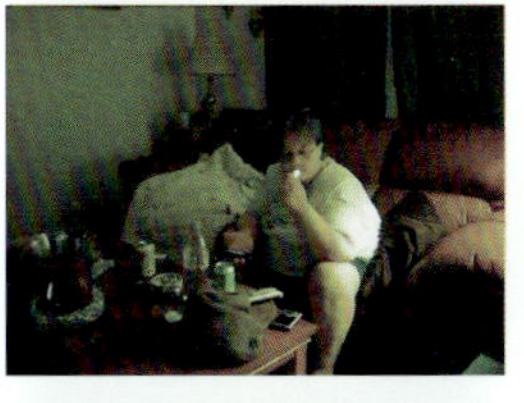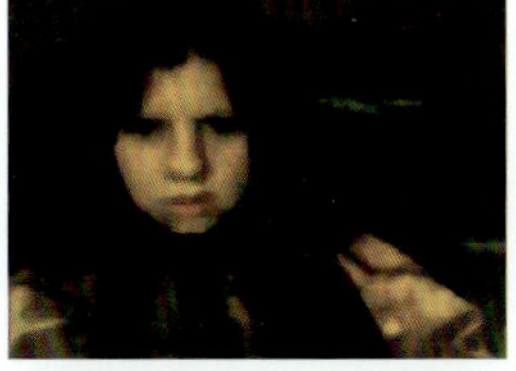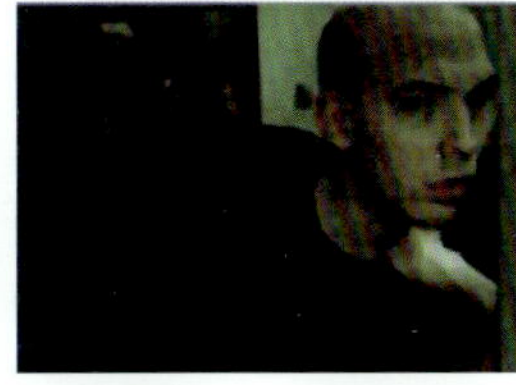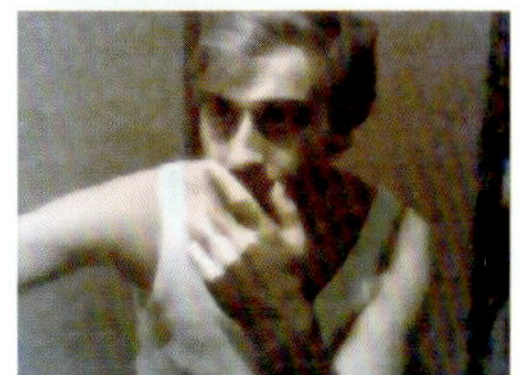

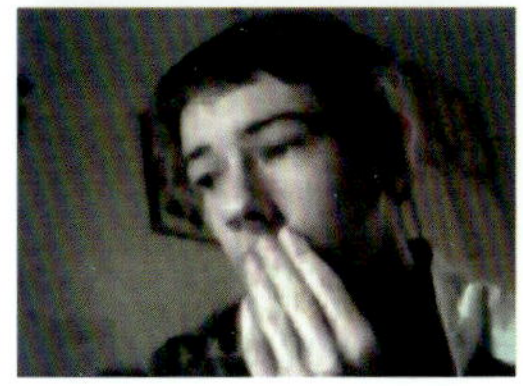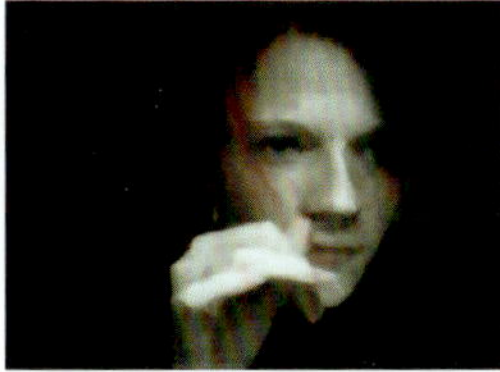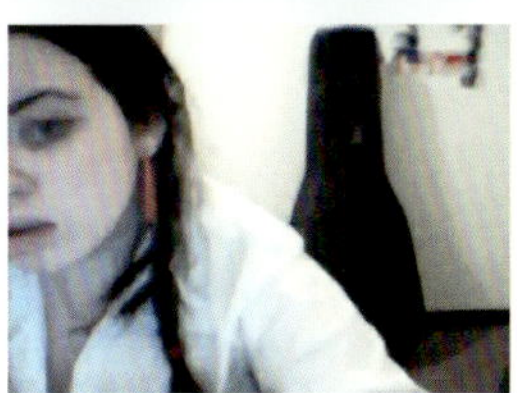

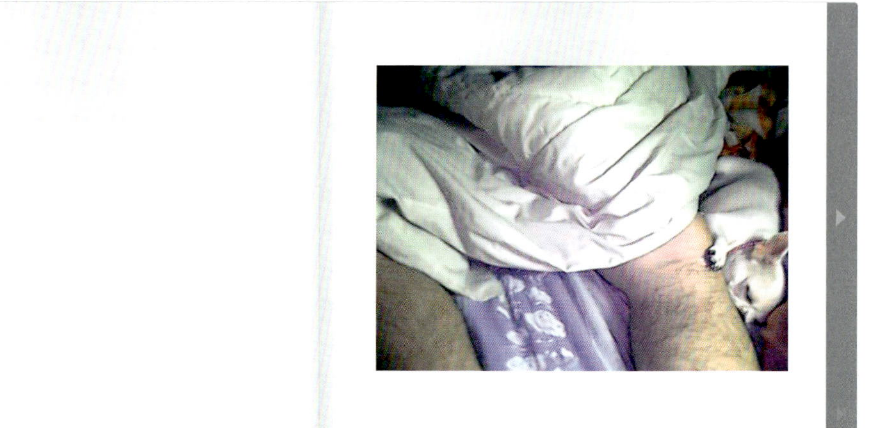

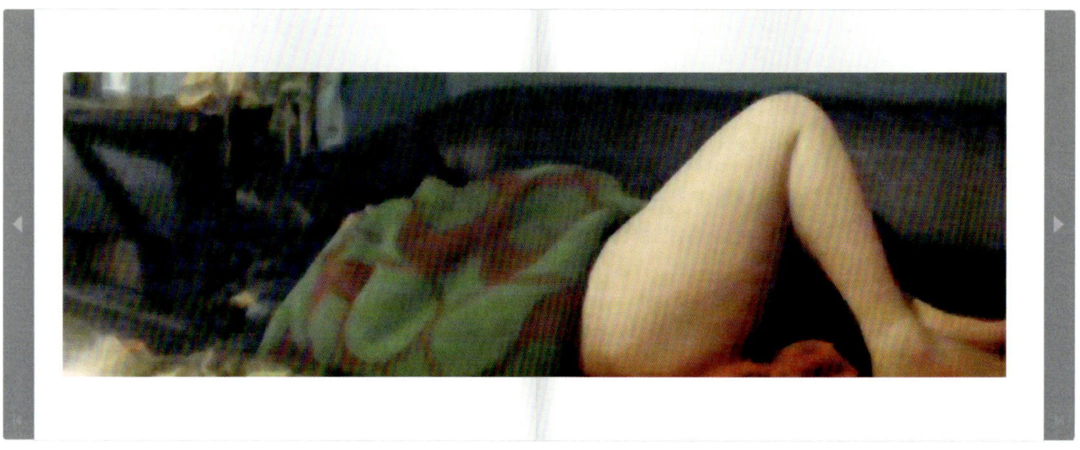

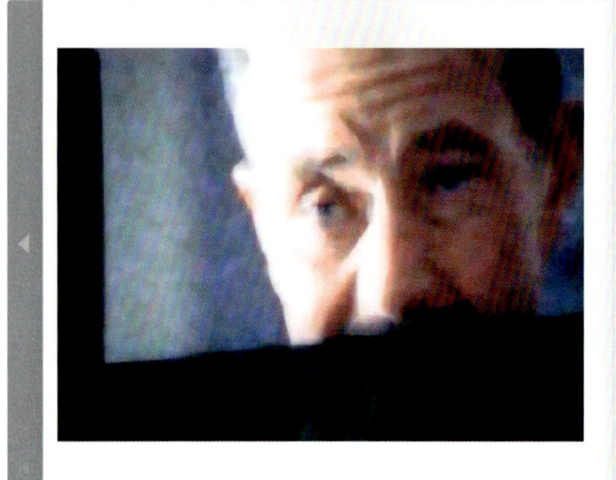

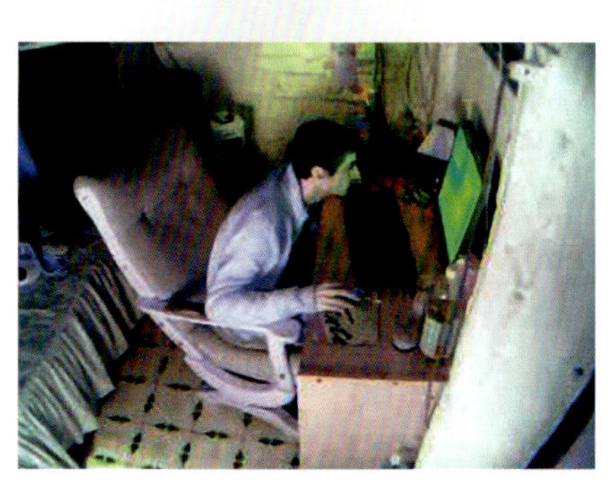

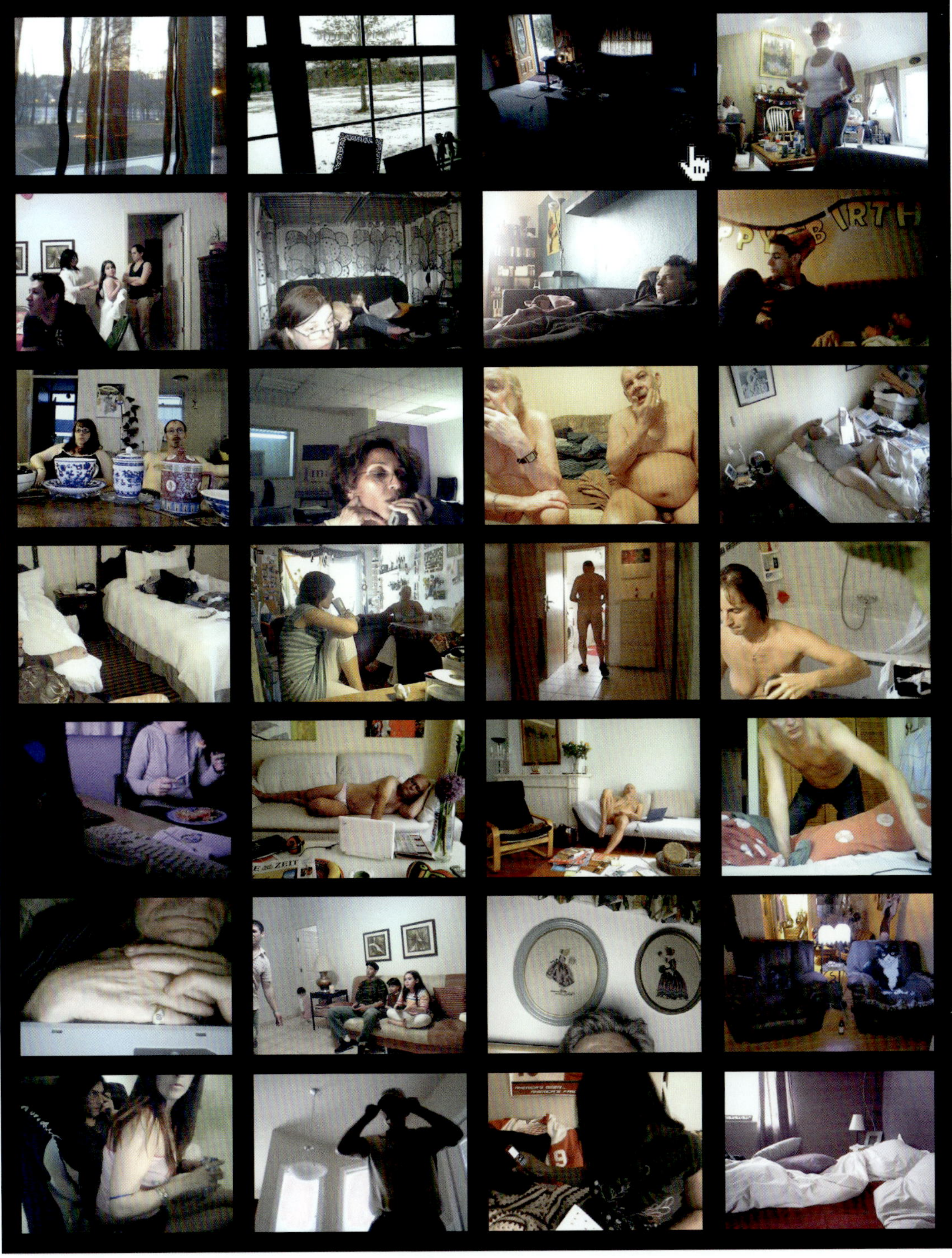

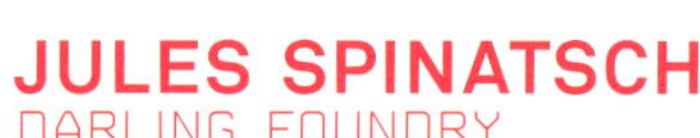

Exhibited Work

Vienna MMIX-17352/7000, Speculative Portrait of a Society, 2009–11

Site-adapted installation of *Surveillance Panorama No. 4*. \ 17,352 images recorded at the 2009 Vienna Opera Ball with interactive network cameras over the entire duration of the evening from 20:32 to 05:17. \ 7,000 participants. \ Exhibited parts: Size 1 to 1 Fragment of the complete panorama with full size of 4.87 x 54 m, with images in chronological order. \ Block *Les Illustres*, 120 single images, arranged in a grid, inkjet prints, 27 x 40 cm each. \ Diagram with timeline, program, and details of the evening, 40 x 50 cm. \ Some inkjet prints, 90 x 120 cm. \ Two book dummies, 33 x 24 cm each.

The Vienna Opera Ball is an annual event that dates back to the mid-nineteenth century at the time of the Austro-Hungarian Empire. Today it celebrates Austria's links to its past imperial power and is seen as the social event of the year. In recent times the ball has taken on a wider social meaning with demonstrations taking place outside the Opera against the opulence of the event. Jules Spinatsch's *Vienna MMIX 17352/7000, Speculative Portrait of a Society* (2009–11) depicts this grand occasion in minute detail. Two computer-controlled cameras, similar to surveillance cameras with telephoto lenses, scanned the event over an eight-hour period to make this expansive society portrait of the great and the good of Vienna.

Born in 1964 in Davos, Switzerland, Jules Spinatsch lives and works in Zurich and Vienna. Spinatsch received an Honorary Appreciation at the Stiftung Buchkunst in Leipzig, the Prix du Livre at Les Rencontres d'Arles in 2005, and the International BMW Photography Prize at Paris Photo 2004. His works have been exhibited at Fotomuseum Winterthur (2012); the Museum of Modern Art in New York (2007, 2012); the Nederlands Fotomuseum in Rotterdam (2011); the Walker Art Center in Minneapolis (2011); the Tate Modern in London (2010); the San Francisco Museum of Modern Art (2010); Kunsthaus Zug in Switzerland (2008); the Centre de la Photographie in Geneva (2008); the NRW Forum in Düsseldorf (2007); and Kunsthaus Zurich (2006), among others. \ www.jules-spinatsch.ch

p. 9, 125 \ Details from *Surveillance Panorama No. 4*: 2 single images from the block *Les Illustres*
pp. 126–27 \ Vienna MMIX – Plan B, Block *Les Illustres*, Blancpain art contemporain, Geneva, 2011

Courtesy of the artist; Blancpain art contemporain, Geneva; and Galerie Luciano Fasciati, Chur

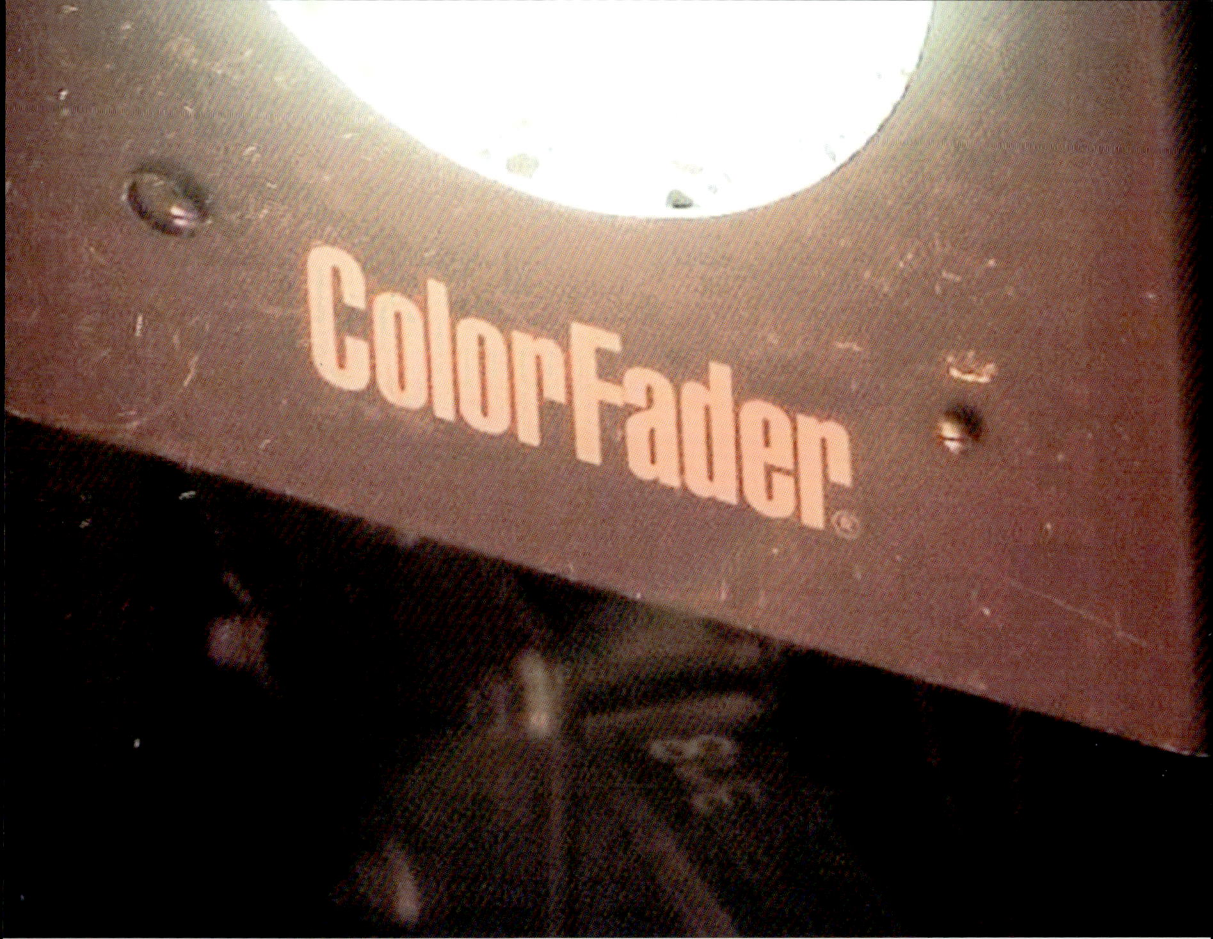

ColorFader

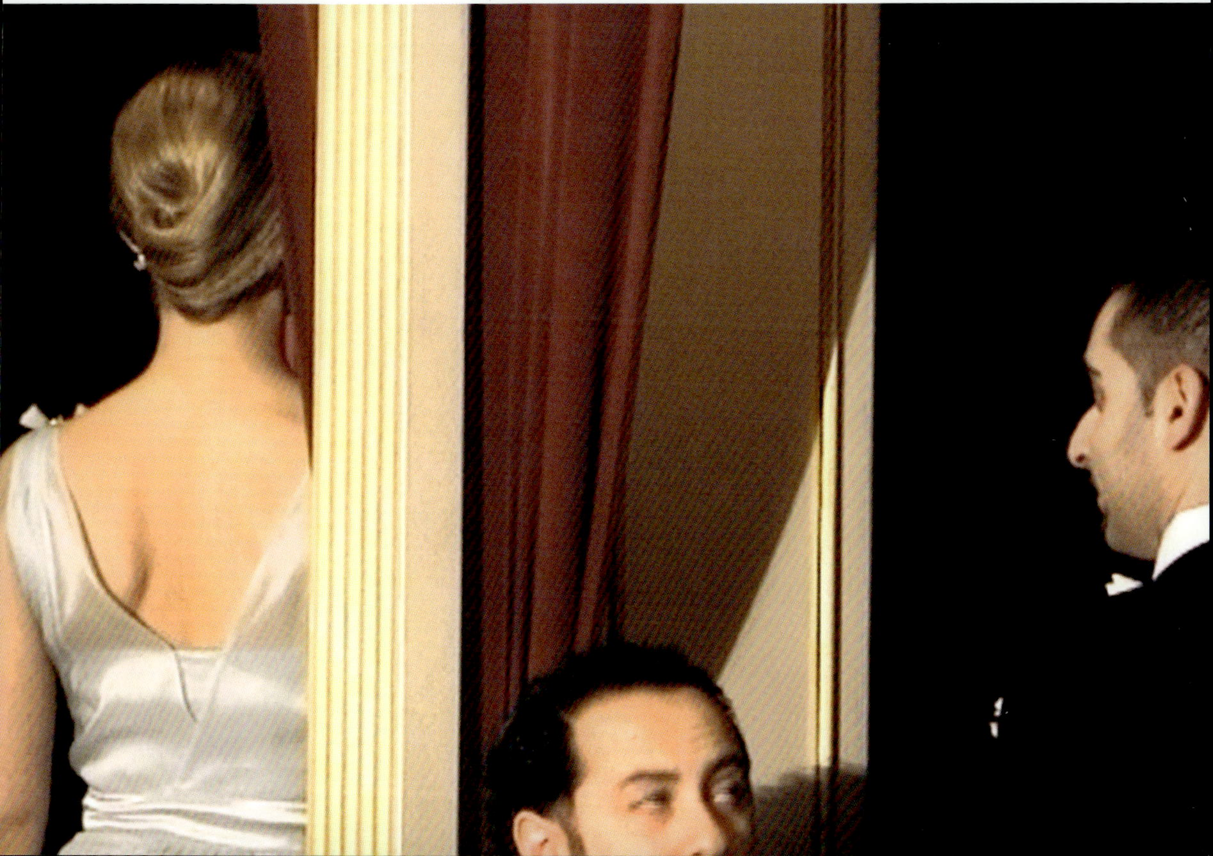

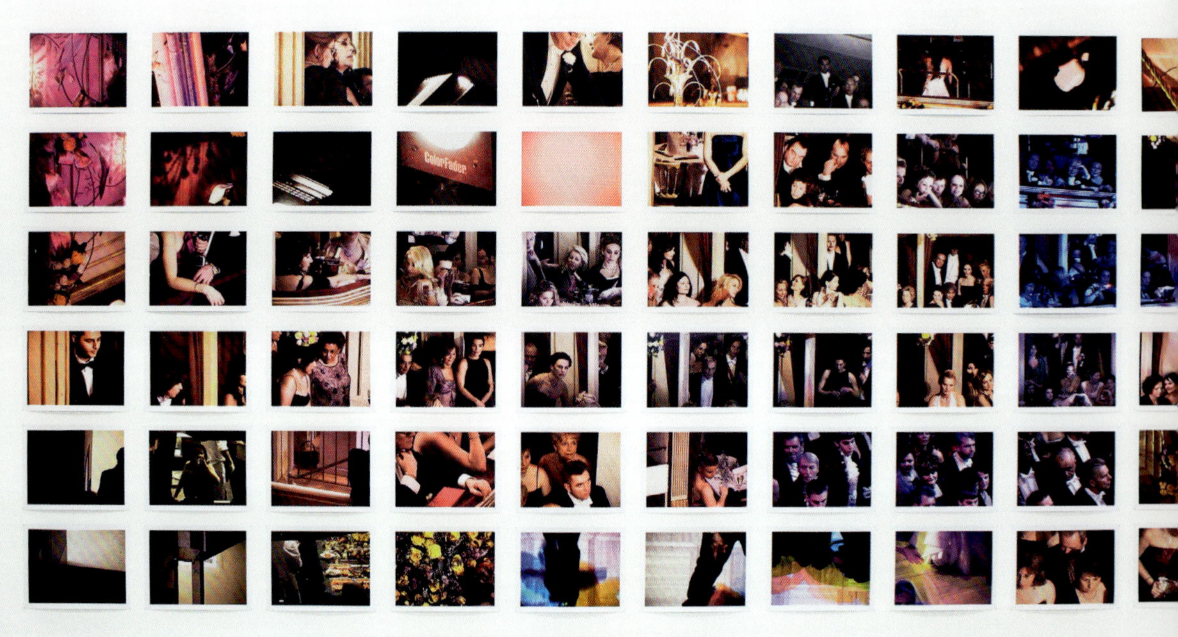

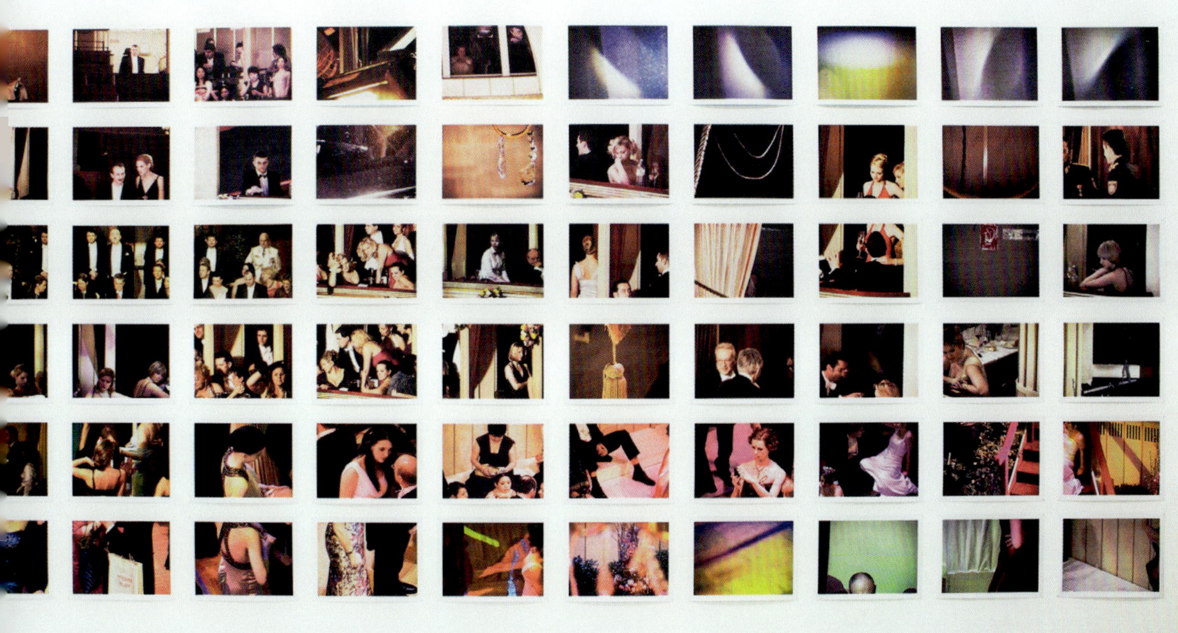

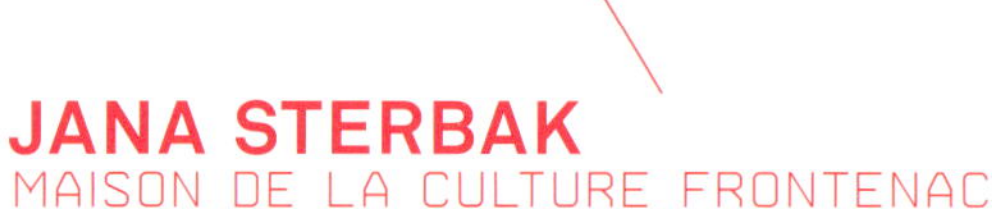

JANA STERBAK
MAISON DE LA CULTURE FRONTENAC

Exhibited Works

From Here To There, 2003
6-channel video installation, 12 min 30 s, colour, sound, loop, 6 video projectors, video server, variable dimensions. Soundtrack: Goldberg Variations by J. S. Bach performed by Glenn Gould (recording 1955).

Stanley Dog, 2010
Sculpture, silver leaf over resin with electronic elements and camera + plexi box, 60 × 85 × 35 cm.

Many of Jana Sterbak's artworks revolve around the themes of power, control, and the use of technology to transcend the limits of the human body. For her video installation *From Here To There* (2003), Stanley, a Jack Russell terrier, was set free to roam the Canadian landscape with a camera mounted on his back. Stanley's vision, based on his size and movement, might seem unstable and jerky, but it directly questions the human view of the world, which is seen to be permanent and steady. This work is an investigation of the relationship between animals and technology grounded on a range of senses that are "natural" and "mechanical."

Born in 1955 in Prague, Jana Sterbak moved to Canada in 1968, and she now lives and works in Montreal. In the past 20 years, she has had solo and group exhibitions in major museums worldwide, including the Musée d'art contemporain de Montréal (2011, 2012); the National Gallery of Canada (NGC) in Ottawa (2008, 2012); the Centre Pompidou in Paris (2009–10); the Museum of Modern Art in New York (1992); as well as at the Venice Biennale (2003). Her solo exhibition *Jana Sterbak: States of Being*, organized by the NGC, toured North America in 1991–92. She has received important awards, including the Governor General's Award in Visual and Media Arts in 2012 and the Chalmers Award from the Ontario Arts Council in 2000. Sterbak is represented by Galleria Raffaella Cortese in Milan, Barbara Gross Galerie in Munich, and Galerie Laroche/Joncas in Montreal. \ www.janasterbak.com

pp. 129–30 \ *Stanley Dog*, 2010. Photo: Lorenzo Palmieri
Courtesy of the artist and Galleria Raffaella Cortese, Milan

pp. 131–33 \ Video stills of *From Here To There*
Courtesy of the artist and Musée d'art contemporain de Montréal

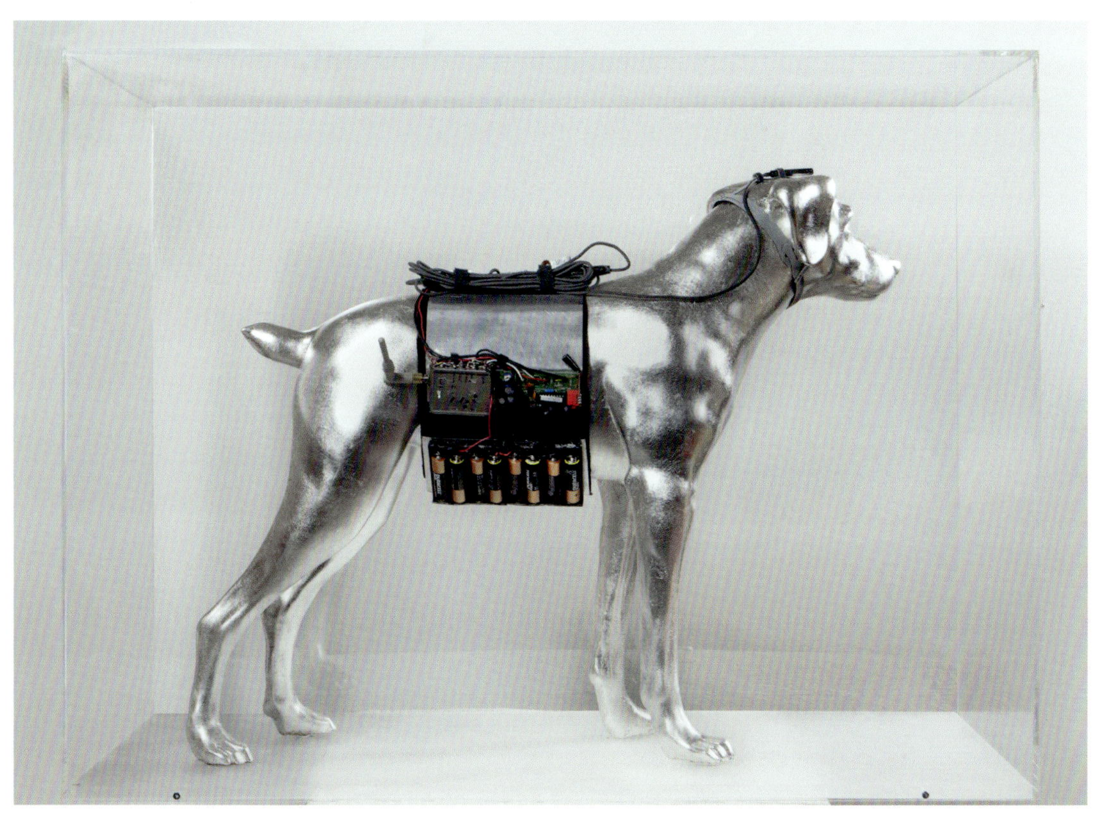

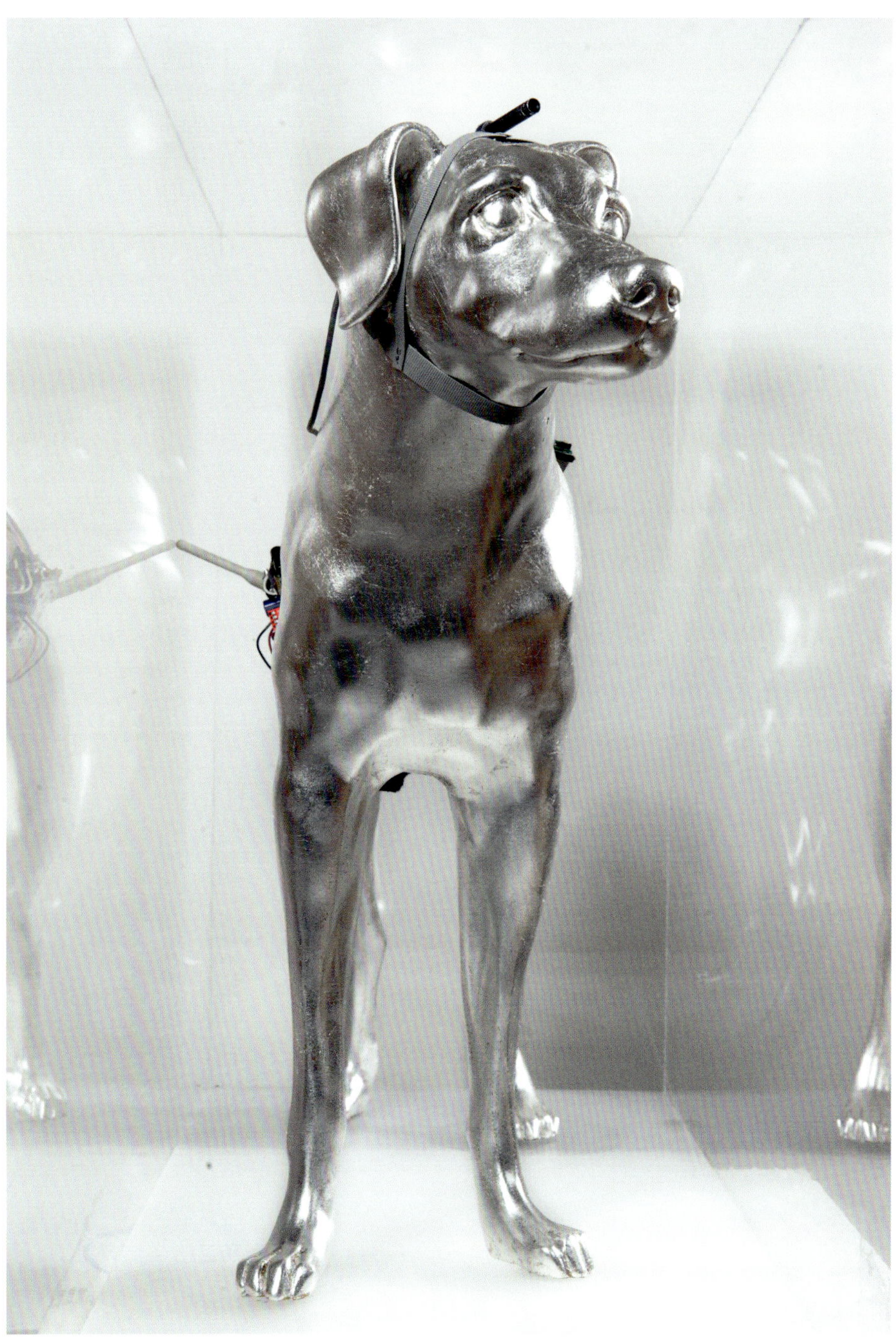

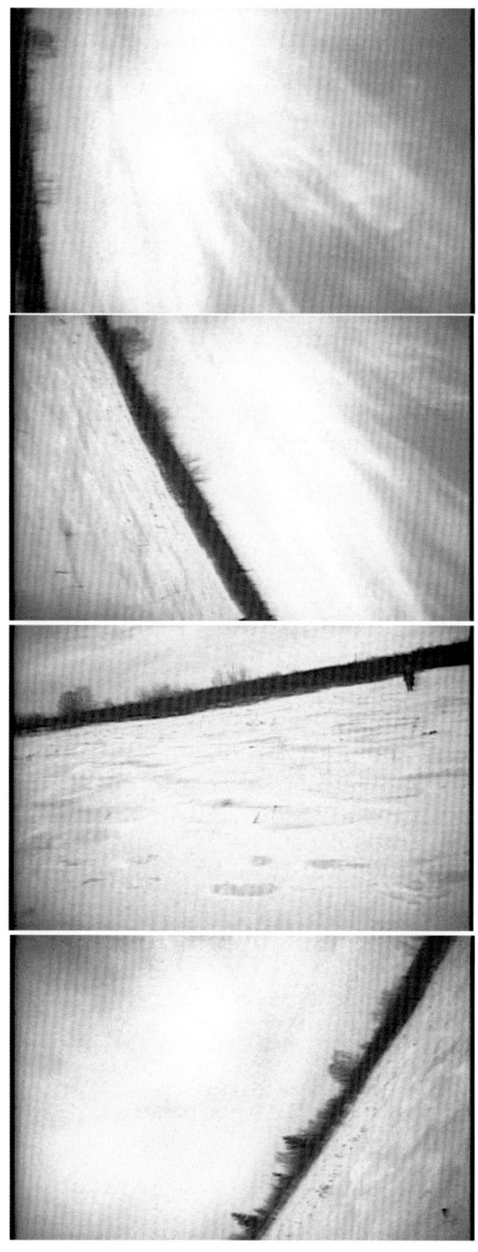

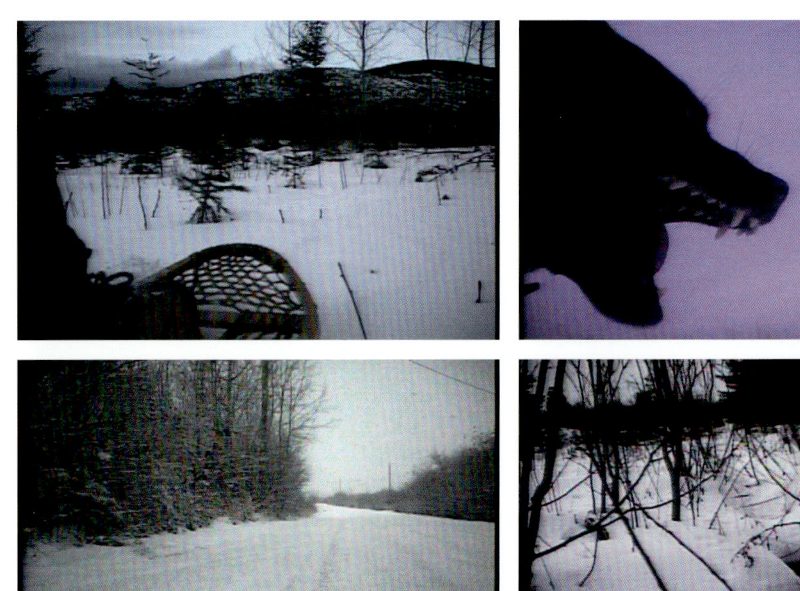

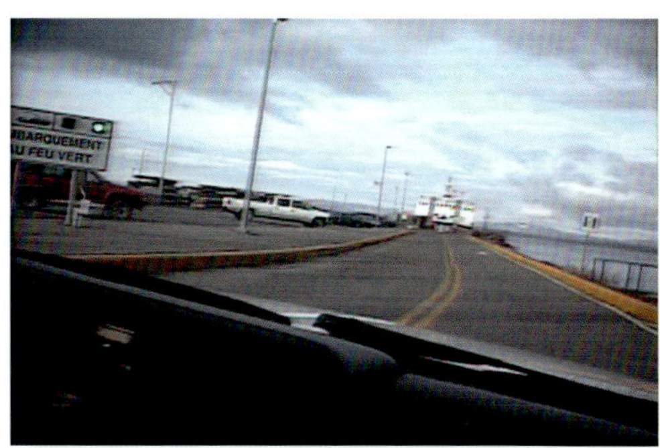
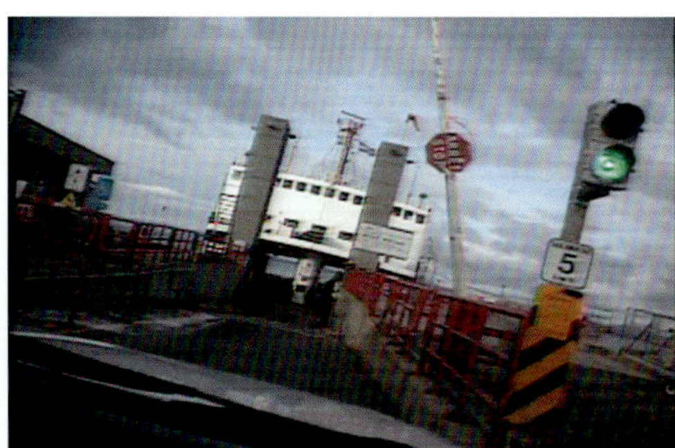
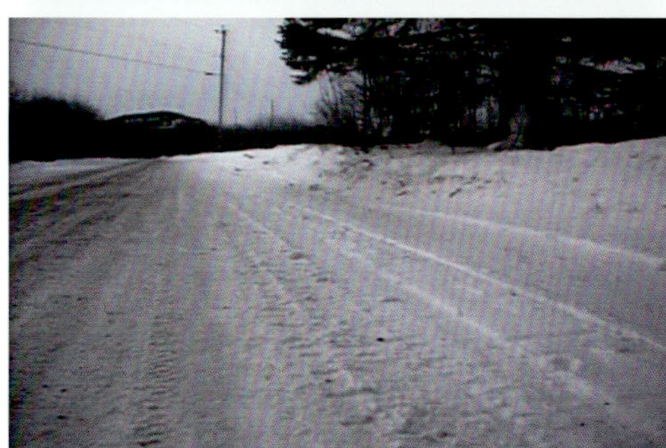
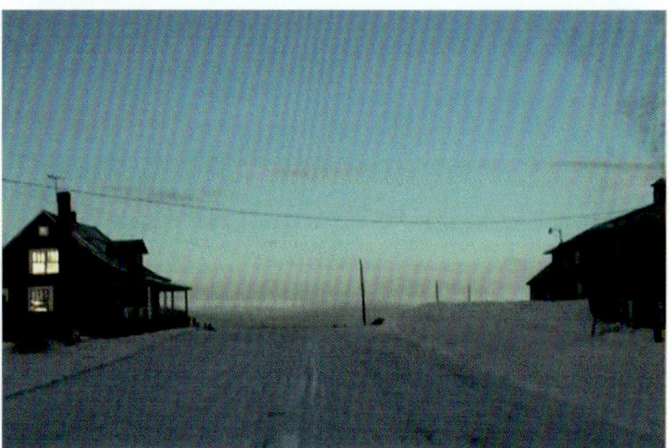

PENELOPE UMBRICO

Exhibited Works

Sunset Portraits from 12,193,606 Flickr Sunsets on 4/25/13, 2013
898 prints, 10.16 x 15.24 cm each.

TVs from Craigslist, 2009–12
78 chromogenic prints on metallic paper, 27.94 x 35.56 to 40.64 cm each.

Penelope Umbrico's work is a reinterpretation of vernacular photography that she has found on the Web or in printed catalogues. In her series *Sunset Portraits from 12,193,606 Flickr Sunsets on 4/25/13* (2013) and *TVs From Craigslist* (2009–12), she suggests that these anonymous images, one set depicting people standing in front of sunsets, the other made for selling televisions, have meanings different from those intended by the photographer or the original publisher of the image. They have a life beyond their original use.

Born in 1957 in Philadelphia, Penelope Umbrico grew up in Toronto. She lives and works in New York, where she received an MFA from the School of Visual Arts. Her works have featured in solo and group exhibitions at the FotoMuseum in Antwerp (2012); The Photographers' Gallery in London (2012); the Aperture Foundation Photography Gallery in New York (2009, 2012); Les Rencontres d'Arles (2011); the San Francisco Museum of Modern Art (2009); and P.S.1 Contemporary Art Center in New York (2009), among others. She has received numerous grants and fellowships, including a Smithsonian Artist Research Fellowship in 2012, a Guggenheim Fellowship in 2011, a New York Foundation of the Arts Fellowship in 2010, an Anonymous Was A Woman grant in 2009, and an Aaron Siskind Foundation Individual Photographer's Fellowship Grant in 2008. \ www.penelopeumbrico.net

p. 10 \ Detail from *Sunset Portraits from 8,462,359 Flickr Sunsets on 12/21/10*, 2010
p. 135 \ *Sunset Portraits from 9,623,557 Flickr Sunsets on 8/22/11*, 2011.
Detail from the installation, Pace Gallery, New York, 2011. Photo: Carly Gabe
pp. 136–37 \ *TVs from Craigslist*. Detail from the installation, Pace Gallery, New York, 2011.
Photo: Carly Gabe

Courtesy of the artist; Mark Moore Gallery, Los Angeles; and LMAKprojects, New York

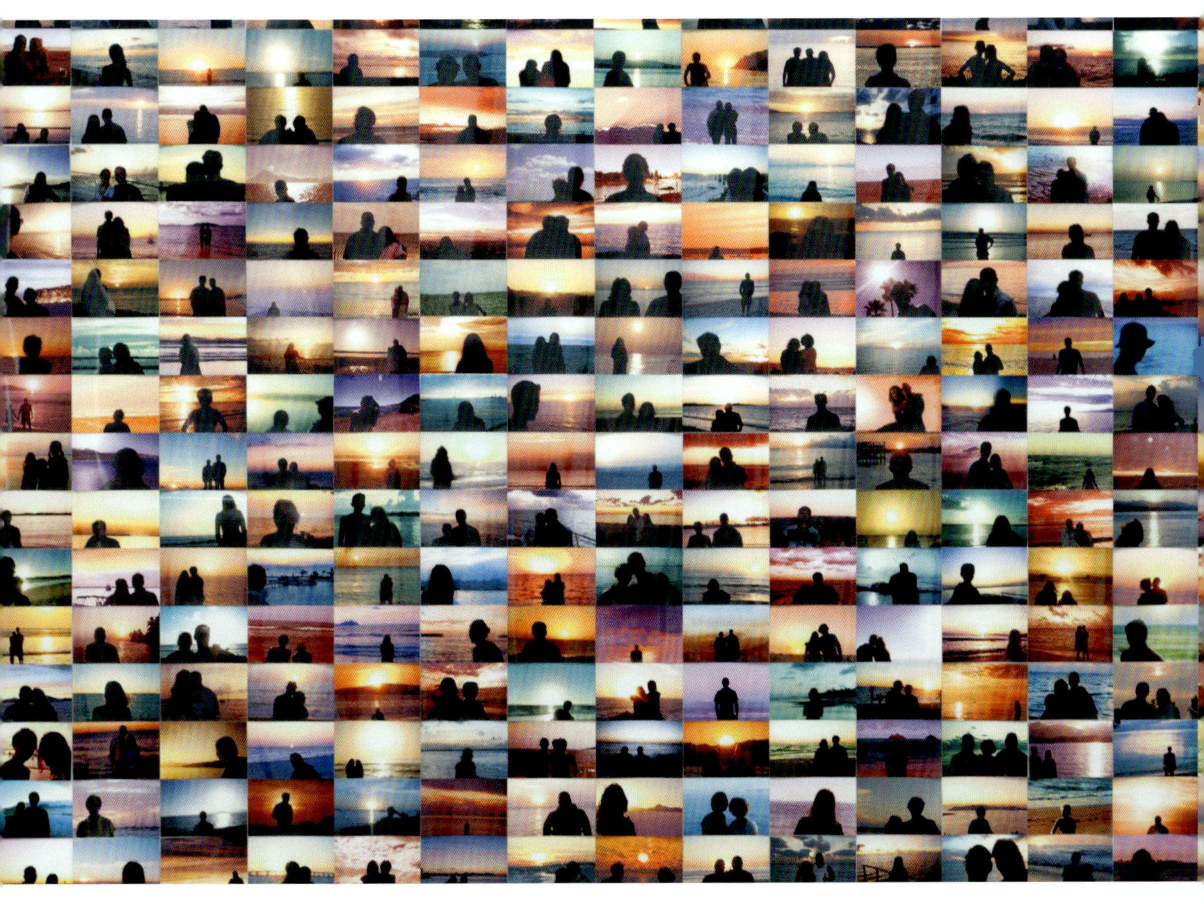

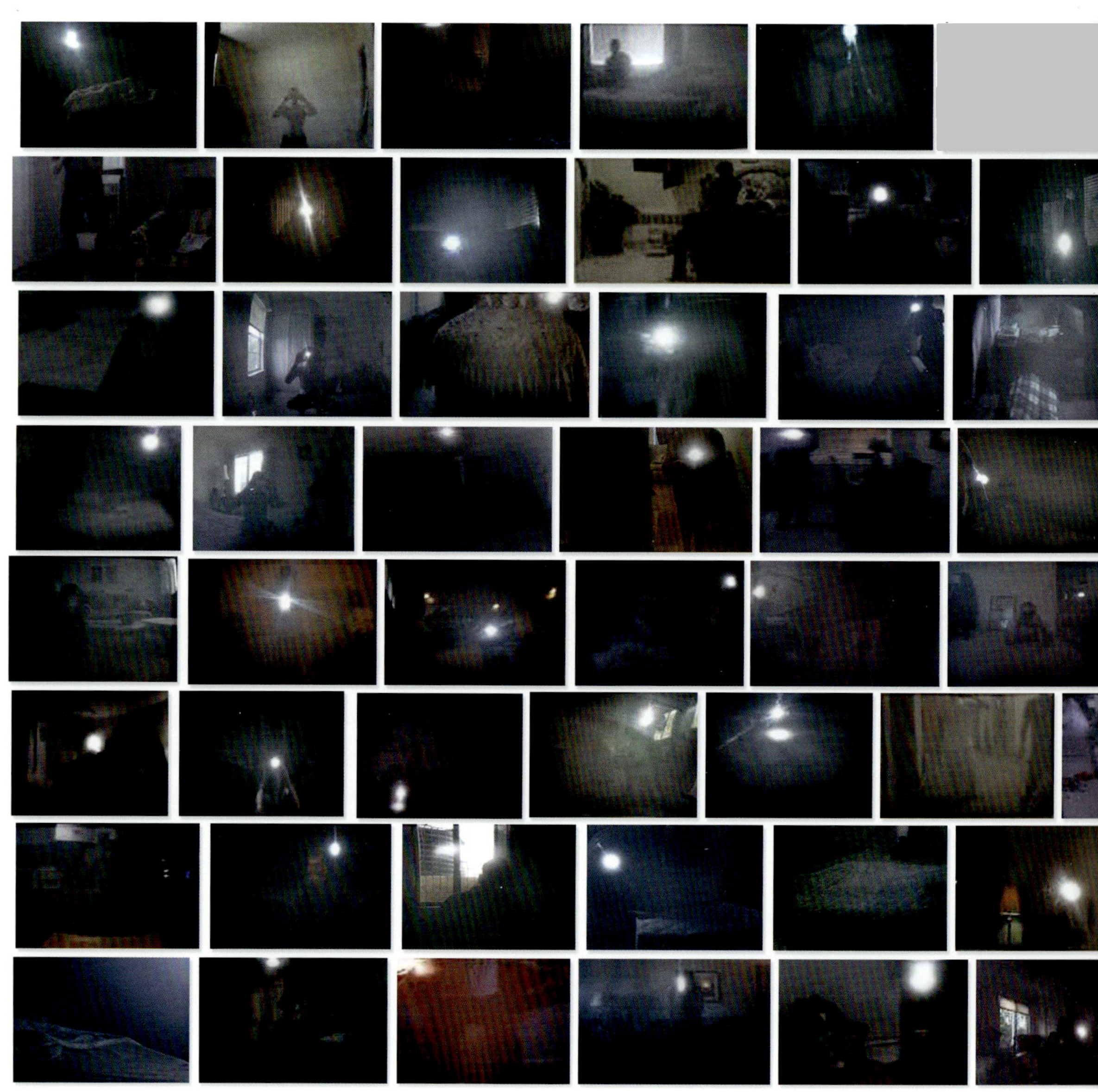

    PENELOPE UMBRICO

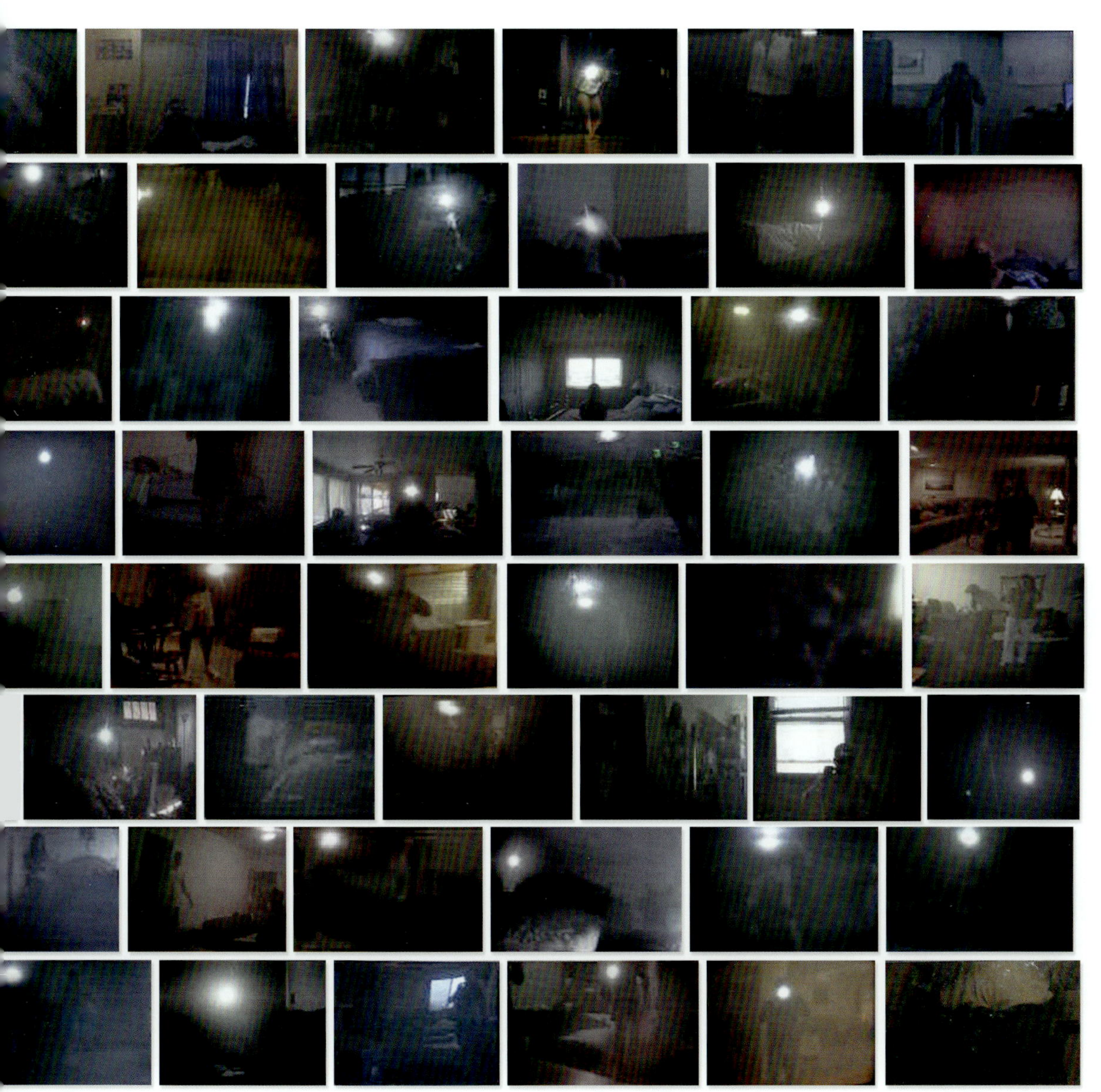

WASSINKLUNDGREN
MAI (MONTRÉAL, ARTS INTERCULTURELS)

Exhibited Work

***Don't Smile Now… Save it for Later!*, 2008**
30 colour Polaroid photographs, 10.2 x 15.2 cm or 10.5 x 11 cm each.

The photo booth was the first automated photographic machine to be used in the public realm and the first camera designed to function without human involvement. Whereas the photo booth is seen as a machine with a limited purpose – to take photographs of the human face – the duo WassinkLundgren (Thijs groot Wassink and Ruben Lundgren) surpassed this constraining role. For their work *Don't Smile Now… Save it for Later!* (2008), they placed a mirror inside photo booths in London, opened the curtains, and fed money into the machines. The result was that, for the first time, the photo booth looked outside and viewed its own surroundings.

WassinkLundgren is a collaboration between Dutch photographers Thijs groot Wassink (born in 1981 in Deventer) and Ruben Lundgren (born in 1983 in Hilversum), who live and work, respectively, in London and Beijing. They are the recipients of numerous awards, including the China Academy Award in 2010 and the Prix du Livre at Les Rencontres d'Arles 2007 for their publication *Empty Bottles*. WassinkLundgren has exhibited in museums worldwide, including Foam Amsterdam (2007, 2013); the Nederlands Fotomuseum in Rotterdam (2010, 2012); the CAFA Museum in Beijing (2011); Fotomuseum Winterthur (2009–10); the Guangdong Museum of Art (2010); the National Media Museum in Bradford, U.K. (2009); and the Stedelijk Museum in Amsterdam (2006). The duo is represented by Van Zoetendaal Collections in Amsterdam, and Pékin Fine Arts in Beijing.
\ www.wassinklundgren.com

p. 139 \ *Asda, Old Kent Road, London*
p. 140 \ *Sainsbury's, Green Lanes, Haringay, London*
p. 141 \ *Whitechapel Underground Station, London*

Courtesy of the artists; Van Zoetendaal Collections, Amsterdam; and Pékin Fine Arts, Beijing

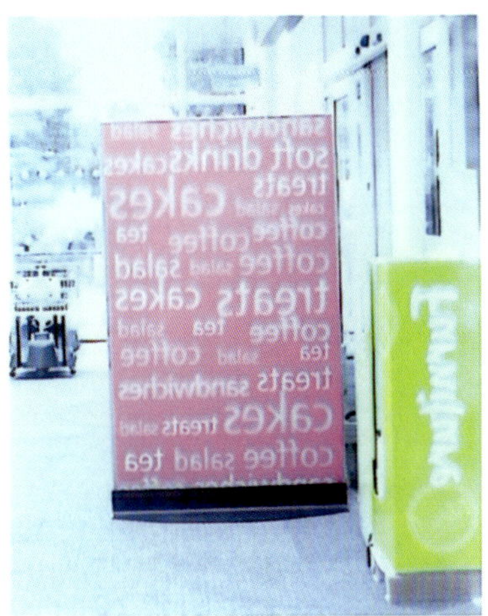

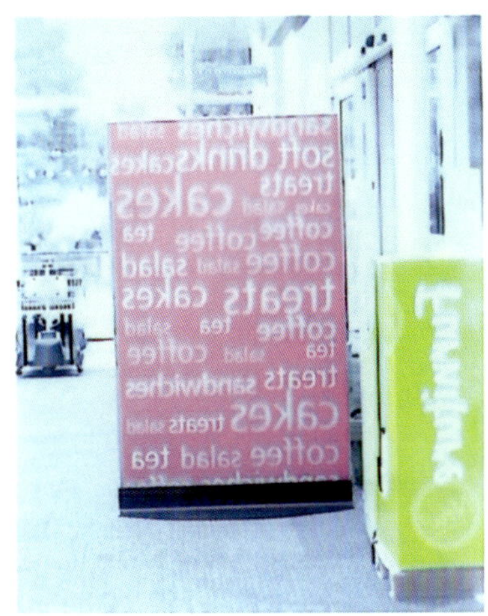

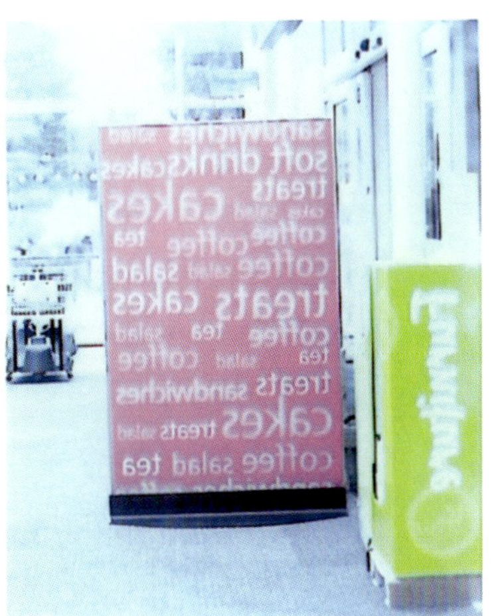

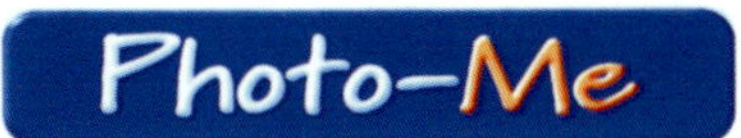

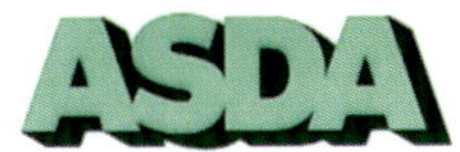

Thank you for using our latest digital technology
£4.00 including VAT at 17.5% - £0.60   17/07/2008 12h13
Photobooth Nbr: 24250   Hotline Nbr: 0845 100 4000

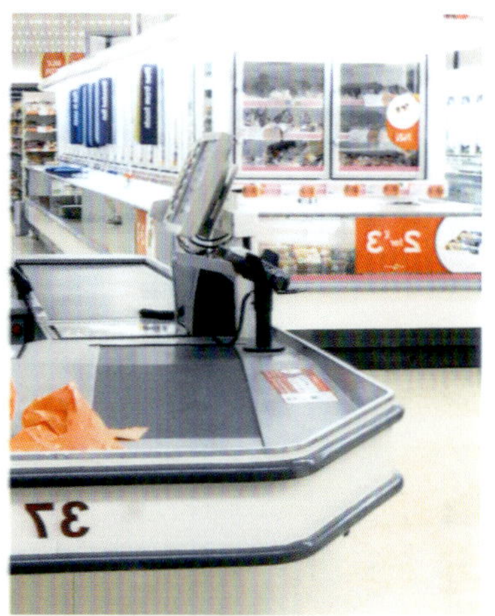
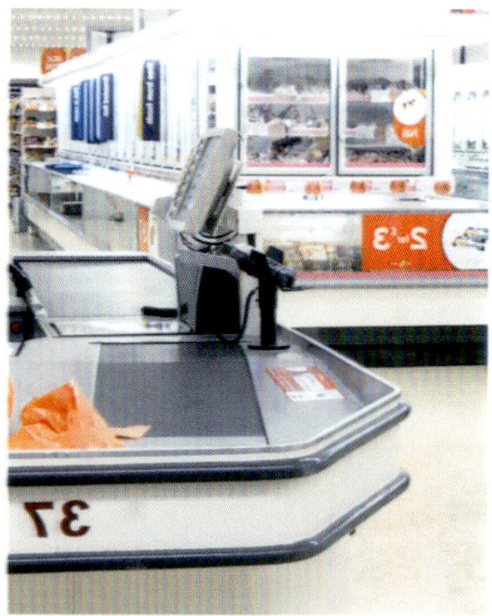
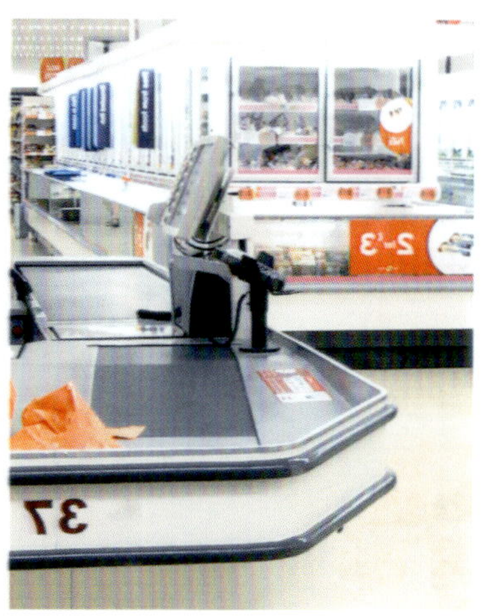
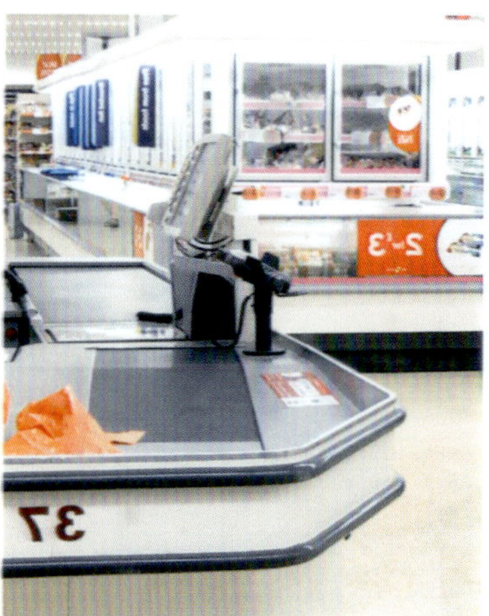

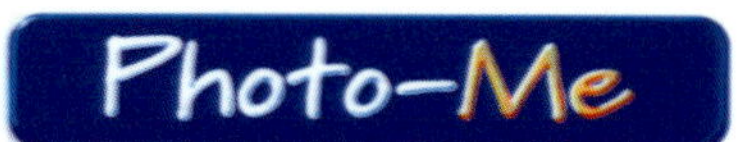

Thank you for using Photo-Me
£4.00
Photobooth Nbr: 43830

SAINSBURY'S

28/07/2008 12h13
Hotline Nbr: 0845 100 4000

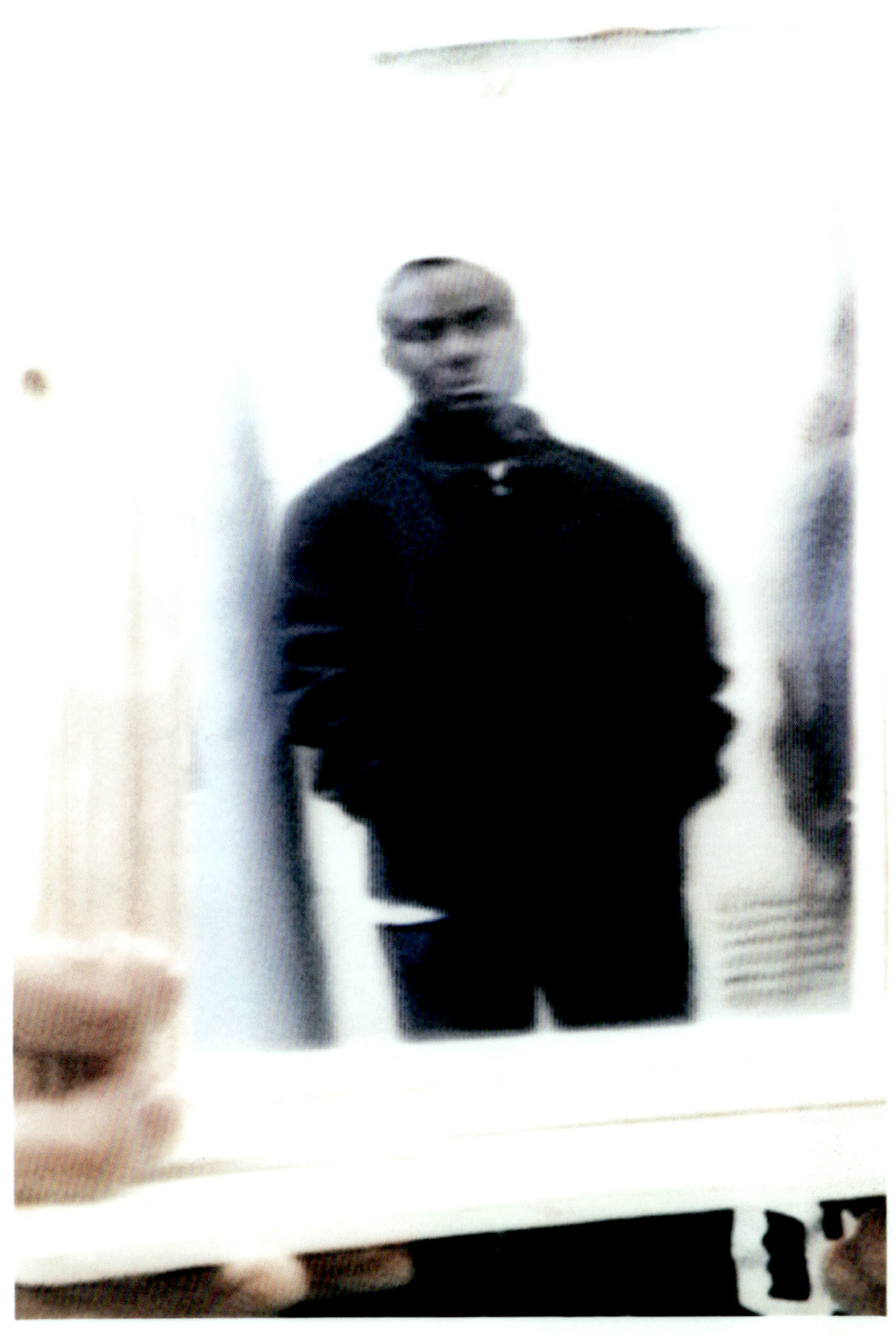

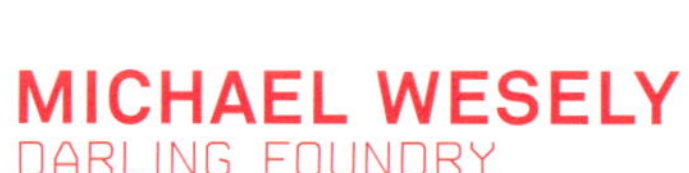

Exhibited Work

Chromogenic prints, Diasec, metal frames, variable dimensions, 1997–2010

Michael Wesely has spent much of his art career working on camera techniques to allow a single exposure of up to twenty-six months. This compression of time into one image creates uncanny photographs, consisting of ghostly buildings that melt like ice, streaks of light that reverberate across the sky, and cars whose fleeting appearance is recorded by a pinch of light. The viewer becomes aware of changes that are too slow to be noticed and of something more profound about time; as Wesely states, "The lines in the sky put our existence, us, our planet into context with the Dance of the Universe, which coexists on an entirely different time."

Born in 1963 in Munich, Michael Wesely lives in Berlin. He attended the Bayerische Staatslehranstalt für Fotografie in Munich and the Akademie der Bildenden Künste München. Wesely's photographs have been exhibited around the world, including at the Centro Cultural São Paulo (2012); the Hamburger Kunsthalle (2011); Fotogalerie Wien in Vienna (2011); PHotoEspaña (2010); the Fahnemann Projects in Berlin (2009); the Kunstmuseum in Magdeburg (2009); the Alte Nationalgalerie in Berlin (2006); the Haus der Kunst in Munich (2006); Martin-Gropius-Bau in Berlin (2005); the Hamburger Bahnhof (2005); the Seoul Museum of Art (2005); and the Museum of Modern Art (MoMA) in New York (2004). Wesely's works are held in various international collections, including MoMA, Neue Nationalgalerie in Berlin, and Kunstmuseum Bonn. \ www.wesely.org

p. 11 \ Detail from *Temporäre Kunsthalle Berlin (31.7.- 3.9.2008)*, 2010, 102 x 140 cm
p. 143 \ *Potsdamer Platz, Berlin (5.4.1997 – 24.9.1998)*, 1997–98, 80 x 110 cm
pp. 144–45 \ *Potsdamer Platz, Berlin (27.3.1997 – 13.12.1998)*, 1997–98, 80 x 110 cm
p. 147 \ *Potsdamer Platz, Berlin (5.4.1997 – 3.6.1999)*, 1997–99, 80 x 110 cm

Courtesy of the artist

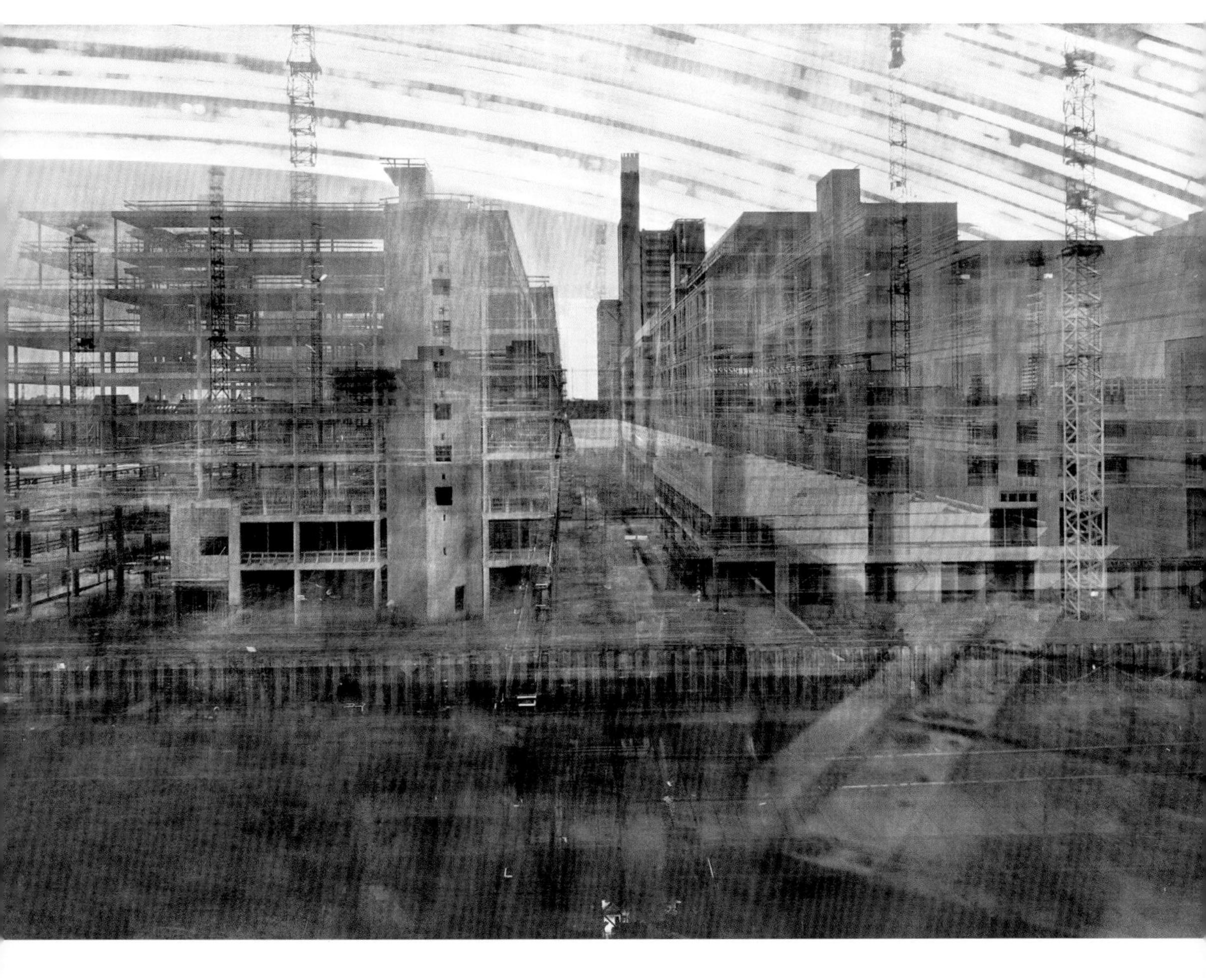

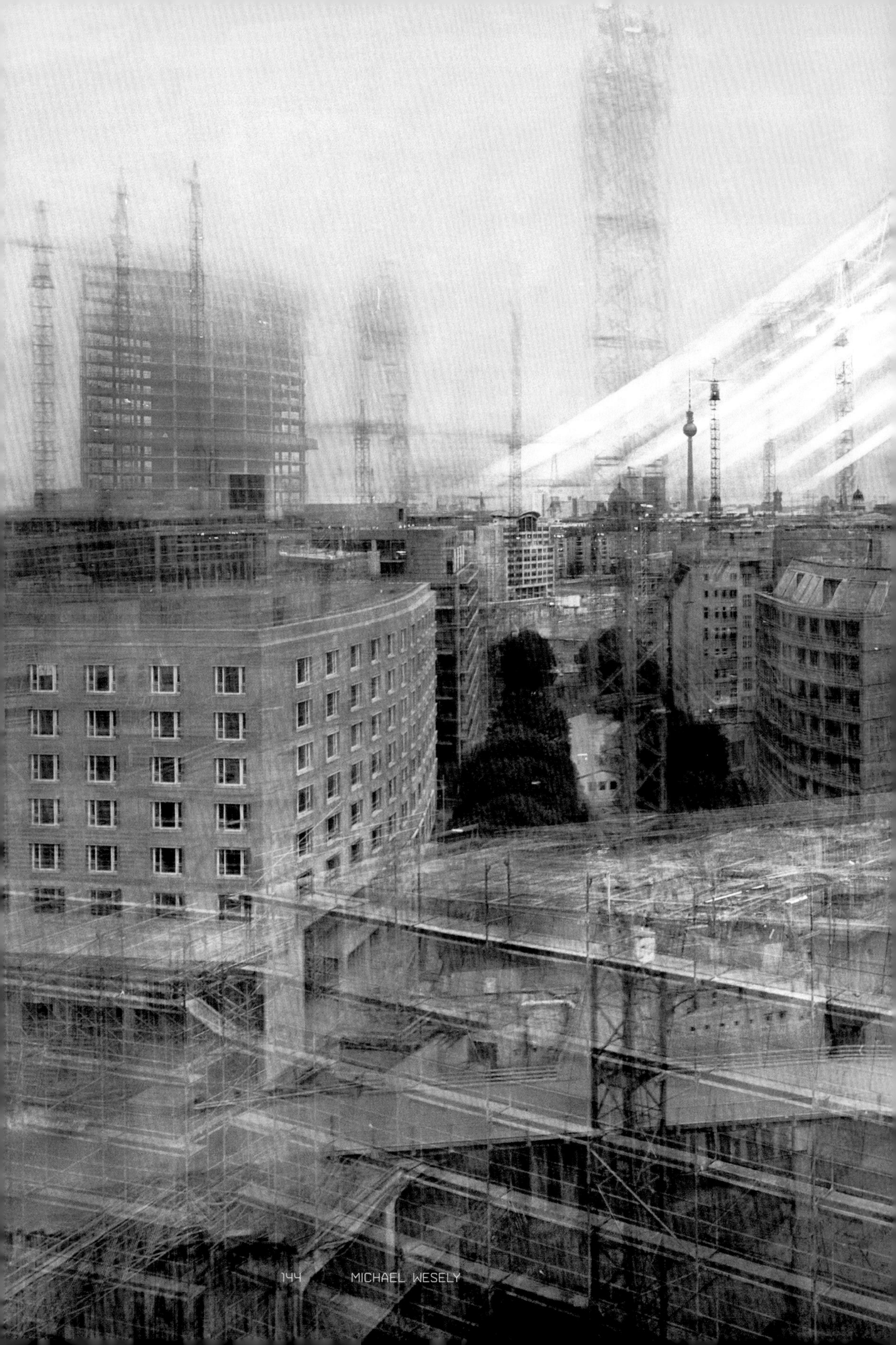

144   MICHAEL WESELY

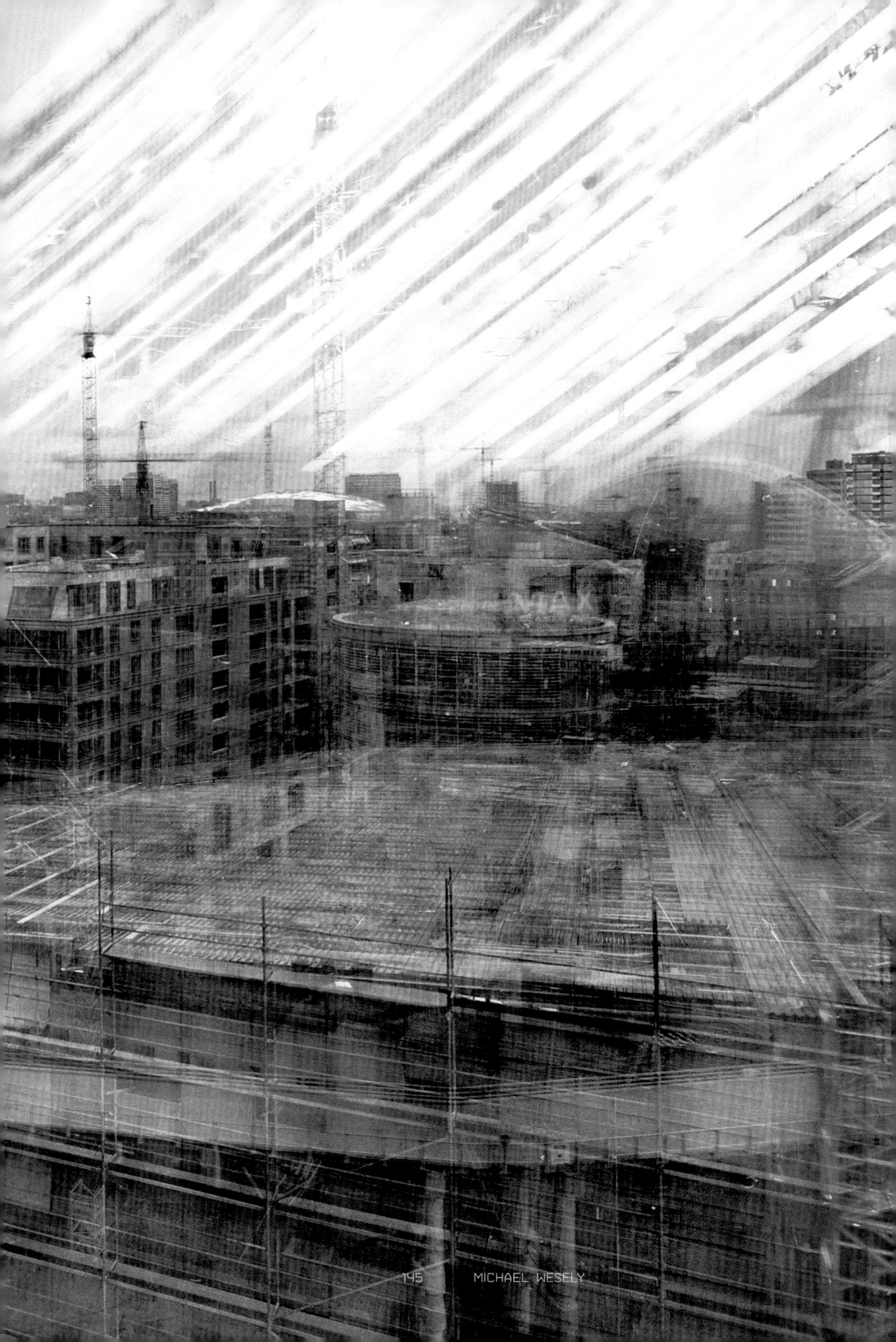

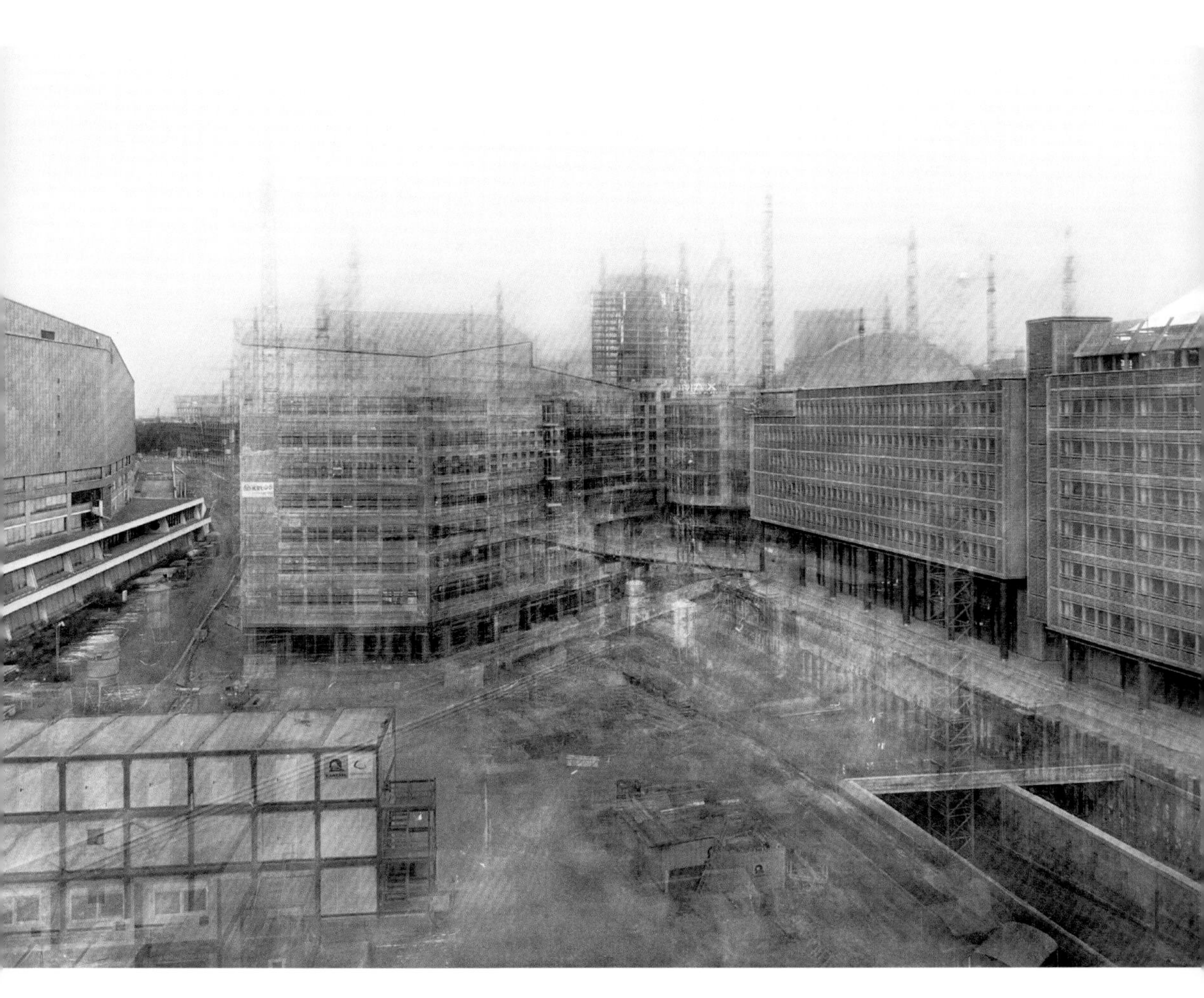

**H-BLOCK.
PRISON HOUSING: DONOVAN WYLIE + SOCIAL HOUSING: ILSE BING**

PRISON HOUSING: DONOVAN WYLIE

Exhibited Work

The Maze, 2003–09
Colour digital pigment prints.
15 prints of Prison Cells. H-Block 5, B-Wing, 2003, 30 x 40 cm each (framed).
4 prints of Walls, Fences, 60 x 70 cm each (framed), and one Google Earth image.

The Maze prison in Northern Ireland opened in 1971 to detain paramilitary prisoners during the Troubles, and closed 29 years later, after the Good Friday Agreement. With the "dirty protest," hunger strikes, and escape attempts, the prison played a prominent role during this difficult period. But it was the prison's architectural element, the H-block buildings, that became the symbol of the Maze and of the protests. Donovan Wylie's photographic survey _The Maze_ (2003–09) focuses on the different layers of imprisonment: the cells in the H-blocks, the various forms of fencing, and finally the perimeter walls. He reveals the vacant cells and interlocking fencing that confined prisoners within a machine of control.

Donovan Wylie was born in 1971 in Belfast, Northern Ireland. In 1998, at the age of 27, he became a full member of the Magnum Photos agency. In 2011 Wylie was awarded the Bradford Fellowship in Photography and in 2010 he was shortlisted for the Deutsche Börse Photography Prize. He has had solo exhibitions at the Imperial War Museum in London (2013); the Royal Ontario Museum in Toronto (2011); the National Media Museum in Bradford, U.K. (2010); the Irish Museum of Modern Art (IMMA) in Dublin (2006); and The Photographers' Gallery in London (2005). His works are in major public collections, including IMMA, the Victoria and Albert Museum in London, and the Centre Pompidou in Paris. Wylie is represented by Magnum Photos. \ www.magnumphotos.com

pp. 150–51 \ _Prison Cells. H-Block 5. Maze Prison. Northern Ireland_, 2003
pp. 152–53 \ _Fence. Deconstruction of Maze Prison. Maze Prison. Northern Ireland_, 2009
pp. 154–55 \ _Demolition of South Perimeter Wall. Maze Prison. Northern Ireland_, 2009

Courtesy of the artist

In collaboration with the CCA

Exhibited Work

Ilse Bing, Photographs from the CCA Collection, 1930
Thanks to Louise Désy, Curator of the Photographs Collection,
for her valuable collaboration in the development of this project.

The 35 mm still camera fundamentally changed
how we view the world. Small and portable, it
was made to be hand-held and placed at eye level.
In 1929, the young German photographer Ilse
Bing bought a Leica and started a photographic
career that took her from Frankfurt to Paris and
on to New York. While Bing was in Frankfurt,
the architect and urban planner Mart Stam
commissioned her to undertake a photographic
survey of the Henry and Emma Budge-Heim
project, a social housing H-block building
designed for elderly people. Bing starts with
an exterior overall view of the building and then
records the interior corridors and rooms. This
gives the impression of a visual narrative that
moves with dexterity from outside to inside
the building, advancing closer to objects, and
taking a microscopic view of the smallest details
within the recently constructed building.

p. 156 \ View of the glass partitions on the balconies of the
Budge Foundation Old People's Home, Frankfurt am Main, Germany, 1930.
Gelatin silver print, 28.0 x 22.1 cm. CCA Collection, PH1984:0288:007
p. 157 \ Interior view of the Budge Foundation Old People's Home showing the architect
Mart Stam closing a window shade, Frankfurt am Main, Germany, 1930.
Gelatin silver print, 28.0 x 22.1 cm. CCA Collection, PH1984:0288:047

Courtesy of the CCA
© Estate of Ilse Bing

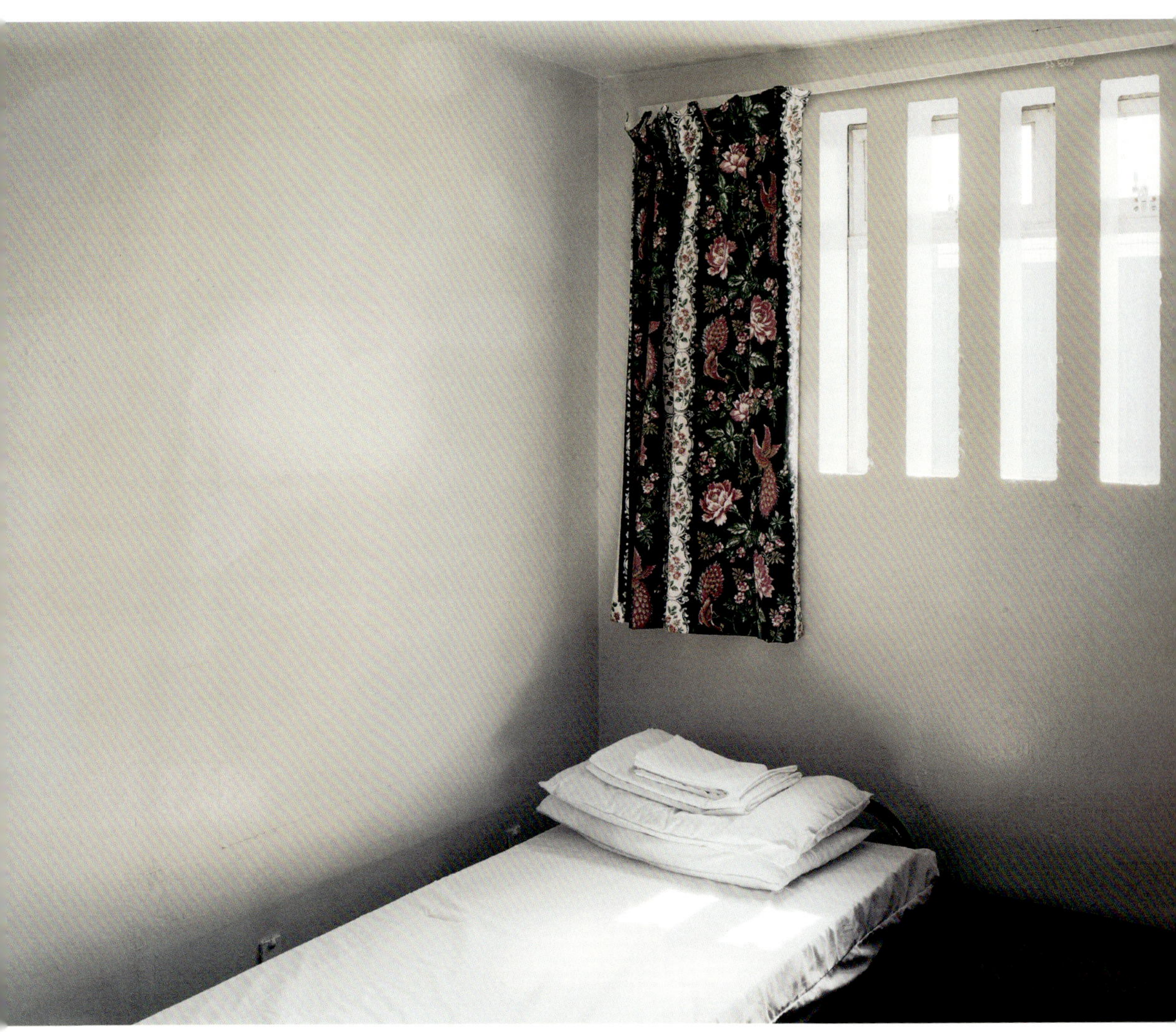

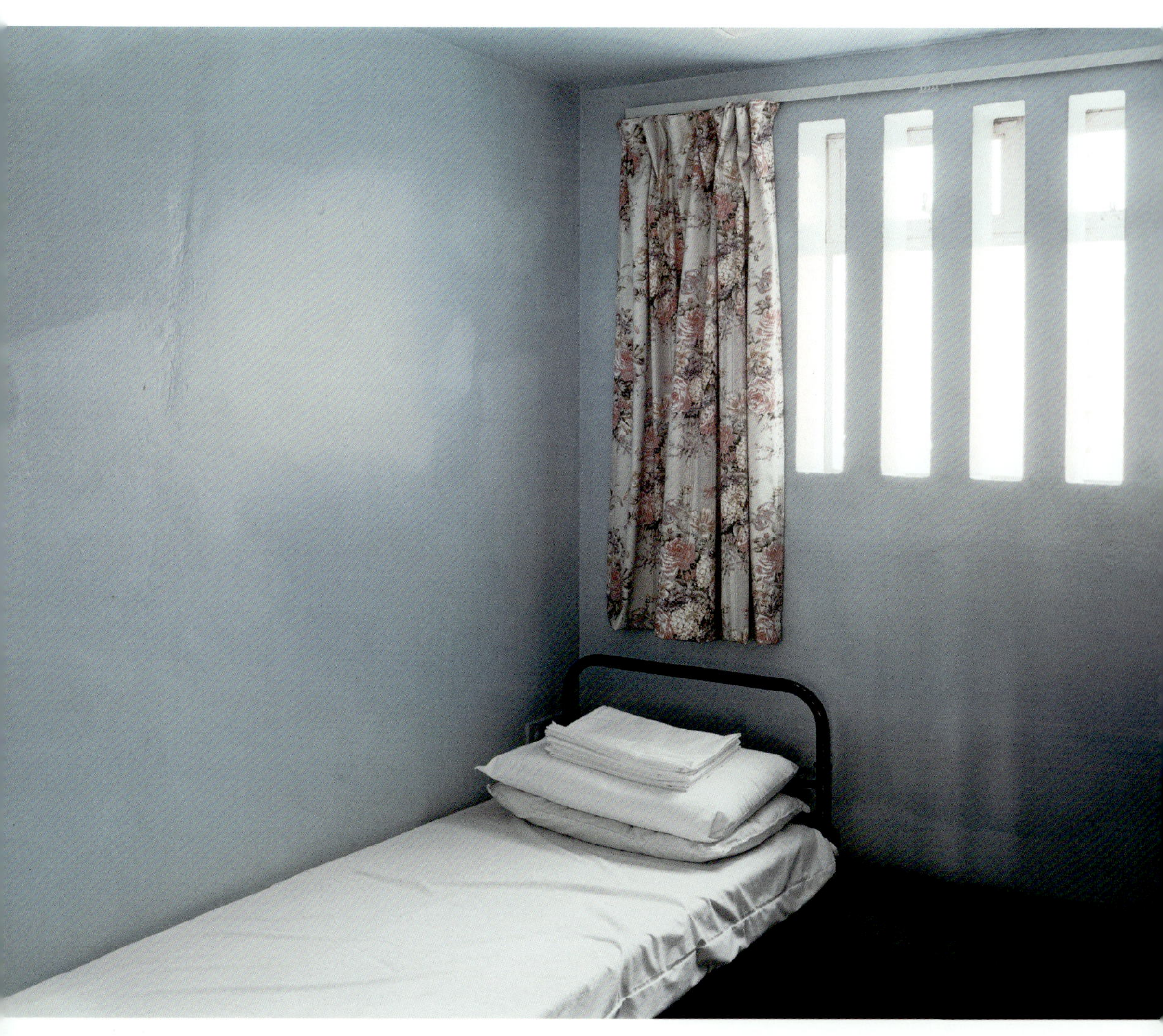

   DONOVAN WYLIE

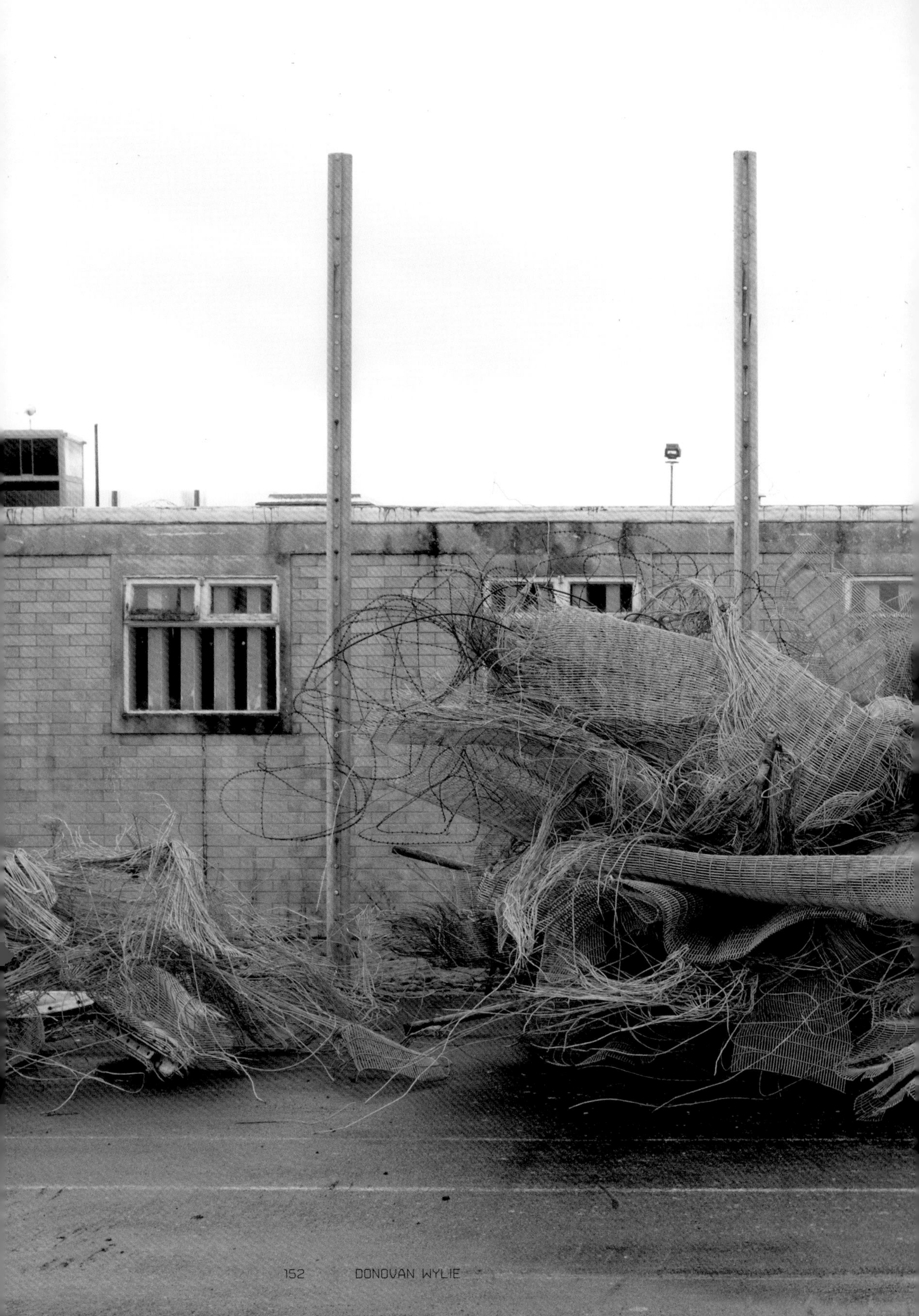

    DONOVAN WYLIE

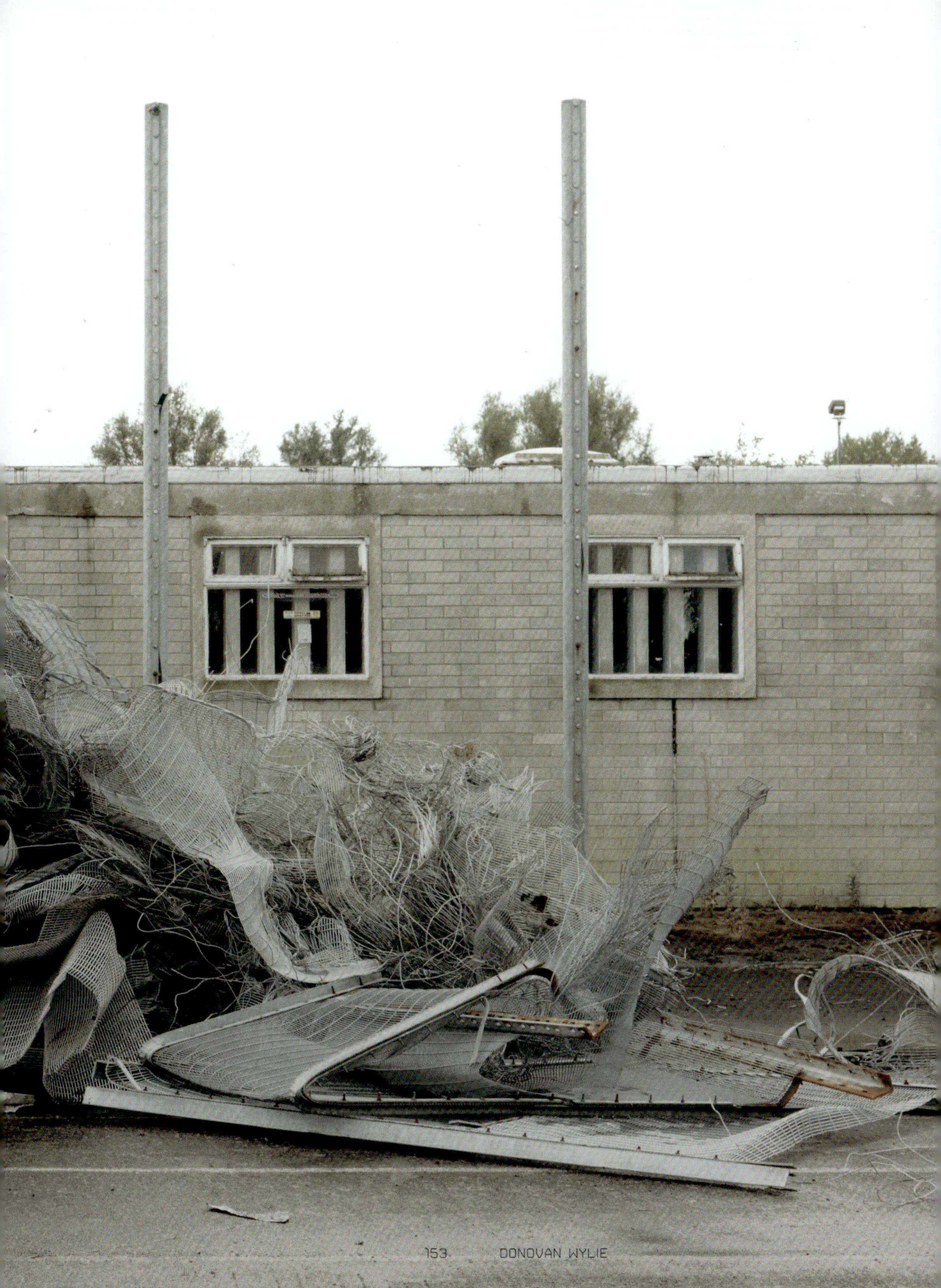

 DONOVAN WYLIE

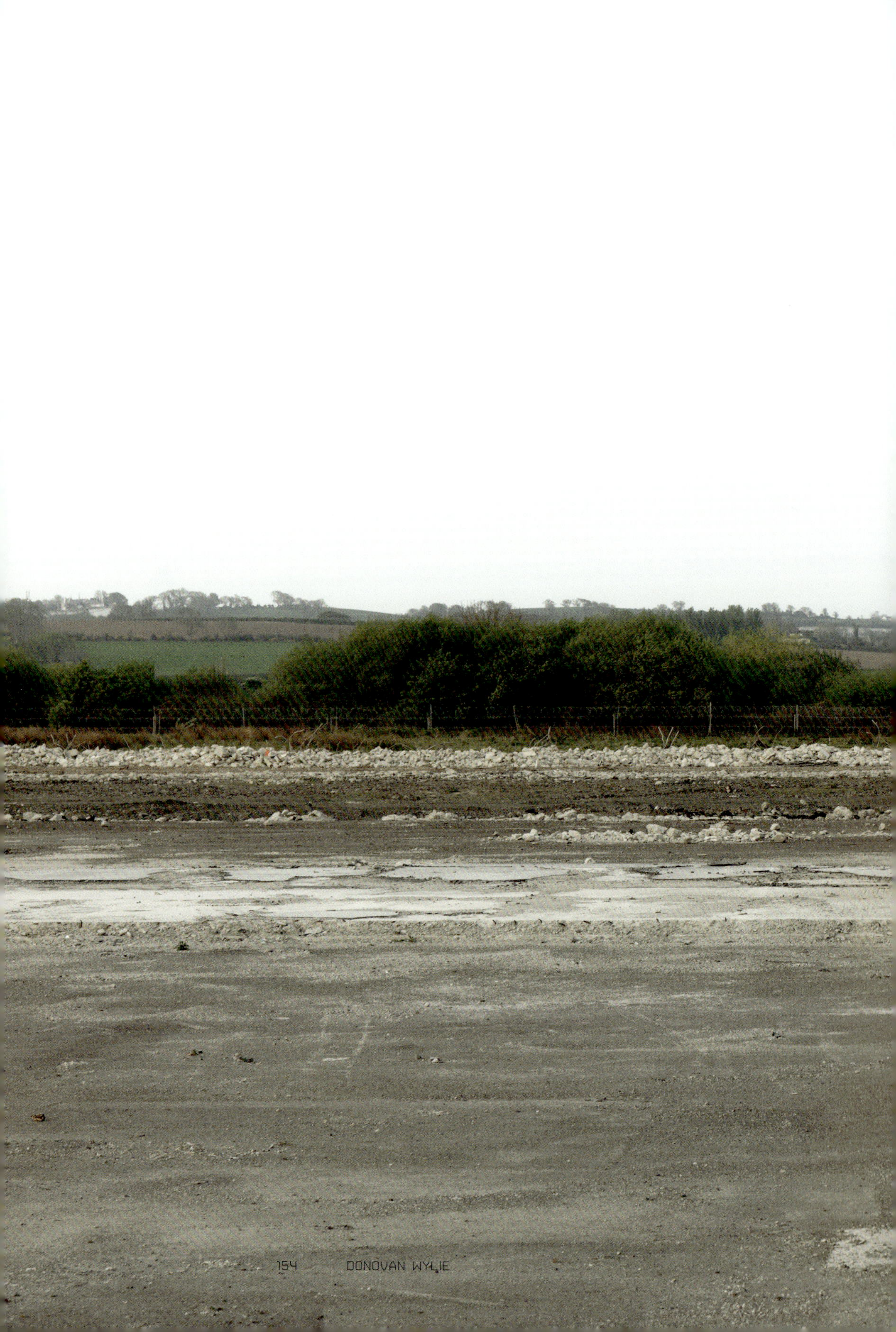

   DONOVAN WYLIE

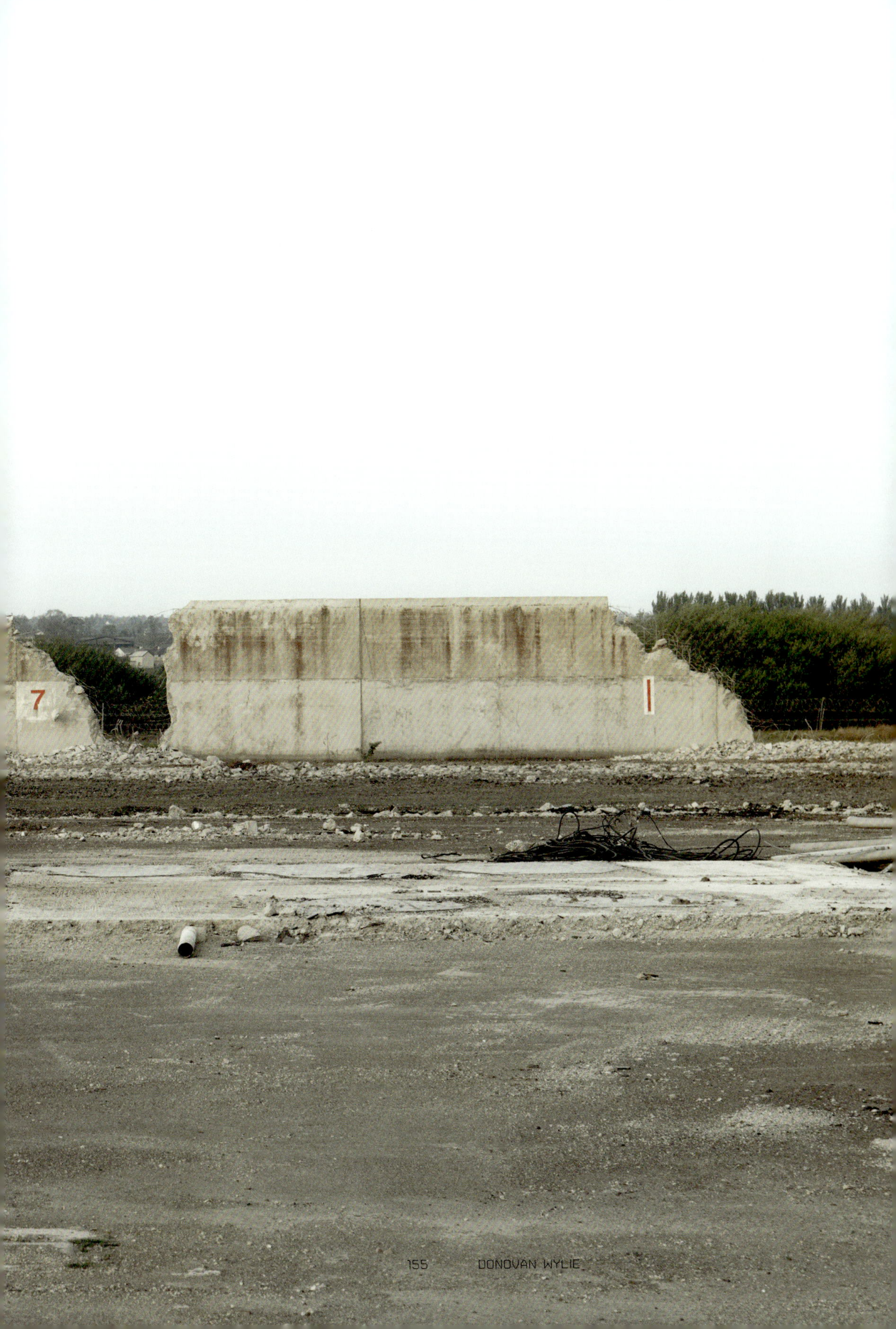
7
1

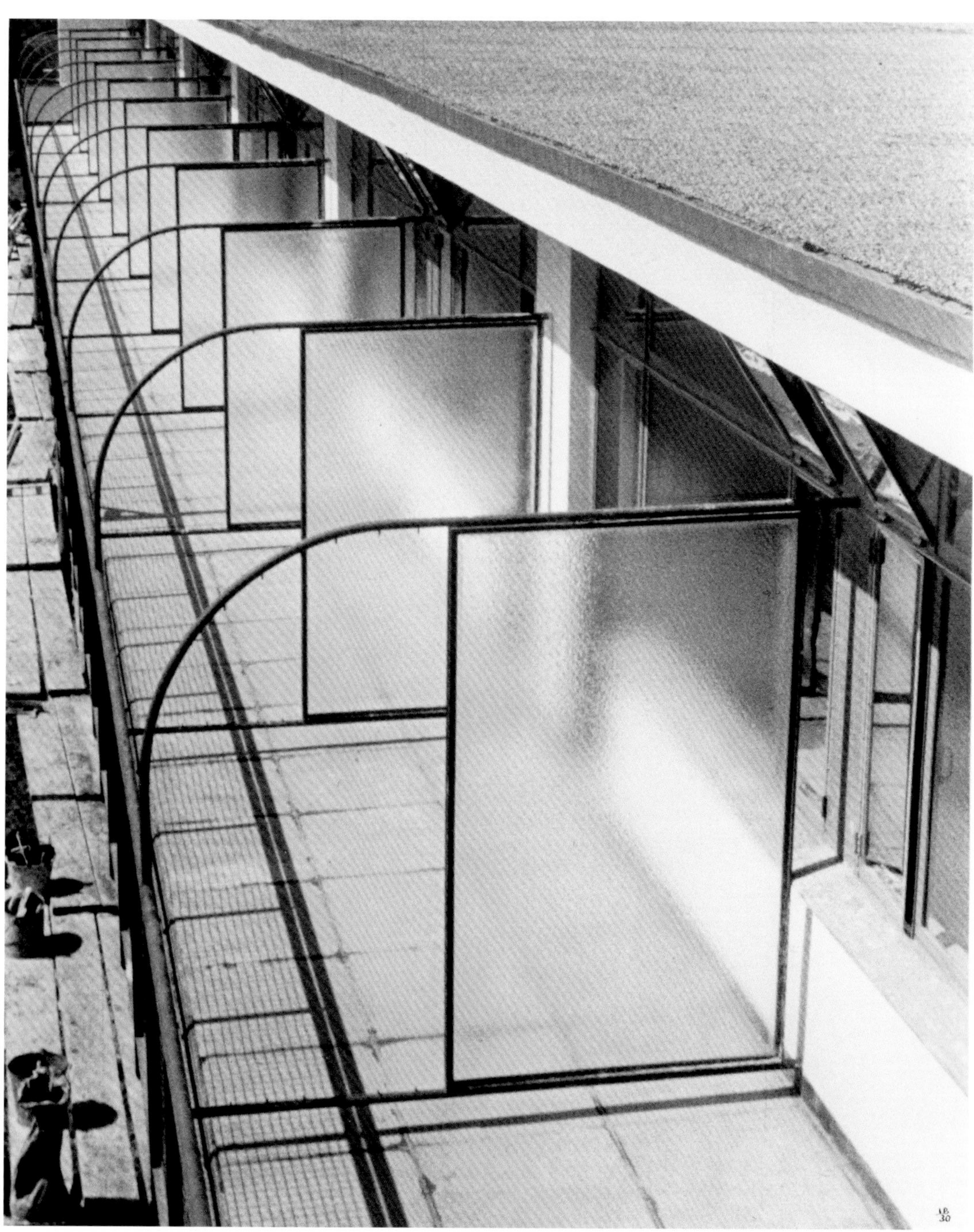

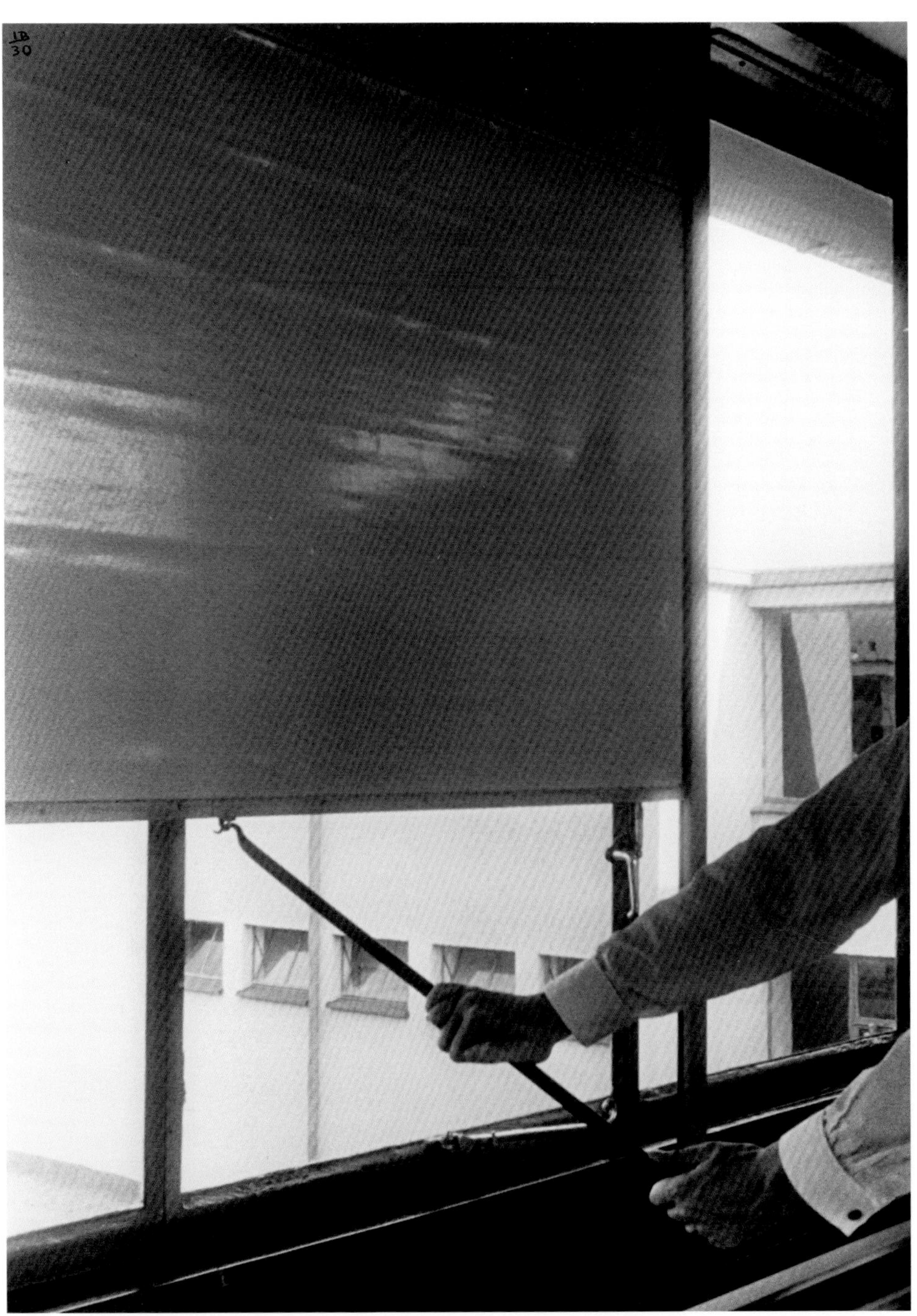

ESSAYS

JOANNA ZYLINSKA

ALL THE WORLD'S A CAMERA:
NOTES ON NON-HUMAN PHOTOGRAPHY

The photographic apparatus lies in wait for photography; it sharpens its teeth
in readiness. This readiness to spring into action on the part of apparatuses,
their similarity to wild animals, is something to grasp hold of in the attempt
to define the term etymologically.[1]
Vilém Flusser

But is it not obvious that the photograph, if photograph there be, is already taken,
already developed in the very heart of things and at all the points of space?[2]
Henri Bergson

1. Vilém Flusser, *Towards a Philosophy of
Photography* (London: Reaktion Books, 2000),
21–22.

2. Henri Bergson, *Matter and Memory*,
trans. Nancy Margaret Paul and W. Scott Palmer
(London: Allen & Unwin, 1911), 31.

Human-driven photography – in which an act of consciously looking through a viewfinder or, more frequently nowadays, at a liquid crystal display (LCD) screen held at arm's length – is only one small part of what goes on in the field of photography, even though it is often made to stand in for photography *as such*. The execution of human agency in photographic practice, be it professional or amateur, is ostensibly manifested in decisions about the subject matter (the "what") and about ways of capturing this subject matter with a digital or analog apparatus (the "how"). Yet in amateur, snapshot-type photography, these supposed human-centric decisions are often affective reactions to events quickly unfolding in front of the photographer's eyes. Such reactions happen too quickly – we could even say *automatically* – for any conscious processes of decision making to be involved, bar the original decision to actually have, bring, and use a camera, rather than not. This automatism in photography is also manifested in the fact that these kinds of "snap" reactions are usually rechannelled through a database of standardized, pre-programmed, pre-existing image-frames, whose significance we are already familiar with and which we are trying to recreate in a unique way, under the umbrella of so-called individual experience: "toddler running towards mother"; "girl blowing a candle on a birthday cake"; "couple posing in front of the Taj Mahal."

Similar representationalist ambitions accompany many professional photographic activities, including those undertaken by photojournalists – who aim to show us, objectively and without judging, what war, poverty, and "the pain of others," to borrow Susan Sontag's phrase,[3] are "really" like – and those performed by photographic artists. Even prior to any moment of making a picture actually occur, the latter remain invested in the idea of an artist as a human agent with a particular vocation, one whose aesthetic and conceptual gestures are aimed at capturing something unique, or at least capturing it uniquely, with an image-making device. And thus we get works of formal portraiture; images of different types of vegetation or geological formations that are made to constitute "landscapes"; still-life projects of aestheticized domesticity, including close-ups of kitchen utensils, fraying carpets or light traces on a wall; and, last but not least, works that can be gathered into the rag-bag called "conceptual photography."

3. Susan Sontag, *Regarding the Pain of Others* (New York: Picador, 2003).

Through the decisions of artists and amateurs about their practice, photography becomes an act of *making something significant*, even if not necessarily *making it signify something* in any straightforward way. It is a practice of focusing on what is, by its very nature, multifocal, of literally *casting light* on what would have otherwise remained obscure, of carving a fragment from the flow of life and turning it into a splinter of what, post factum, becomes known as "reality." Traditionally, this moment of selection – referred to as "decisive" by followers of the documentary tradition in photography – was associated with the pressing of the button to open the camera's shutter. However, with the introduction of the Lytro camera to the market in 2012, the temporality of this seemingly unique and transient photographic moment has been stretched into both the past and the future. Lytro captures the entire light field rather than a single plane of light, thus allowing the photographer to change and readjust the focus on a computer in postproduction. Interestingly, Lytro is advertised as "the only camera that captures life in living pictures" – a poetic formulation that is underpinned by the ongoing industry claim to "absolute novelty" but that merely exacerbates and visualizes the inherent instability of *all* photographic practice and *all* photographic objects. Lytro is thus just one more element in the long-term humanist narrative about "man's dominion over the earth" – a narrative that drives the progressive automatization of many of our everyday devices, including cameras, cars, and refrigerators. Giving us an illusion of control over technology by making cameras smaller and domestic appliances more user-friendly, the technoscientific industry actually exacerbates the gap between technology and the human by relieving us of the responsibility of getting to know and engage with the increasingly software-driven "black boxes."

In light of the dominance of the humanist paradigm in photography – a paradigm that is premised on the supposed human control of both the practice of image-making and the equipment – it is important to ask what gets elided in such conceptualizations. This is where the interventionist force of *Drone: The Automated Image*, an event in which non-human photographic agency is directly engaged, comes to the fore. The uniqueness of this event lies not so much in highlighting the machinic aspect of photographic and video practice, as this aspect was already mobilized in the early days of photography – for example, in the works of Alexander Rodchenko and László Moholy-Nagy. *Drone* takes one step further on the road toward non-humanist photog-raphy by actually departing from the human-centric visualization process. In many of the works shown, the very act and process of capture is relegated to a computer, a camera mounted atop a moving vehicle, a robot, or a dog. Through this, *Drone*

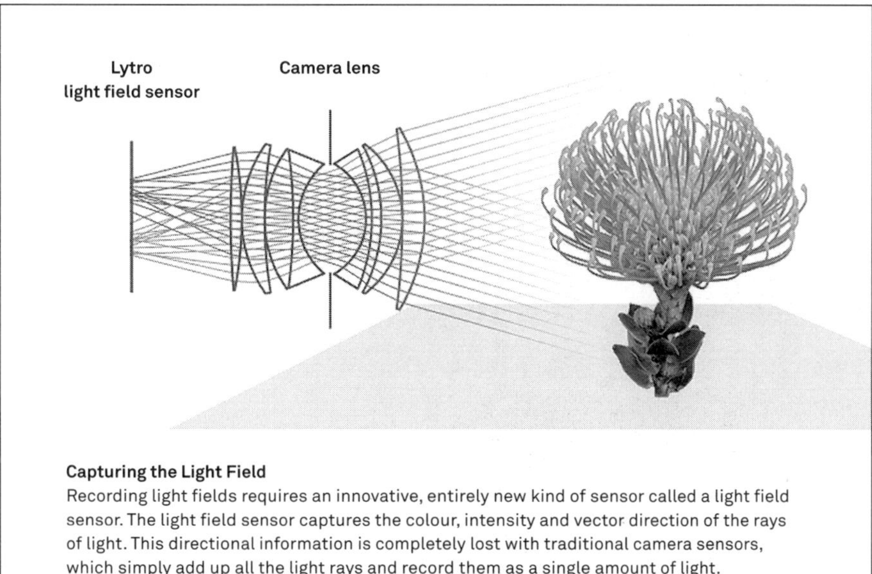

Lytro camera light field sensor.

seems to be showing us that art practice is merely a part of the wider *photographic condition*, with things photographing themselves, without always being brought back to the human spectrum of vision as the ultimate channel of perception and of things perceived. Naturally, humans form part of the photographic continuum on display at Le Mois de la Photo à Montréal – as the event's organizers, artists, engineers, printers, and spectators. However, the guest curator and the artists have let themselves – and us – be a part of that photographic flow of things being incessantly photographed, and of trying to make interventions from within the midst of it. In this way, they have put together an event that focuses on what we could term "insignificant photography" – not in the sense that it is irrelevant and of no consequence, but in the sense of allowing us to see things that have been captured almost incidentally and in passing, with the thematic "what" not being the key impulse beyond the execution of the majority of the still and moving images on display.

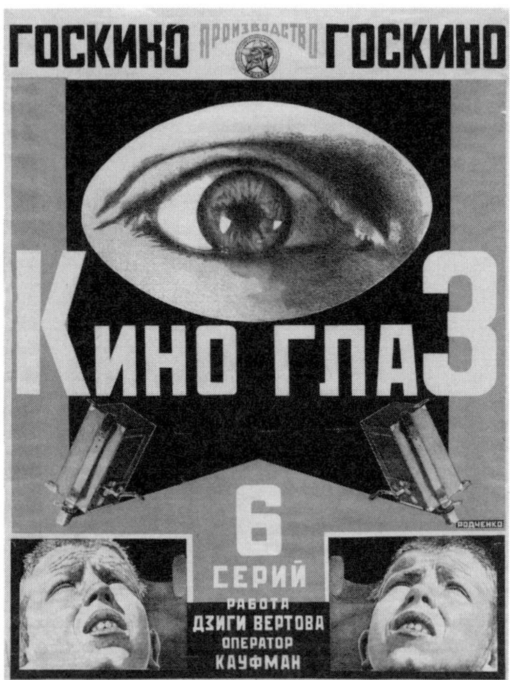

Alexander Rodchenko (1891–1956), *Kino Glaz* [Kino-Eye], 1924.
Lithograph.

But what is actually meant by this *photographic condition*, and does the postulation of its existence stand up to philosophical and experiential scrutiny? To explore these questions, let us start from a very simple proposition: *there is life in photography*. If living in the so-called media age has become tantamount to being photographed on a constant basis, with our identity constituted and verified by the ongoing development of our photo galleries and photo streams on mobile phones, tablets, and social media platforms such as Facebook, Tumblr and Pinterest, not to mention the thousands of security cameras quietly and often invisibly registering our image when we pass through city centres, shopping malls, and airports, then, contrary to its more typical Barthesian association with the passage of time and death, photography can be understood more productively as a life-making process. As Sarah Kember and I argue in our book *Life after New Media: Mediation as a Vital Process*, it is "precisely in its efforts to arrest duration, to capture or still the flow of life – beyond singular photographs' success or failure at representing *this* or *that* referent – that photography's vital forces are activated."[4] Photography lends itself to being understood in a vitalist framework due to its positioning in a network of dynamic relations between present and past, movement and stasis, flow and cut. In making cuts into duration, in stabilizing the temporal flow into entities, photography is inherently involved with time. Significantly, for vitalist philosophers such as Henri Bergson and Gilles Deleuze, time, duration, and movement stand precisely for life itself. Photography's proximity to life is therefore revealed in the temporal aspect of photography, which is enacted in its dual ontology: it can be seen as both object and practice, as both snapshot and all the other virtual snapshots that could have potentially been there, and as being both something here and now and something always unfolding into something else. It is also in this dual ontology that the non-human side of photography comes to the fore, enacted as it is through agents as diverse as closed-circuit television (CCTV), aerial camera systems, satellites, endoscopy equipment, webcams, and Google Street View.

Its on-off activity, which carves life into fragments while simultaneously reconnecting them to the imagistic flow, may allow us to conclude not only that *there is life in photography*, but also that *life itself is photographic*. Claire Colebrook explains this process of creative becoming in and of life by drawing on the very concept of image production, or "imaging." She writes, "All life, according to Bergson and to Deleuze after him, can be considered as a form of perception or 'imaging' where there is not one being that apprehends or represents another being, but two vectors of creativity where one potential for differentiation encounters another and from that potential forms a relatively stable tendency or manner."[5] This idea has its root in Bergson's *Matter and Memory*; according to Bergson, our experience of the world, which is always a way of sensing the world, comes in the form of images. "And by 'image,'" explains Bergson, "we mean a certain existence which is more than that which the idealist calls a representation, but less than that which the realist calls a thing – an existence placed half-way between the 'thing' and the 'representation.'"[6] It is precisely through images that novelty comes into the world, which is why images should be understood not as representations but as creations, "some of which are philosophical,

4. Sarah Kember and Joanna Zylinska, *Life After New Media: Mediation as a Vital Process* (Cambridge, Mass.: MIT Press, 2012), 72.

5. Claire Colebrook, *Deleuze and the Meaning of Life* (London and New York: Continuum, 2010), 11.
6. Bergson, *Matter and Memory*, vii.

some artistic, some scientific."[7] To put it another way, the creative impulse of life takes it beyond representation as a form of picturing what already exists: instead, life is a creation of images in the most radical sense, a way of temporarily stabilizing matter into forms. Photographic practice as we conventionally know it is just one instantiation of this creative process of life.

If all life is indeed photographic, the notion of the photographic apparatus that embraces yet also goes beyond the human becomes fundamental to our understanding of what we have called the *photographic condition*. To speak of the photographic apparatus is, of course, not just to argue for a straightforward replacement of the human vision with a machinic one, but rather to recognize the mutual intertwining and co-constitution of the organic and the machinic in the production of vision, and hence of the world. In her work on the use of apparatuses in physics experiments, the philosopher and quantum physicist Karen Barad argues that such apparatuses are not just "passive observing instruments; on the contrary, they are productive of (and part of) phenomena."[8] We could easily apply this argument to photography, in which the camera as a viewing device, the photographic frame both in the viewfinder and as the circumference of a photographic print, the enlarger, the computer, the printer, and the photographer (who, in many instances, such as surveillance or speed cameras, is replaced by the camera-eye) are all active agents in the constitution of a photograph. In other words, they are all part of what we understand by photography.

It is not just philosophy that can be of use in helping us envisage this non-human, machinic dimension of photography: photographic and, more broadly, artistic practice is even better predisposed to enact it (rather than just provide an argument *about* it). A series of works by British artist Lindsay Seers provides a case in point. Exhibited, among other places, at Matt's Gallery in London as *It Has To Be This Way* (2009), and accompanied by an aptly titled book, *Human Camera*, Seers's ongoing project consists of a number of seemingly autobiographical films. These are full of bizarre yet just-about-believable adventures occurring to their heroine, all verified by a body of "experts" – from doctors and critics to family members – who appear in the films but also leave behind "evidence" in the form of numerous written accounts, photographs, and documentary records. In one of the films, a young girl, positioned as "Lindsay Seers," is living her life unable to make a distinction between herself and the world, or between the world and its representations. The girl is gifted with exceptional memory so, like a camera that is permanently switched on, she records and remembers

7. Colebrook, *Deleuze*, 23.

8. Karen Barad, *Meeting the Universe Halfway: Quantum Physics and the Entanglement of Matter and Meaning* (Durham, N.C.: Duke University Press, 2007), 142.

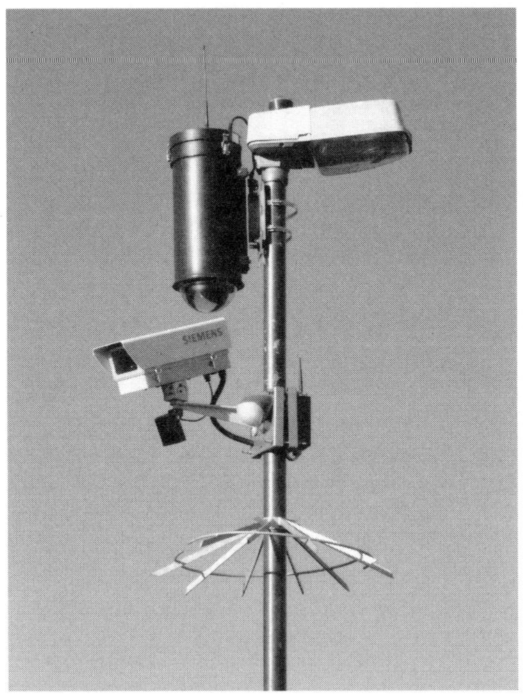

A collection of CCTV security cameras attached to a lamp post
in North London, December 7, 2008.

practically everything. "It is as if I was in a kaleidoscope, a bead in the mesmerising and constantly shifting pattern. Everything was in flux, every single moment and every single object rewritten at every turn," as "Lindsay Seers" recalls in a short piece called "Becoming Something" included in *Human Camera*.[9] This terrifyingly magnificent gift is lost once the girl sees a photograph of herself. She then spends her adult life clothed in a black sack, photographing things obsessively. In this way, she is literally trying to "become a camera" by making photographs on light-sensitive paper inserted into her mouth, with the images produced "bathed in the red light" of her body. This ambition is later replaced by an attempt to "become a projector" by creating things ex nihilo through the emanation of light. Some of Seers's films

9. Lindsay Seers, *Human Camera* (Birmingham:
Article Press, 2007), 36, http://www.lindsayseers.
info/sites/seers-dev.dev.freewayprojects.com/files/
publications/human_camera.pdf.

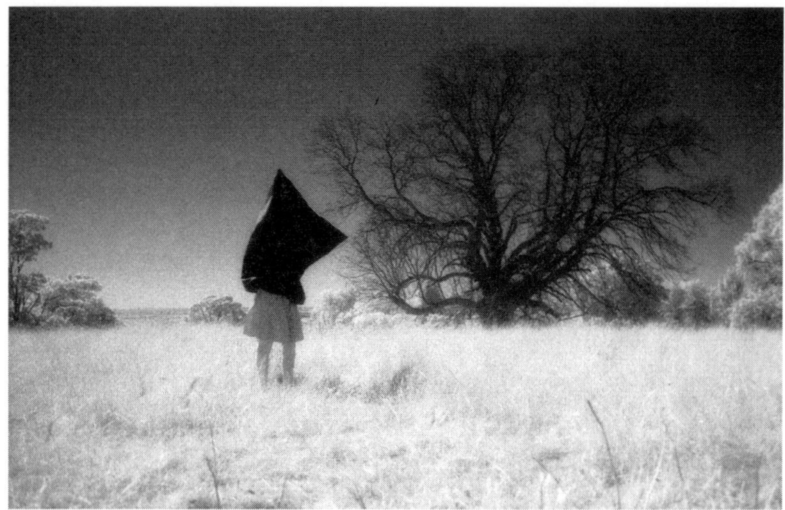

Lindsay Seers, *Extramission 6 (Black Maria)*, 2009. Video still.

presented in the show at Matt's Gallery are screened in a black hut modelled on Thomas Edison's Black Maria, his New Jersey film studio that was used for projection as well as photography. With this, Seers invites us not just to witness her process of becoming a camera but also to enter a giant camera ourselves, to literally step into the world of imaging, to reconnect to the technicity of our own being.

Although Bergson's argument about life as a form of imaging is posited as trans-historical, we can add a particular inflection to it by turning to Flusser's *Towards a Philosophy of Photography*, and, in particular, his study of the relation between the human and the technical apparatus. For Flusser, that relation changed significantly after the Industrial Revolution, a state of events in which "photographers are inside their apparatus and bound up with it. . . . It is a new kind of function in which human beings and apparatus merge into a unity."[10] Consequently, human beings now "function as a function of apparatuses,"[11] limited as they are to the execution of the camera's program from the range of seemingly infinite possibilities that are nevertheless

10. Flusser, *Towards a Philosophy*, 27.   11. Ibid., 26.

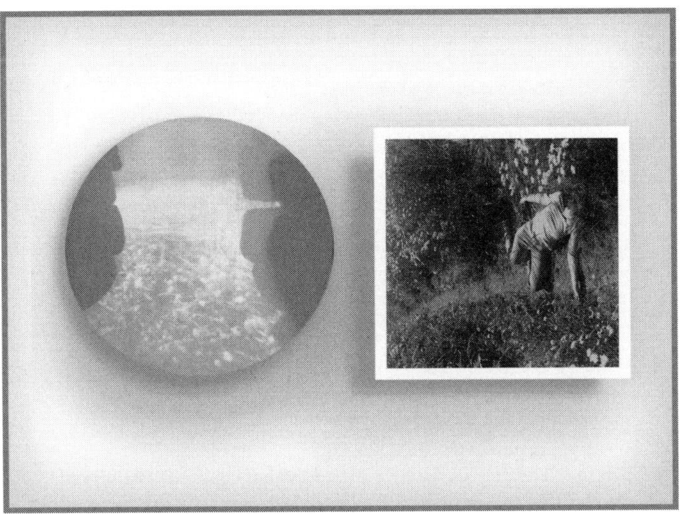

Lindsay Seers, *Pushing Daisies*, 2001. Pinhole photograph and gelatin silver print.

determined by the machine's algorithm. Arguably, humans themselves are enactors of such a program, a sequence of possibilities enabled by various couplings of adenine, cytosine, guanine, and thymine, arranged into a double helix of life. To state this is not to postulate some kind of uncritical technological determinism that would remove from "us" both any possibility of action – as artists, photographers, critics, or spectators – and any responsibility for the actions we are to take. It is merely to acknowledge our kinship with other living beings across the evolutionary spectrum, with our lives remaining subject to biochemical reactions that we cannot always understand, control, or overcome (from blushing to ageing and dying). Just as "the imagination of the camera is greater than that of every single photographer and that of all photographers put together,"[12] the imagination of that program called life in which we all participate far exceeds our human imagination. Such recognition of our entanglement in complex biological and technical networks is necessary if we are to become involved, seriously and responsibly, in any kind of photography, philosophy, or other critical or everyday activity in which we aim to exercise "free will."

12. Ibid., 36.

By reconnecting us to the technical apparatus, by letting us explore our machinic kinship, artists such as the appropriately named Seers and the image-makers in the *Drone* event are all engaged (even if they are not always up-front about it or, perhaps, entirely aware of it) in exploring the fundamental problem that many philosophers of technology who take science seriously have been grappling with: given that "there is no place for human freedom within the area of automated, programmed and programming apparatuses," how can we "show a way in which it is nevertheless possible to open up a space for freedom"?[13] Such an undertaking is very much needed, according to Flusser, "because it is the only form of revolution open to us."[14] This is to say that any prudent and effective way of envisaging and picturing a transformation of our relation to the universe must be conducted not in terms of a human struggle against the machine but in terms of our mutual co-constitution, as a recognition of our shared kinship. This recognition of the photographic condition that encompasses yet goes beyond the human, and of the photographic apparatus that extends well beyond our eyes and beyond the devices supposedly under our control, prompts us human philosophers, photographers, and spectators to mobilize the ongoing creative impulse of life, in which the whole world is a camera, and put it to creative rather than conservative uses. The conceptual expansion of processes of image-making beyond the human can also allow us to work toward escaping what Colebrook calls the "privatization of the eye in late capitalism,"[15] in which what starts out as a defence of our right to look often ends up as a defence of our right to look at the small screen. In challenging the self-possessive individualism of the human eye, *Drone: The Automated Image* is therefore a truly *revolutionary* event.

\ **Joanna Zylinska** is a professor of new media and communications at Goldsmiths, University of London (U.K.). She is the author and editor of many books on technology, culture, and ethics, including *On Spiders, Cyborgs and Being Scared* (Manchester University Press, 2001), *Bioethics in the Age of New Media* (MIT Press, 2009), and *Life after New Media: Mediation as a Vital Process* (MIT Press, 2012, with Sarah Kember), and an art photographer. Her current projects involve writing on critical vitalism, photographing media entanglements, and serving as artistic director of Transitio_MX05 "Biomediations," the 2013 edition of the Festival of New Media Art and Video held in Mexico City. \ www.joannazylinska.net

13. Ibid., 81–82.
14. Ibid., 82.

15. Colebrook, *Deleuze*, 17.

MELISSA MILES

PRIVACY IN GOOGLE STREET: WEBCAMS, STREET VIEW, AND THE TRANSFORMATION OF PHOTOGRAPHY AND PRIVACY IN PUBLIC

In 2009, angry residents of Broughton, a village in Buckinghamshire, United Kingdom, surrounded a Google Street View vehicle and, berating the driver about the "invasion of privacy," blocked the vehicle from entering their town.[1] Street View[2] has surveyed countless public streets in thousands of cities and towns around the world since its launch in 2007, using vehicles mounted with a series of cameras positioned to take overlapping photographs. By stitching the photographs together to form a 360-degree image, linking them to geospatial data, embedding them into Google Maps and Google Earth,[3] and making them available online, Street View allows Internet users to step into the mapped locations and virtually stand on the streets. The obstructive Broughton residents were concerned that criminals might be among those Internet users and that a recent spate of local burglaries could increase if Google made photographs of their streets and houses available online. Despite police reassurance that there was no evidence of a connection between Street View and an increased risk of burglary, the residents' desire to protect their private property, and more widespread anxieties about photography and the limits of privacy in public, compounded and erupted.

1. Murad Ahmed, "Village Mob Thwarts Google Street View Car," *Times* [London], April 2, 2009.

2. http://www.google.com/streetview.

3. http://maps.google.com, http://earth.google.com.

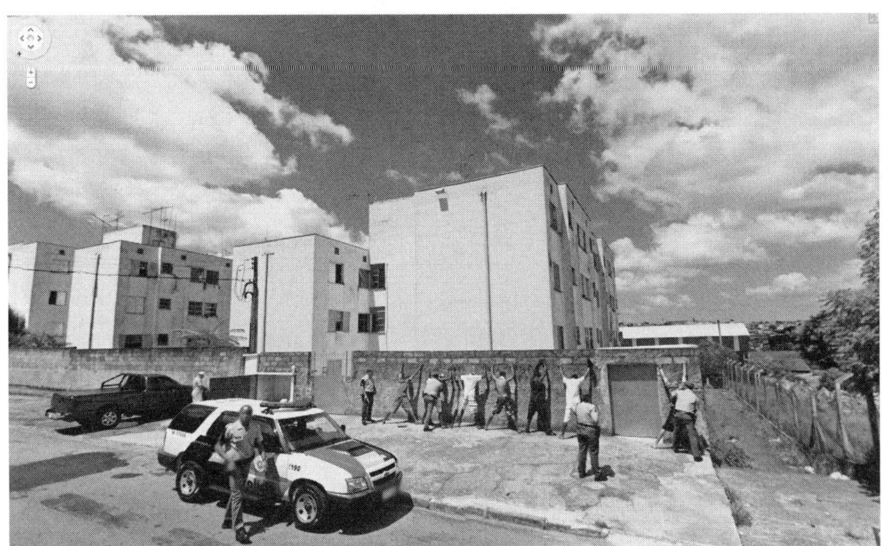

Jon Rafman, *125 Rua Maestro Benedito Olegário Berti*, Mogi das Cruzes, São Paulo, Brazil, 2010. From the project *The Nine Eyes of Google Street View* (2008–ongoing).

Although Google is not the only company to offer this type of mapping,[4] it has received the most attention and criticism, largely around issues of privacy. This focus on Street View's cameras is particularly curious in the United Kingdom, where an estimated 1.85 million closed-circuit television cameras (CCTV) watch over the public every day.[5] Other privacy-related confrontations with Street View have taken place in the media and in courtrooms in the United States, Japan, South Korea, China, Italy, Germany, Switzerland, Spain, and the Czech Republic, and the relationship between photography, privacy and the public is being hotly debated. As in comparable controversies concerning publicly mounted webcams, the repercussions of these debates extend well beyond the parameters of individual disputes. The perceived boundaries between public and private have long been traversed by photography. However, in the era of the automated image and its mass consumption online, it has again become necessary to reassess photography's relationship with privacy and reconsider its wider implications for public life today and into the future.

4. See Bing Maps Streetside (http://www.bing.com/maps) and Mapjack (http://www.mapjack.com).

5. Paul Lewis, "You're Being Watched: There's One CCTV Camera for Every 32 People in the UK," *Guardian* [London], March 3, 2011, http://www.guardian.co.uk/uk/2011/mar/02/cctv-cameras-watching-surveillance.

Court cases instigated against Google over Street View speak to the issues at hand. For example, Pennsylvania residents Aaron and Christine Boring brought a lawsuit against Google in 2008, claiming that the company violated their privacy rights and caused them mental suffering when it took images of their residence from a private road and published them online. The case was dismissed, but it is indicative of larger trends in which private property rights are conflated with classic American definitions of personal privacy as "the right to be let alone."[6]

Such concerns about privacy and Street View follow similar disputes over publicly mounted webcams in the early 2000s. Unlike Street View, which presents images from a fixed moment in time, webcam images are continually refreshed. Thousands of webcams installed in airports, restaurants, beaches, shopping malls, cruise ships, zoos, churches, public squares, gardens, train stations, and ski resorts, in every continent in the world – including Antarctica – allow us to view these sites remotely twenty-four hours a day. In 2001, one such webcam was installed on a private house overlooking the Block Island Ferry terminal, approximately twelve miles off the Rhode Island coast in the United States. The camera uploaded photographs of the ferry dock automatically every fifteen minutes, allowing travellers to check weather conditions and confirm whether the ferries were running. The objections to the camera that arose, similar to those in the Borings' case, fused an assertion of rights over private property with notions of individual privacy. The ferry company, Interstate Navigation, reported "serious concerns" about the camera and the privacy of its business operations and passengers, even though the camera was installed at a distance that made it impossible to identify anyone in the pictures.[7] Under threat of litigation, the local businessman who had installed the webcam removed it.

Anxieties around the public use of these photographic technologies must be understood in a larger context in which our privacy is perceived as being under increasing threat. Since the 1990s, commentators in the United States, the United Kingdom, and Australia have decried the "end of privacy" and the "death of privacy" in response to issues as diverse as the electronic distribution of personal information and receiving unwanted phone calls from telemarketers.[8] This anxiety about the loss of personal privacy is coupled with a growing desire for privacy in public, fostered in part by the proliferation of surveillance technologies and the accumulation and circulation of personal information by private and public bodies. Calls for privacy in

6. Samuel D. Warren and Louis D. Brandeis, "The Right to Privacy," *Harvard Law Review* 4 (1890), 193, http://www.jstor.org/stable/10.2307/1321160.
7. Paul Zielbauer, "Webcam's Scenic View Raises a Privacy Issue," *New York Times*, May 3, 2001, http://www.nytimes.com/2001/05/03/technology/webcam-s-scenic-view-raises-a-privacy-issue.html?pagewanted=all&src=pm.

8. Richard Spinello, "The End of Privacy," *America* 176, no. 1 (1997), 9–13; David Brin, *The Transparent Society: Will Technology Force Us to Choose Between Privacy and Freedom?* (Reading, Mass.: Perseus Books, 1998); Reginald Whitaker, *The End of Privacy: How Total Surveillance is Becoming a Reality* (New York: New Press, 1999); Charles J. Sykes, *The End of Privacy: The Attack on Personal Rights at Home, at Work, On-Line, and in Court* (New York: St. Martin's Press, 2000).

public are made more complex by the privatization of once-public spaces, including train stations, shopping malls, and some entire communities. The small private community of North Oaks, Minnesota, won its dispute with Google on these grounds. After proving that the Google vehicle was in violation of the private town's trespassing ordinance, the mayor of North Oaks ensured that the town was wiped from Street View altogether in 2008.

The ever-increasing focus on individualism in contemporary Western cultures and our related withdrawal from the public realm as a shared social space are other significant factors that inform this rising anxiety over privacy. More than two decades after Margaret Thatcher proclaimed, "There is no such thing as society,"[9] this culture of individualism encourages us to conceive of ourselves not as members of a public with shared responsibilities and obligations, but as competitive individuals, perpetually vulnerable to perceived threats against our properties and ourselves. Rather than engaging actively in the public sphere, we retreat into private domains and remain largely content to have the world beamed into our homes through computers and television sets.[10] Ironically, by allowing us to explore the streets of the world from the privacy of our own homes, Street View both responds to and reinforces the demand for privacy that Google is now defending itself against.

Ongoing disputes over Street View's approach to privacy have led to significant changes in its online publication practices. People are now able to request the blurring of images of their own properties and the removal of "inappropriate content," and images of faces and vehicle licence plates are routinely blurred. Google is also embracing less controversial options for image gathering, including incorporating into Street View user-contributed photographs from Panoramio, a geocentric photo-sharing site purchased by Google in 2007.

Despite Google's claims that Street View imagery "is no different from what you might see driving or walking down the street,"[11] it is important to acknowledge how Google's organization and presentation of those sights using photography changes the privacy implications considerably. Photography has long operated in the murky borderland between the public and the private. The invention of the Kodak camera in 1888 allowed the camera to leave the formal settings of the studio and bourgeois home and be taken into the streets. The subsequent proliferation of cameras in

9. Margaret Thatcher interviewed by Douglas Keay, "Aids, Education and the Year 2000!," *Woman's Own*, (October 31, 1987), 10, http://www.margaretthatcher.org/document/106689.

10. Alastair Hannay, *On the Public* (New York and London: Routledge, 2005), 78.
11. http://maps.google.com.au/help/maps/streetview/privacy.html.

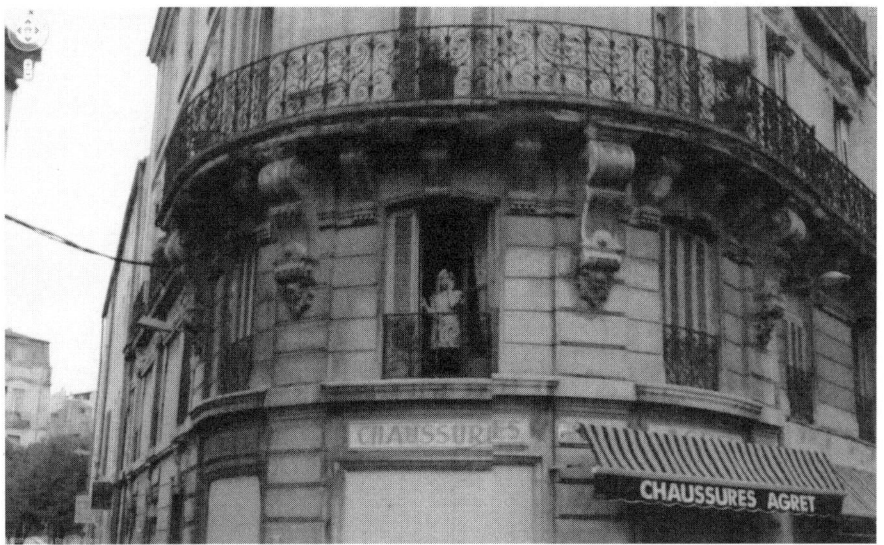

Jon Rafman, *Place Alexandre Laissac / Rue de l'Ancienne Poste*, Montpellier, France, 2010.
From the project *The Nine Eyes of Google Street View* (2008–ongoing).

public spaces created suspicions in the United States about "camera fiends" and led to the banning of photography at the Washington Monument and at some beaches.[12] Samuel Warren and Louis Brandeis made their famous calls for greater legal protection of privacy in the United States in 1890 in direct response to photography. They expressed the fear that "instantaneous photographs and newspaper enterprise" would invade the domestic sphere and argued that "the sacred precincts of private and domestic life" had to be defended.[13] In their view, a legal defence was required "to protect the privacy of the individual from invasion either by the too enterprising press, the photographers, or the possessor of any other modern device for recording or reproducing scenes or sounds."[14]

Warren and Brandeis recognized photography's unique ability to intensify invasions of privacy. As it fixes a moment in time, the camera has the ability to overcome the temporal limitations of experienced moments and allow for the scrutiny of those moments to continue indefinitely. Photographs also allow us to study details that

12. Robert E. Mensel, "'Kodakers Lying in Wait': Amateur Photography and the Right to Privacy in New York, 1885–1915," *American Quarterly* 43, no. 1 (1991), 28–29, http://www.jstor.org/stable/2712965.

13. Warren and Brandeis, "Right to Privacy," 195.
14. Ibid., 206.

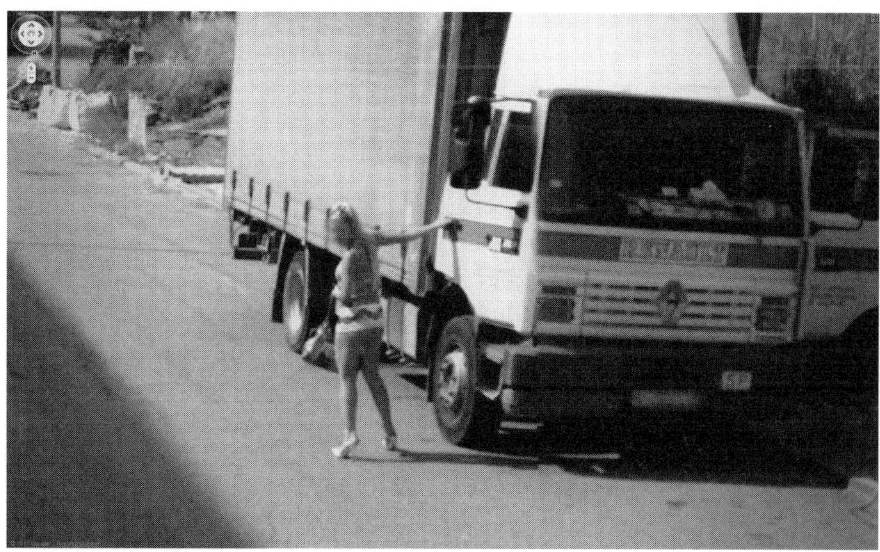

Jon Rafman, *Calle de Osona*, Santa Perpètua de Mogoda, Spain, 2010.
From the project *The Nine Eyes of Google Street View* (2008–ongoing).

may not have been noticed in real time, making once marginal or overlooked sights available for much closer inspection. Moreover, the ability to disseminate photographs, now done instantaneously online, makes it possible for the sight to be made available to a much larger audience and in many contexts different to those that the subjects may have intended when they appeared in public. These qualities of photography underpin many of the controversies over moments captured and disseminated worldwide on Street View, including images of dead bodies in the streets of Brazil,[15] a man entering an adult video store in the United Kingdom,[16] and a woman's underwear hanging on a washing line in Japan.[17] The Japanese owner of the underwear attempted to sue Google, claiming psychological distress for this exposure of her intimate apparel to the world.

Although such cases can be seen as a continuation of photography's long, tense historical entanglement with privacy and the public, there are some crucial new developments. Today, the "camera fiends" of the 1890s have been replaced

15. Andrew Hough, "Google Forced to Remove 'Dead Body' Images from Brazil Street View Service," *Telegraph* [London], October 6, 2010.
16. Matthew Moore, "Google Street View: Private Moments Captured," *Telegraph* [London], June 19, 2008.

17. Kerry Cunningham, "Google Street View: Other Cases where the Web Giant Has Been Questioned over Privacy," *Telegraph* [London], January 18, 2011.

with automated machines operated by faceless figures and corporations. The development of such mechanized modes of image production and viewing led to much discussion in the 1980s and 1990s about the decentring and disembodiment of vision. However, debates about privacy and the online publication of automated images have shifted focus back onto the body. The mass media may invoke abstract terms – such as "user," "consumer," and "demographic" – to describe its viewers, but those anxious about privacy and the automated image are all too aware that these online images may potentially be seen by millions of embodied individuals just like them. Contemporary concerns about privacy on Street View and webcams are thereby intimately bound up with relations between the visible and the invisible, as those who look but are not looked at do their looking from the security of an anonymous private domain.

This pervasive sense that our privacy is under threat from invisible sources and viewers has created paranoia that is also directed at more visible signs of public photography. Individual photographers working in public in the United Kingdom and in Australia frequently experience verbal abuse and threats of violence or arrest, usually from fellow citizens and over-zealous security guards.[18] Fuelled by fears of terrorism, sexual predators, and pedophiles, and bolstered by more formal restrictions on photography, the increasing hostility toward photographers working in public is leading to their practising self-censorship, as well as limiting the way that they work in public and the types of photographs that they produce.[19] The impact on the future historical record is a very real concern, as more and more photographers turn away from public life to construct work in the studio or with found photographs. Nonetheless, many photographers are fighting back: in Australia, they have formed the lobby group Arts Freedom Australia, and in the United Kingdom, photographers have come together under the banner "I'm a Photographer, Not a Terrorist!" These groups' protest activities in 2010 drew attention to the wider implications of restrictions on public photography and the culture of privacy that they support.

In an apparent paradox, tensions around public photography are rising in a period in which people are more willing than ever to post photographs of themselves on the Internet, often sharing the most intimate parts of their lives. As debate continues about the privacy of individuals captured in public in Street View, Facebook pages and personal blogs are multiplying like never before, millions are taking up YouTube's invitation to "broadcast yourself," and teenagers are circulating sexually explicit

18. Melissa Miles, "Photography, Privacy and the Public," *Law, Culture and the Humanities*, 19–20 (prepublished January 19, 2012, doi:10.1177/1743872111430277).

19. Ibid., 20.

images of themselves on their mobile phones in a phenomenon known as sexting. This culture of mediated voyeurism also thrives in the form of reality TV, celebrity gossip magazines, media scandals over politicians' sex lives, and confessional TV talk shows.

The tensions between voyeurism and a desire for privacy reflect the important role that photographic practices play in demarcating public–private boundaries in advanced media cultures.[20] The camera's power to invade privacy is mirrored by its function as a tool for authenticating the private realms of personality and self-definition. Privacy itself plays a central role in facilitating self-definition. It enables us to present edited versions of ourselves to different audiences, and to expose only those parts of our lives that we want others to see. Our colleagues at work may be invited to see one side of us, while our family and friends may see another.[21] Photography aids in this process by allowing us to produce images of our ideal selves as self-possessed and individual. Whereas discrete, formal photographic portraits may have borne the weight of such image production in the nineteenth century, today large archives of personal digital photographs, documenting even the most banal aspects of daily life, produce a more fragmented and malleable image of the self. Photography nonetheless remains central to the notion of individualism that underpins the very concept of privacy. As well as producing images of particular individuals, the proliferation of personal photographs continues to dramatize the larger concept of individualism that is so central to privacy.

At the same time, as we have seen with Street View and webcams, photography's power to make the world visible is central to our negotiation of the public. According to Paul Frosh, photography in this context is "both the index and agent of publicness itself."[22] Voyeurism is controversial because it draws attention to the ultimate pre-cariousness of the distinctions between the public and the private. In voyeurism, writes Frosh, the gaze of the private viewer becomes integral to the field of public visibility, but also distances the viewer from that field. The boundary between public citizen and private person is therefore revealed to be porous, unstable, and in need of continual reiteration.[23]

Controversies over Street View and webcams are additional manifestations of this ongoing tension between the public and the private, which photography has long made visible. In an effort to resolve the tension, more firmly demarcate these terms,

20. Paul Frosh, "The Public Eye and the Citizen-Voyeur: Photography as a Performance of Power," *Social Semiotics* 11, no. 1 (2001), 43, doi:10.1080/10350330123316.

21. Christopher Slobogin, "Public Privacy: Camera Surveillance of Public Places and the Right to Anonymity," *Mississippi Law Journal* 72, no. 1 (2002), 264, http://dx.doi.org/10.2139/ssrn.364600.
22. Frosh, "Public Eye," 43.
23. Ibid., 49.

and establish clear boundaries around the private, some critics have proposed that we adopt international privacy standards that respond to the global consumption of online images and cut across the diversity of national privacy laws.[24] However, this is an unlikely solution as it fails to recognize that privacy is not a universal human right but a historically and culturally specific concept that has different connotations in different contexts. Fears about privacy in Germany, with its history of the Stasi secret police in communist East Germany, will have an inflection different to American notions of privacy, which are grounded in the protection of individuality and personhood and tied to the defence of capitalism in liberalism.[25] Efforts to enshrine a universal right to privacy in law will inevitably result in dominant cultures imposing their own approaches to privacy on others.

Instead of attempting to fix this inherently fluid concept, we need to recognize that privacy is a very complex set of ideas and expectations that must be weighed against other rights and responsibilities that we have as members of a public. If we stop struggling to fix photography's fraught relationship with privacy and acknowledge that privacy is intimately tied to the construction of certain social norms and values, debate can be shifted away from specific technologies and toward the deeper social and cultural anxieties that lie at the heart of these controversies.

\ **Melissa Miles** is a senior lecturer in the Faculty of Art, Design and Architecture at Monash University (Melbourne, Australia). Her research has been published in the world's leading journals, including *Journal of Visual Culture, History of Photography, International Journal of Art and Design Education, Photographies*, and *Law, Culture and the Humanities*. Miles is the author of a book on photography, *The Burning Mirror: Photography in an Ambivalent Light* (Australian Scholarly Press, 2008). She is currently completing a large-scale Australian Research Council–funded project, *Photography and Crime*, with colleagues from her own faculty, the Faculty of Law, Monash University, and the Centre for Contemporary Photography.

24. Lauren H. Rakower, "Blurred Line: Zooming In on Google Street View and the Global Right to Privacy," *Brooklyn Journal of International Law* 37, no. 1 (2011), 317–47, http://www.brooklaw.edu/intellectuallife/lawjournals/brooklynjournalofinternationallaw/volumes/volume37/Issue1.aspx.

25. See "Privacy, Photography, and the Press," *Harvard Law Review* 111, no. 4 (1998), 1087, http://www.jstor.org/stable/1342012; Nicholas Abercrombie, Stephen Hill, and Bryan Turner, *Sovereign Individuals of Capitalism* (London: Allen & Unwin, 1986), 36; Christopher Slobogin, "Public Privacy," 264.

FRANCINE DAGENAIS

THE BIOMACHINIC PHYLUM:
THE DRONES IN THE HIVE, IMPLICATIONS
FOR CONTEMPORARY ART

In physics, the term *singularity* refers to a point at which, usually in a black hole, it is no longer possible to predict the outcome of the interaction between various forces and matter (or antimatter in this case). Similarly, technological singularity refers to a point at which interaction between artificial intelligence (AI), artificial life (Alife), and humans will produce technological change so rapid that it will no longer be fathomable by pre-singularitarian humans – a sublime technological state often referred to as the "nerd rapture." Through the 1940s and 1950s, a number of theorists conceived of the singularity. Isaac Asimov, Alan Turing, Stan Ulam, and John von Neumann, among others, imagined a kind of melding of human and non-human DNA with AI, the blending of data (organic code + machinic code) becoming a new super-entity. Judging by the artists whose works I am about to discuss, it is perhaps not so counterintuitive to conceive of the singularity as a sociological event affecting our behavioural patterns, in which the act of self-discipline and self-surveillance becomes our bridge to a new *biomachinic phylum, Machina Chordata.*

We are emerging from a long era of individuality that took hold during the Renaissance, when the experience and consciousness of an individual human being was viewed as not only central in the universe but exemplary of all others: *Homo universalis*. Increasingly, we are being immersed in an era of the collective, in which a constantly interconnected *hive* of distributed humans is jacked into a multipartite, virtual, ubiquitous network composed of text- and voice-based devices that drive social media and the Internet, a *hive mind*. The hive mind was initially conceived as a knowledge base and set of beliefs prevalent at a given point in history and shared by a collective community. In the early twentieth century, French sociologist Émile Durkheim studied the hive mind, or, as he coined it in French, the "*conscience collective*";[1] he concluded that it found its strength in group dynamics and that the sharing of values and information that it generated was crucial to the well-being of those within it. In this metaphorical structure, the division of labour within a community follows the roles within a real hive – queen, worker, drone, and so forth. Durkheim viewed the hive mind as a rational complex with, as was the case in his era, a slow reaction time. He did not foresee its current incarnation, which, in addition to reason and faith, is driven by emotion and instinct. What can be said of today's construct, which reacts instantaneously to messages or events by staging flash mobs that may address superficial dance, fashion, or lifestyle trends on the one hand, or important political ideals on the other hand? What is this hive mind about? Does it obliterate the individual or does it free it by allowing a perpetual state of flux? How we view it depends entirely to the degree to which we are plugged into it.

The image of the hive mind is certainly convenient; it serves to form a bridge between the real, the virtual, and the cyber, on the one hand, and communications systems and devices such as the Internet and social media, on the other hand, forming one overarching structure. Post-9/11, this structure has also been a means of acquiring control over and intelligence on individual members of the hive. As theorist Ollivier Dyens points out, "[The hive] redefines the territorial borders that isolate (or do not isolate) living beings. . . . A hive is both unique and multiple, one and several."[2] Since 9/11, there has been an explosion of surveillance technologies, and as they become smaller and more polyvalent our most intimate boundaries become increasingly permeable.

1. Émile Durkheim, *The Division of Labor in Society*, trans. George Simpson (New York: The Free Press, 1947), 73–80.

2. Ollivier Dyens, *Metal and Flesh: The Evolution of Man: Technology Takes Over*, trans. Evan J. Bibbee and Ollivier Dyens (Cambridge, Mass.: MIT Press, 2001), 45.

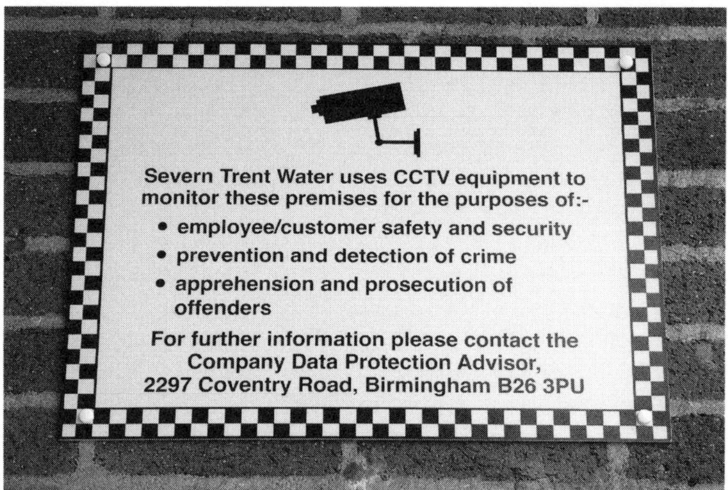

CCTV advisory sign at the Severn Trent Water company in Birmingham, U.K., on October 14, 2005.

Not surprisingly, artists from around the world have taken notice of this push toward surveillance and developed a number of strategies to critique it. A debate has raged for over half a century now on whether we live in a society of *spectacle* (1967)[3] or one of *surveillance*. In a book titled *Suspensions of Perception*,[4] however, art historian Jonathan Crary concludes that surveillance and spectacle intertwine. Indeed, if we look at the proliferation of reality television shows in which subjects interact under laboratory conditions for the entertainment of a voyeuristic mass audience, we can clearly see both dynamics at play. This phenomenon was strongly reflected in the work of a crop of artists' groups and hackers who emerged in the late 1990s, when *sniffing*, a means of accessing surveillance image databanks, became a strategy for bringing this topic to mass attention. In some cases, artists used the technology even more directly. For instance, the Surveillance Camera Players staged plays in front of closed-circuit television (CCTV) cameras, and artist Manu Luksch accumulated five years' worth of personal surveillance footage from databanks in order to produce a film titled *Faceless* (2007).

3. Guy Debord, *The Society of the Spectacle*, trans. Donald Nicholson-Smith (New York: Zone Books, 1994).

4. Jonathan Crary, *Suspensions of Perception: Attention, Spectacle, and Modern Culture* (Cambridge, Mass.: MIT Press, 2001), 73–76.

A sign informing residents of the presence of a video surveillance system in the area close to Boulogne-Billancourt, a western suburb of Paris, on January 16, 2012.

Some artists and designers are proponents of sousveillance, a means of subverting surveillance through appropriation. Steve Mann has been at the forefront of this trend, donning increasingly discreet wearable computing devices (from a large helmet and camera devised in 1980 at the Media Lab at the Massachusetts Institute of Technology (MIT) to his most recent device, the EyeTap digital eyeglass).[5] For decades now, Mann has stayed constantly connected in an endless 24/7 feedback loop, living in augmented reality, plugged into networks at all times, and providing real-time sound and images of his experiences. Sousveillance is a strategy of one-upmanship in which surveillance is itself confronted and surveilled, as the subject of surveillance provides a mass of information so overwhelming that it becomes impossible to comb through it.

Many others have followed Mann's example and, particularly in the past decade, sousveillance has caught on as a means of taking back control. Hasan M. Elahi is a well-known case in point in his response to an incident that took place at the

5. For more information, see http://www.eecg.
toronto.edu/~mann/.

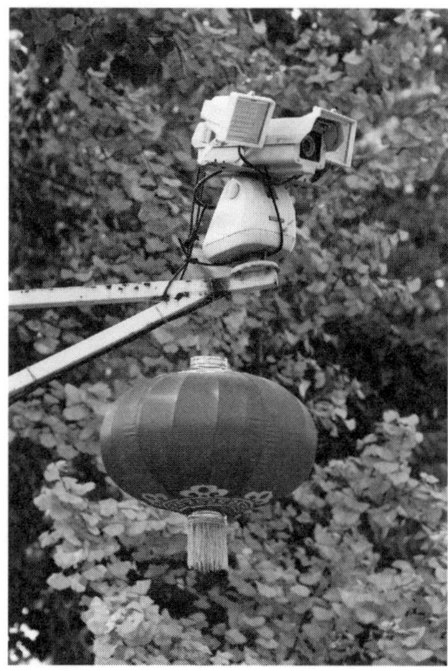

A security camera watching Ai Weiwei's home on
November 7, 2011.

Detroit airport in June of 2002, when he was forced to provide the Immigration and Naturalization Service with a wealth of information on his whereabouts before and after the incidents of 9/11.[6] Visiting his Web site is like entering several episodes of his private world, categorized according to a specific taxonomy (travel meals, hotel washrooms, and so on), in which the sheer abundance of automated images renders them meaningless.

Perhaps the most famous international artist to have embraced the strategy of sousveillance is Ai Weiwei. In April of 2012, after his detention and months of subsequent surveillance, the artist decided to ironically mark the one-year anniversary of his arrest.[7] In response to the state's fifteen cameras already surveilling the outside

6. Hasan M. Elahi speaks of his ordeal in "You Want to Track Me? Here You Go, F.B.I.," *New York Times Sunday Review*, October 29, 2011. Elahi's work can be viewed at the University of Maryland Web site, http://elahi.umd.edu.

7. In April of 2011, Ai was detained by Chinese authorities without formal charges for eighty-one days and then released under what is essentially house arrest.

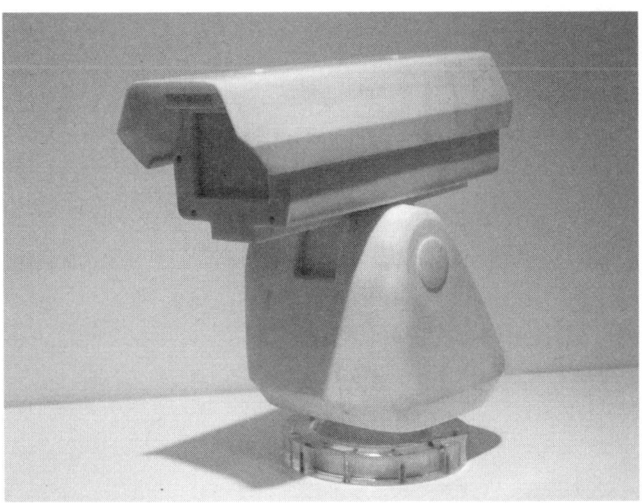

Ai Weiwei, *Surveillance Camera*, 2010. Installation view at the Hirshhorn
Museum and Sculpture Garden, Washington, D.C., 2012.

of his house, Ai placed four additional cameras around his home and in his bedroom.
Given the David-and-Goliath struggle that he has had to wage with Chinese authorities,
it is not surprising that the topic of surveillance has emerged as a mainstay in his
work. Following his detention, self-surveillance images of the artist started to surface
on the social media application Google+ and, for a few days in April 2012, on his
Web site, weiweicam.com, before it was shut down by authorities.

If we examine a photograph taken outside Ai Weiwei's home on November 7, 2011, a
few months before the Chinese authorities shut down his Web site, we see a generic
surveillance camera – a rather old model, one that most people in cities worldwide
would recognize. Indeed, most icons representing surveillance cameras, or the
presence of surveillance, show an old-fashioned configuration of the device – a long
rectangle with either an overhang to shield the lens from the elements or a cylinder
representing the lens itself protruding from the rectangle – despite the fact that

semi-spherical models now abound in institutional and commercial applications. Ai Weiwei's *Surveillance Camera* (2010) is a faithful replica, made of marble, of the particular model that was documented outside his home. *Surveillance Camera* is a dummy, an object shaped like a surveillance camera but without functional application – in other words, a skeuomorph standing in for the concept of surveillance itself.

Through the weiweicam.com Web site and through his various sousveillance statements, Ai is showing the world the reality of his daily life and the constant scrutiny that he has had to endure. He is also speaking for the large number of people in his country who are surveilled but do not have the power or status to fight back. Given how much attention the story garnered from print and electronic media all over the world and the fact that it took less than two days for Chinese authorities to shut the Web site down, Ai has given a tangible demonstration of just how effective sousveillance can be.

The strategy of sousveillance in effect inverts the polarity of what Donna Haraway has called the "informatics of dominance,"[8] a hierarchical system with an established set of power relations built in to computer systems, the Internet, and social media. The hive mind is too multipartite to be truly governable. The feedback loop of user/ interface device/systems of dominance/hive mind/systems of dominance/interface device/user has inadvertently brought about surprising social changes in a very short period – changes that have been met with immediate pushback from economic powers and old systems of governance. This underscores the difficulty of dealing with the hive mind and its lack of boundaries. We have all, to a lesser or greater degree, embraced our new status as hive members, or fractions of a whole in which it becomes increasingly difficult to define where member entities end and the hive mind begins.

Of course, the centrality of living organic beings has been gradually encroached upon since Cartesianism; the fact that it is now challenged on a daily basis simply presents us with a more pressing need to examine our understanding of what is still considered natural. Informatics machines now rule almost all functional apparatuses. Intensive research into AI, graphene, molecular manufacturing, nanobiotechnology, nanocomposite plating, nanorobotics, and silicon nanowires has led to ever-smaller circuitry and biotech components. Communications are increasingly machine mediated,

8. Donna Haraway, "A Cyborg Manifesto: Science, Technology, and Socialist-Feminism in the Late Twentieth Century," in *Simians, Cyborgs, and Women: The Reinvention of Nature* (New York and London; Routledge, 1991), 161. In this famous essay, the author devotes a section to the "informatics of dominance," in which she establishes a hierarchical chart of categories of domination, comparing "comfortable old" dominations to "scary new networks" of domination.

to the point that social media serve an important function in mass decisions, movements, and trends. The collective consciousness, or hive mind, is predicated on a form of interaction in which rapid response time is key, leading to a behavioural model in which, like a laboratory subject, the hive member is perpetually punished or rewarded for clicking the wrong or right button. This stimulus-response connection between the hive member and the hive mind has become unruly and unpredictable. Virtual/machinic entities seem to have developed a mind of their own and are edging ever closer to passing the Turing test, at which point it will become impossible to distinguish humans from computers.

In *The Human Use of Human Beings*,[9] Norbert Wiener pondered the distinctions between humans and animals and between humans and computers, and he developed a communications model that encompasses possible combinations: human to human, machine to machine, human to machine. Wiener concluded that whereas, for instance, ant behaviour is hardwired with no self-selection possible, no such boundaries need limit humans and machines.[10] He conceived a theory that combined the machinic with the human and that would comprise the "study of language, the study of message as a means of controlling both machinery and society, the development of computing machines and other such automata, [and] certain reflections upon psychology and the nervous system."[11] This description closely approximates the biomachinic entity that is the current hive mind. Theorists Gilles Deleuze and Félix Guattari – and, later, Manuel De Landa – wrote about the concept of the *machinic phylum*. De Landa takes this logic to the extreme, imagining a blurring of boundaries between the organic and non-organic, the virtual and the real worlds.[12] He defines the machinic phylum as "the set of all the singularities at the onset of processes of self-organization – the critical points in the flow of matter and energy, points at which these flow spontaneously acquire a new form or pattern."[13] The history of information analysis and machinic control, he suggests, reflects the process of cognitive structures shifting from humans to machines, a process that has become more evident in the past few decades.

With Michel Foucault's *Discipline and Punish*,[14] we were made more aware of how panopticism functions and how a surveillance system establishes an expectation of surveillance. According to Foucault, the naturalization of surveillance ultimately

9. Norbert Wiener, *The Human Use of Human Beings: Cybernetics and Society* (Cambridge, Mass.: Da Capo Press, 1988).
10. Ibid., 16.
11. Ibid., 15.

12. Manuel De Landa, *War in the Age of Intelligent Machines* (New York: Zone Books, 1991).
13. Ibid., 132.
14. Michael Foucault, *Discipline and Punish: The Birth of the Prison*, trans. Alan Sheridan (New York: Vintage Books, 1995).

serves as a means of imposing self-discipline. Foucault suggested that those who are surveilled eventually comply without question, whether someone is watching or not. He posited that this technology led to a new ontology for the body whereby humans were viewed as machines.

The structure of panopticism in the age of the hive mind differs somewhat from its architecture in the eighteenth century, when the building itself imposed a technology of surveillance. Today, the sheer array of available surveillance systems and devices, along with their decreasing size, makes them ubiquitous. It is the machinic, however, that brings humans and their hive mind under one rule. The word *hive* immediately brings to mind multiplicity, a collective of very small animals, generally insects, that live according to a prescribed social order in which individuality has no place and the priority is the fulfilment of a destiny, unencumbered by subjecthood, agency, or conscience. We even refer to these surveillance devices as insects. Old-fashioned cold war microphones were called bugs, and today the term *drone* clearly evokes a mindless fractional entity linked to a greater social order and colony.

Unmanned aerial vehicles (UAVs, or drones) have been in use since the end of the Second World War, but only in the past decade has the market for such devices exploded in both military and commercial markets. Customers are now expecting smaller and smaller drones, some weighing twenty grams or less. One example, the Monolithic Bee (Mobee), emerges from a self-assembling origami nanomatrix. Because of its pop-up-assembly scaffolding, the Mobee can easily be massed-produced in exponentially smaller sizes with no risk of human error. This will make it all the more appealing to profit-driven drone makers, much to the world's detriment. Whereas bugs were usually planted in locations where the surveilled were known to live or work, biomimicking stealth drones can follow and kill the surveilled wherever they go. It is significant that the term "bugsplat"[15] was coined by the Pentagon and CIA drone operators to refer to collateral damage in Pakistan, Somalia, and Yemen. The term was subsequently associated with a computer program designed to estimate casualties during drone attacks. As drones in the 'hood will soon become as common as surveillance cameras are now, they will clearly have to undergo a makeover, as their public image leaves much to be desired; advertising giant Saatchi & Saatchi has taken on this task.

15. Bradley Graham, "Military Turns to Software to Cut Civilian Casualties," *Washington Post*, February 21, 2003. A version of this article has been reprinted in the *Baltimore Sun*: http://articles.baltimoresun.com/2012-01-01/news/ bs-ed-koehler-20120101_1_civilian-toll-civilian-deaths-drone-strikes.

During the 2012 edition of the New Directors' Showcase — an event organized by Saatchi & Saatchi under the "Meet Your Creator" theme at the Cannes Lions International Festival of Creativity — a troupe of sixteen quadrotors flew in perfect formation in a short performance. The drones buzzed like lovely fireflies, dancing and hovering to a snappy techno beat.[16] The carefully choreographed show, which directed light beams across a darkened room, fulfilled the stated goal of achieving a "fusion of sound, technology and light" and the "ambience of a [wired] Church of Creativity."[17] Despite Saatchi & Saatchi's attempts at making drones seem harmless, however, the art world's general take on them is focused less on the playful aspects and much more on their effects on the lives of those whom they surveil and attack. In the realm of warfare and intelligence, drones have become ubiquitous and their names conjure up images of animals stealthily watching, hunting, and attacking their prey. Here are a few names that demonstrate this: Global Hawk, Hunter, Predator, Puma, Rascal, Raven, Reaper, Scan Eagle, Shadow, Spyder, Tiger Moth, Vigilante, Warrior, and Wasp.

Perhaps in response to the lack of attention by the mainstream media, some artists, designers, photojournalists, and writers have addressed the issue of drones. Most notably, Noor Behram has made it his mission to show the world what drones actually do. He painstakingly documents the impact of U.S. Air Force drone strikes in his native Waziristan.[18] Intended as a means of hunting down al-Qaida and the Taliban, U.S. drone strikes also have an impact on civilian populations, and Behram is there to draw our attention to this fact. His images of dead children resonate in a way that few written reports can. The term *bugsplat* may have become commonplace since its first use ten years ago, but there is no offhand or mitigating terminology that can do away with the pain conveyed by these images.

Drones extend our hive mind in ways that we have only begun to realize. The Internet was developed by the Defense Advance Research Projects Agency (DARPA), and DARPA is also behind the production of a variety of *unhumanned* — remote-controlled or remote-guided — vehicles.[19] In the view of many artists, the drone is edging us that much closer to an Orwellian version of constant connectedness with the machinic phylum, in which intelligence is intrinsically linked with warfare. In Paul Virilio's view, the inception of each new technology brings with it a foreseeable accident, its inherent

16. The designers of the quadrotors, Alex Kushleyev and Daniel Mellinger, are the founders of Kmel Robotics, one of the fifty or so companies involved in producing UAVs in the United States.
17. See http://www.saatchi.com/news/archive/ saatchi__saatchi_new_directors_showcase_2012.

18. Saeed Shah in Islamabad and Peter Beaumont, "US Drone Strikes in Pakistan Claiming Many Civilian Victims, Says Campaigner," *Guardian* [London], July 17, 2011.
19. Autonomous ground vehicles (AGVs), autonomous underwater vehicles (AUVs), biologically inspired AI for micro-aerial vehicles (BioMAV), and UAVs are just a few of these.

self-destruct button.[20] The original sin that would come of the mating of two phyla, *Machina* and *Chordata*, would result in our being turned away from the paradise of nature, condemned to a world of intelligence gathering, surveillance, and warfare. One of the great fallacies in the drone metaphor, however, is the seeming erasure of humans from the process.[21] There are humans all along the way – in the development, maintenance, operation, guidance, and decision-making processes. Whether or not we are nearing mutation and inching closer to a new biomachinic phylum, *Machina Chordata*, humans are still endowed with consciousness and conscience, and artists such as Ai Weiwei and photojournalists such as Noor Behram are urgently working to raise awareness of the reality of surveillance systems and devices, and their real and virtual effects on our world.[22]

\ **Francine Dagenais** is an author, theoretician, and art historian who has been writing about visual and media arts for more than twenty years. Her essays have recently appeared in *Art Tomorrow* and *Intermédialités*. As a curator, she has organized a number of events and exhibitions for artist-run centres, universities, and organizations such as ISEA International (formerly Inter-Society for the Electronic Arts). She has also participated in numerous colloquia and congresses, including, in 2011, the Conference on Religion and Spirituality in Society at the University of Illinois at Urbana-Champaign, in Chicago. She lives in Montreal and teaches at Université Laval, in Quebec City.

20. Paul Virilio, *The Original Accident*, trans. Julie Rose (Cambridge, U.K.: Polity Press, 2007).
21. One of the few articles in the mainstream press came out in the summer of 2012: Elisabeth Bumiller, "Drone Pilots Are Changing, and Changed by, Remote Warfare," *New York Times*, July 30, 2012, http://atwar. blogs.nytimes.com/2012/07/30/drone-pilots-are-changing-and-changed-by-remote-warfare.

22. Artists, designers and thinkers discussed in this paper have been at the forefront of an effort to raise awareness about human (mind and body) augmentation technologies and their impact on our lives. A new initiative at the University of Cambridge is indicative of how pressing the issue has become and how seriously we should all be taking technological advancements that edge us closer to the singularity: philosopher Huw Price, astrophysicist Martin Rees, and Skype co-founder Jaan Tallinn are planning to launch the Centre for the Study of Existential Risk in 2013. Its stated goal is to initiate a reflection on machinic evolution in humans and, if possible, limit the risk of human extinction due to new developments in AI, biotechnology, nanotechnology, robotics, and other anthropogenically induced changes to our planet and climate. For more information on the Centre for Study of Existential Risk, visit http://cser.org.

JORDAN CRANDALL

ONTOLOGY OF THE DRONE

We begin this analysis from the tail end, rather than the front. Not with the eyes, but with the ass. We start at the bottom and work our way up. When we finally arrive at the helm, we may be a bit greasy.

When seen from below, the tiniest component can assume large-scale relevance, can have the biggest effects. We ignore it at our peril. A Global Hawk – the largest unmanned plane in the U.S. military's arsenal – was once brought down by a *rudder*. As the hulking, ungainly vehicle rumbled through the sky, resembling a strange sea creature with no eyes, this lowly steering device swerved back and forth at the tail end, lodged within the fin. Its motion was irregular, owing to the fact that it had become loosened during a previous mission. During the fatal flight, it began flapping uncontrollably. Its excessive flailing created, over time, a sufficient degree of destabilization to cripple the mammoth plane and send it plummeting to earth.

In the event of a failure, inquiries are launched, explanations set into motion. Probes are conducted into – in this case – the maintenance of the rudder, the programming of the mission, the writing of the code. They reveal the drone's concealed infrastructures, its systems of operation, logistics, and maintenance. When delving into this subterranean level, parts take on new relevancies and meanings, for they are always linked with other components in shared functions that complicate their discreteness. The roles that they play are always contingent, connected across scales in relational couplings that are hard to fathom. Even the smallest coupling can be of paramount importance.

In certain cases, the rudder might be viewed as an autonomous entity. A human observer might isolate the form, regard it in terms of its material and functional specificity, marvel at the contours of its design. Its smooth, curved shape is the material outcome of the need to harness the properties of moving air – to maximize the efficiency of the interactions between air and the solid bodies that move through it. Yet without the input of information or power, the device does nothing. It is simply a control platform, a surface that awaits command. The control is provided by an actuator (a motor). The rudder is attached to its output hub and secured in place with hinges.

At the most basic scale, the rudder's job is very simple. It moves back and forth along a set range of motion in accordance with received instruction. When we move up in scale, this action stays the same, but the task changes. At a larger scale, its job is to change the shape of the tail fin's surface and subsequently vary the amount of force that it generates. At a still larger scale, its job is to control movement of the plane about its vertical axis – to change the horizontal direction in which the nose is pointing.

In order to accomplish these tasks, the rudder must work in conjunction with the plane's other directional control surfaces. The cooperation occurs across a number of fronts. Actuators drive control platforms at their own local scale (such as at the tail or wing), in ways that alter their aerodynamic features, and these movements, in turn, alter the aerodynamic characteristics of the larger-scale platform of the plane. The overall cooperative job is to provide stability for the aircraft – to keep it straight in flight.

The actuator assumes command based on the control signals that it receives. It converts these control signals to physical actions. Its ability to drive its platform well requires that it receive *informed* operational instructions. In order for this to occur, environmental conditions must be detected and measured, the data processed by the flight computers, and the necessary information exchanged via transmitters and receivers. The flight computers send relevant information to operating crews and other teams of actors who might be involved with launch and recovery elements, maintenance and logistical support systems, mission command and control, or image processing and dissemination. Flight engineers at ground control stations monitor operational states via technical data arrayed on displays. Pilots navigate by Global Positioning System (GPS) signals and other locational data downloaded by satellite transmission and translated as coordinates on geographic information systems.

The correct data, once assembled into coherent control signals, instruct the actuators to drive their respective control platforms. The plane is steered and its relative position, speed, and attitude are adjusted in accordance with this instruction, and a cohesive flight is (it is hoped) produced.

The plane's actuator-platform *affiliation*, then, works in conjunction with a multiplicity of *actors* whose functions are to sense, process, and communicate the relevant information. The vehicle's countless other affiliations, working across various scales of operation, are all dependent upon the kinds of couplings that they seek out or afford. Because of the rudder's properties – its material quality, density, curvature, and texture – it has the capacity to deflect and contour the air that flows into it. When coupled with a motor that has the capacity to move it, the rudder-actuator is endowed with the more complex property of back-and-forth motion. When it is coupled with an instructor capable of commanding it, the mechanism activates its potential to change the shape of the tail fin's surface. It now achieves its capacity to vary the amount of force it generates. When working in conjunction with the plane's other directional control mechanisms, with their different capacities to vary force levels, it has the capacity to control the movement of the plane around its vertical axis.

The unmanned aerial system operates as an affiliation of maintained and monitored states through the activity of actors that might be human, mechanical, informational, environmental, or institutional. These actors operate at various scales and levels of complexity, whether at the level of hardware, software, image, data, controls, or flight or ground crews, or at the scale of logistical support, service, or operator and maintenance training. The affiliations that they constitute are practices as much as object-configurations, systems as much as parts. As data flows connect the flight crew to the plane, they also connect the plane and flight crew to intelligence teams and arrangements of commanders and troops on the ground or in the air. Their links and flows are determined through existing connections, platforms, and procedural agencies, yet at the same time they help instantiate them. Transmitted signals are modulated and rendered discrete as code, in concert with the programs, hardware, organizations, and personnel that rely on them. As they flow through such actors, the signals are filtered, constrained, related, and interpreted, and in the context of this activity the bounds and locales of materiality are enacted.

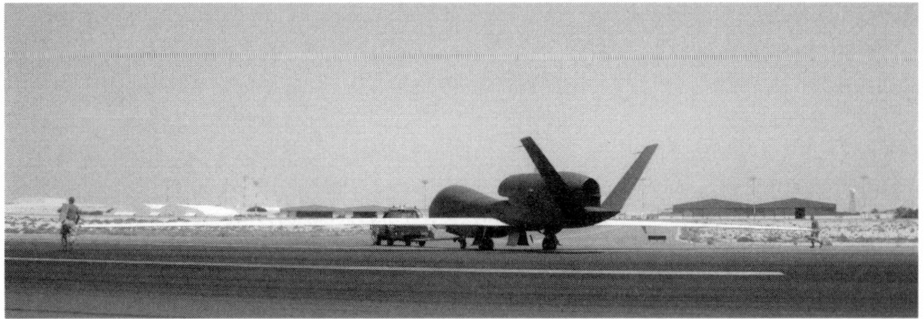

Pilots of the 12th Reconnaissance Squadron and the 380th Expeditionary Maintenance Group tow a Global Hawk back to its hangar after a mission.

Through it all, the rudders remain stable. The transmissions are cleared, the connections enabled. Collective intelligence and skill emerge for operation. Hardware, personnel, and supplies are integrated into tactical formations. Communication protocols and pathways fit together in stable systems. Ideas fit together in doctrines. The component actors within these ecologies are relatively discrete and stabilized. Yet they are active: they band and disband, accumulate and release, extend and consolidate. Some links are weak and some more durable. A dispatch is simple, whereas a doctrine is complex. Even internally, composites that would seem to be solid are embroiled in bandwidth battles and interservice rivalries. All must be actively maintained, with varying levels of frequency and force.

Even though they operate at different scales and levels of complexity, these components and ecologies are somehow integrated into coherent, stable formations that can be replicated and relied upon. Contexts are created, communication among components facilitated, and inferences from data drawn. They stabilize and cohere because of the procedural structures and standards of the higher-order affiliations into which they fit — networked, scalar concealments that might exist at the algorithm, hardware, or logistics level, or at the local, regional, or national scale. The tasks performed, whether at the small scale of control surfaces or the large scale of control infrastructures, are accomplished by linking to other affiliations and functioning in accordance with them in terms of common programs.

It is a matter of the modality of the linking. It is a process of bonding, synchronization, calibration, and agreement that, occurring across components and systems functioning at different speeds, scales, magnitudes, and levels of complexity, does not involve simply a conventional relational structure. The difficult question is not how actors relate to one another, but how they gather together to stabilize in cohesive wholes that are more than the sum of their parts. It is a matter of how, once sufficiently stabilized, they replicate, become redundant, and standardize, at various scales, across various platforms of endeavor.

The functions of sensing, processing, communicating, and actuating are distributed, shared, and consolidated across a number of ontological platforms. Many biological and machinic assemblages perform all of these functions. At the most basic level, all component actors are sensors and transmitters of energy. They emit and absorb electro-chemical signals, vibrations, and electric or nervous impulses. They filter and calibrate affective, rhythmic, and linguistic flows in ways that increase or diminish their ability to apprehend, act, and materialize. The foundational structure of this relationality is not based solely on difference. Actors may consolidate as discrete entities, yet they also vibrate in terms of constrained transmissions and modulated thresholds, however approached, attained, or crossed. Relationality involves the correspondence of elements, yet also involves the limitation of flows.

Conventional ontological categories recede and performative functions rise to the fore: the scalar roles that agencies perform. Functions are always consolidated in the specificities of actors, which might be human, institutional, technological, spatial, or representational in nature. These actors achieve a level of discreteness, in concert with external agencies that rely on them. But the challenge is to hold specificity and distribution together – placing part and practice, component and system, together on the same analytical plane. The drone is a rigid flying platform, yet it is also a dynamic system defined by the atmospheric, technological, and institutional systems that it moves through.

The rudder's direction in manned aircraft was once manipulated by a pilot who moved a pair of foot pedals. Although most of the Global Hawk's operations are the result of programming and commanding the autopilot's computers – a rudder command is sent encrypted via fibre optic overseas cable and satellite and takes about three seconds to reach the plane – this does not mean that the agency of the pilot has been fully replaced by a program or relocated in one human crew member at one site. It is a matter of looking at the distribution and embeddedness of the piloting function – understanding how its capacities have been redistributed in sensing, processing, and actuating affiliations at various scales and consolidated in new clusters of ontological significance.

It is messy work, which only increases our workload. It drags us further downward, just when we are ready to ascend. Often we undertake it only when something goes wrong – the necessity of the endeavour propelled by the advent of the failure.

At the onset of the Global Hawk crash, the investigation was set into motion. It located the rudder-actuator as the faulty agent – its excessive flapping was identified as the cause of the plane's demise. But where, exactly, was the fault located? Perhaps it lay deep within the mechanics of the actuator itself. No matter how stable and correct the command, the component may have responded only partially, or not at all, to the instruction's demand.

Or perhaps it was located in the instructions themselves, or in their transmission. It could have been located in the program through which these instructions were compiled, or in the agency that programmed them. Because the loosening of the rudder-actuator complex was not detected, the fault could have been located in the performance of the sensor that monitored the actuator's output hub.

The output of each set of components at each scale of organization provides units of assembly for the next level up. Data may be processed correctly at one scale but incorrectly at another. Faulty measurements alter the measurements required by controllers, and, depending on their severity, may scale up to degrade the overall feedback loop. One contingent fault may lead to another, cascading upward through the levels of the system to affect its overall performance. The small-scale fault can lead to the large-scale failure.

There are no hard-and-fast boundaries between fault and failure, but there is a transition point. Failure comes when a fault cascades up to cross a critical threshold. It is a matter not of eliminating fault, but of developing a control system equipped with an adequate degree of robustness.

The drone's components and systems take shape in degrees of coalescence and disruption, at various frequencies, rhythms, magnitudes, and scales of endeavour. They are subject to external forces, to the environmental stress placed upon them. How much can a part take before it fails, decouples from its job, spins out of synch?

Forces of temperature, mass, and vibration conspire against it. Discursive pressures, too. The drone works as a platform because the agents that it helps to assemble, however organic or inorganic, material or linguistic, together stabilize a sufficient degree of operational commonality – agreement that the thing works. The agreement happens through a setting of the terms: the ascendance of the organizing principles, or programs, that allow sustained affiliation to be achieved.

Perhaps now, having worked our way up from the greasy mechanics on the lower decks, we can arrive at the top. We can clean up and assume our rightful place at the helm, clicking through the drone's images, its views from above – its control panels, the representational constructs through which it sees, through which we see, and through which we seek to understand its operations and politics. However, this is not so easy, for in the analytical orientation that drone ontology demands, the cockpit is gone.

If there is a dominant genre of image, it is perhaps the simulation. Its interface is familiar to any aficionado of video games and high-tech adventure films. Like the control panels of actual flight crews, it bears the traces of the commercial game formats from which it is derived. Yet, like the actual drones of which they are a component, the coherency and discreteness of these interfaces dissolve upon scrutiny, scattering into arrays of component actors that are shared by other affiliations. These actors – visual and rhythmic motifs, behavioural conventions, perspectival formats, codes, tags, controllers, users, procedures, game architectures, rules – circulate and bond across multiple domains of experience, traversing the divides between corporation and government, operation and training. The particular applications in which they accumulate, developed largely by the game industry and influenced by its formats of cognitive and affective engagement, are made to excite the player and must be adjusted in accordance with the velocities, magnitudes, and textures of the real world.

The component actors of these gaming, control, and simulation ecologies relate as discrete entities, yet they also modulate and constrain flows at various scales of experience. They are relatively stabilized, consolidated platforms but also dynamic systems defined by the environments that they move through. As they configure and fluctuate, they require continuous adjustments across the various scales, magnitudes, and rhythms at which they are active. From which ontological "side" does the agency of this adjustment derive? The differentials, commonalities, and alignments that are negotiated do not involve hard-and-fast separations. The action

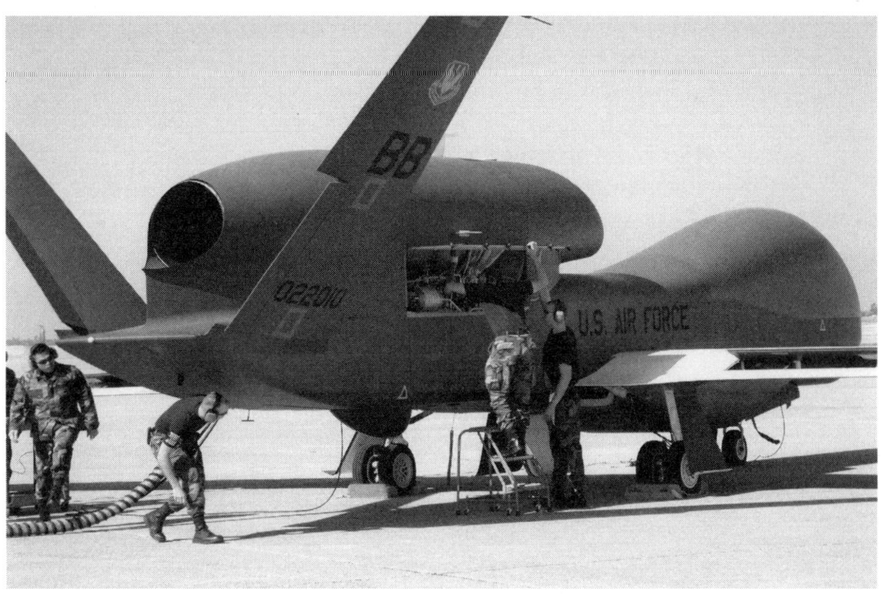

Avionics specialists with the 12th Aircraft Maintenance Unit prepare a Global Hawk for a runway taxi test at Beale Air Force Base in California.

courses through all of the actors in attendance, as these actors perform – performatively enact – within the dynamics of the various situations that arise, in various degrees of attunement to the shared priorities that are revealed.

Agency manifests by way of its action and maintenance: through the ways it comes to perform, at various speeds and degrees of complexity, and the extent to which this performance is recognized, valued, and maintained. An actor endeavours to be an adequate player of the game. What is deemed adequate performance, and how is it sustained? Some aspects of practice, prioritized, congeal into higher-order principles. Sufficiently stabilized, they replicate, become redundant, and standardize, at various scales, across various platforms of endeavour. They perpetuate their standards such that other actors come to move in accordance with their terms.

It is a matter of maintaining sufficient stability at numerous scales of practice, to the extent that these shared formats, agreements, and standards can come to exist: potential alliances that can offer propagation and endurance over time.

As simulations often require nothing more than a joystick and portable computer, the same high-end environments that are found in stationary systems can be taken directly into the field. Some simulations are plugged directly into actual ground control stations, allowing operators to toggle between simulation and actuality, rehearsal and mission, within a functional crew station. Game-based training becomes an essential precursor to deployment, increasingly integrated into actual operations in real time.

Ground control stations, training simulations, and video games occupy a common cognitive and affective terrain: sites of data rendered actionable. Together they constitute an interlocking complex, harnessing the imaginary, that conditions orientation in the world. Along with the infrastructure of the bases and training facilities within which they unfold, the enacted routines of this complex play a large materializing role: as affiliations of monitored and maintained states, they stabilize and entrain the material agencies of crew members and flown drones.

Across these dynamic, entraining affiliations, functional organizations of knowledge and skill are redistributed and reconstrained, along with positions, categories, and divisions of labour. As agencies circulate and bond across multiple domains of experience, traversing the divides between combat and entertainment, research and commerce, unlikely bedfellows are brought together through economic need. The redistribution of manpower – the shift from soldiers in battlefields and fighter planes to those in high-tech ground control units and command centres – challenges the stances, positions, and qualifications that have defined previous generations. The values and dispositions of unmanned warfare do not always align with the gendered roles, imaginaries, and concepts of adequacy that were present in the heroic ideals of the past. Displacement from the mastering console of the cockpit, haven of modernist subjectivity, does not come easy.

Nor do the incessant demands for new adequacies. As unmanned systems gain the ability to record activities on the ground over much longer timeframes, the vast amounts of data that they absorb can easily outrun the capacities of personnel. Cameras and sensors become ever more sophisticated, yet they are of limited value unless they can be accompanied by improved human intelligence and skill. The task of interpreting what the drone is seeing falls partly into the hands of the flight crew, and video and sensor feeds are also sent to analysis and dissemination sites at bases around the world. Inside their cavernous rooms, analysts filter vast streams of data. They, too, are hard-pressed: staring for hours on end at their monitors, nearly inert at their chairs, they try to ferret out the single, telling deviance in the normalized flow. Armed with the skill of extracting relevant data from image flows and information arrays, they attempt to organize those data into patterns from which extrapolations can be made.

The unmanned system, as an affiliation of components and practices, relies on analysis and dissemination sites like these. They are vital platforms of the drone in its shared perceptual and analytical capacities, its sensing, processing, communicating, and actuating functions – nodes through which its data are streamed, formatted, tagged, and rendered searchable across networks of datasets. As the image and sensor data are organized and stored, they become the primary site through which correlations can be made and inferences drawn. Databases, activated through search algorithms, become the primary repository of knowledge.

The challenge is that of tracking vehicles, objects, and humans on the ground with a higher degree of precision, in ways that lessen the demands on human decision making: to amplify the overall intelligence and skill of the system. This often takes the form of enhancing the capacity of tracking and search algorithms, along with the network processing capability required to parse and coordinate the data. It involves increasing the ability of drones to sense, reason, learn, and make decisions, and to collaborate and communicate, with a minimized degree of direct human involvement.

Such systems are often described as automated or autonomous. Yet the unmanned system does not eliminate the human: it redistributes the agencies of warfare. The capacities of sensing, analyzing, and alerting – the intelligence and skill required to interpret information and act on the results – are shared by an affiliation of actors, however algorithmic, organic, or systemic. Their ontological statuses arise from their performative practices within the functional organization of the system.

It is a matter of how they are maintained as dynamically stable entities – sustained, naturalized, and rendered discrete – and the programs through which this is accomplished. It is a matter of the priorities that come into play: the patterns and flows that are deemed most appropriate to the circumstances, as they are stabilized and maintained in practice.

As intelligence migrates into unlikely, shared sources, even those that are spatial and atmospheric, and agency is understood to be distributed and embodied in all manner of organic and inorganic actors, a sense of skill emerges whose source is in negotiation rather than domination. Here, an actor works with a material rather than against it, cultivating an existing, emergent meaning rather than externally imposing one. Unforeseen intimacies arise. It requires an agile practice attuned to the unexpected, an excessive proximity to that which cannot be contained or possessed. Analytical notions of power diminish, along with the control consoles that provide their supports.

Below the decks the rudders swerve.

\ **Jordan Crandall** is a media artist, theorist, and performer, and a professor in the Visual Arts Department at the University of California, San Diego (UCSD). He is the 2011 winner of the Vilém Flusser Theory Award, given by the Transmediale in Berlin in collaboration with the Vilém Flusser Archive of the University of Arts, Berlin. His current project, *UNMANNED*, explores new ontologies of distributed systems and the status of the human in a militarized landscape increasingly dependent on automated technology. Crandall is a researcher at the California Institute for Telecommunications and Information Technology (CALIT2) at UCSD, a collaborator at Eyebeam Art and Technology Center in New York, and founding editor of the online journal *VERSION*. \ http://jordancrandall.com

GEORGE LEGRADY

REFLECTIONS ON THE COMPUTATIONAL PHOTOGRAPH

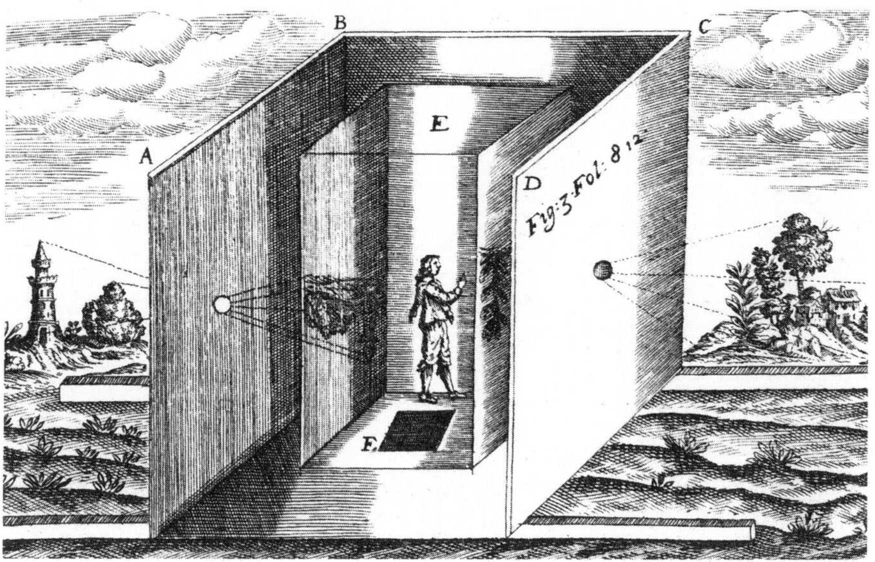

Camera Obscura, 1671. From *Ars Magna* by Athanasius Kircher (Amsterdam, 1671).

The optically reflected image has been part of our cultural evolution since the dawn of history. One can only imagine the amazement that people felt, thousands of years ago, when they saw images of outdoor scenes projected on cave surfaces or in darkened nomadic tents. Such projections were eventually scaled down and made visible in portable, darkened boxes with light waves entering through a pinhole or lens at one end, and being projected onto a ground glass at the opposite end. The challenge of capturing and retaining the optically projected image was first resolved in 1826 by the French inventor Nicéphore Niépce (1765–1833), whose eight-hour exposure of an image of a rooftop was preserved on a sheet of pewter coated with a mixture of bitumen and lavender oil.

During the twentieth century, chemically processed photographic and cinematic images became the dominant form of visual representation, transforming Western society into an image-based culture. Our understanding of the photographic image as a chemical-based technological medium emerged and crystallized over a 170-year period, resulting in conventions of visual representation; cultural definitions, applications, and functions; and an epistemological understanding of the photographic image. Over the past two decades, with the transition to digital and increased computer functionalities, photography is in the process of being reinvented.

Eastman Kodak, which dominated the photographic supplies industry internationally throughout the twentieth century, filed for bankruptcy protection in early 2012,[1] some thirty-seven years after one of its engineers, Steven Sasson, invented the digital camera in 1975 (US Patent 4131919).[2] His prototype machine consisted of an electronic still camera that employed a basic audio-grade magnetic tape to record the data captured by a charged-couple device (CCD) that converted incoming photons into electron charges, which were then translated into pixel values. It wasn't until the early 1990s that the digital camera fully entered the market.

My first interaction with digitized images occurred in the mid-1980s, when an affordable imaging system, the AT&T Truevision Targa frame buffer placed inside an IBM AT computer, became available. The card could grab a colour image from a video stream and turn it into a bitmap image composed of a matrix of pixels at a 16-bit resolution of 32,768 colours for each pixel. Once digitized, the image could then be processed computationally or through an onscreen interactive paint program. The digital camera and related imaging technologies shifted the processing of the image

1. Kodak plans to complete its reorganization and emerge from Chapter 11 of the U.S. Bankruptcy Code in the first half of 2013. The Rochester-based company will be focusing its future business on commercial imaging. See Associated Press [New York], November 28, 2012, http://bigstory. ap.org/article/kodak-reaches-improved-financing-deal-worth-830m.

2. http://www.google.com/patents/US4131919? printsec=abstract#v=onepage&q&f=false.

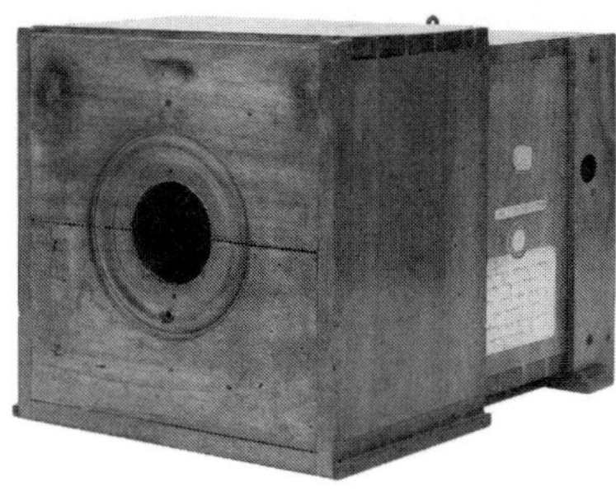

The world's first camera, known as the "chambre de la
découverte" (the chamber of discovery), made by Nicéphore
Niépce before 1826. Sliding box camera. 30.5 x 31.5 x 25 cm.

from development and reproduction with chemicals to a mathematically based
algorithmic operation, in which focus, contrast, tonal range, sharpness, and other
parameters could be corrected by adjusting pixels' numerical red, green, and blue
colour values.

Digital images can be processed in any number of ways and encoded with additional
data not visible to the viewer. Every digital image today has encoded exchangeable
image file format (EXIF) information about its origins. EXIF is used by most digital
cameras to add descriptive data to the image file such as creation date and time
and camera settings; some cameras also include Global Positioning System (GPS)
coordinates. The field of steganography, which involves concealing data so that only
sender and intended recipient are aware of them, has evolved to a significant extent
with techniques to encode messages in unused bytes in the data files of digital images,
sounds, and texts. Such techniques are commonly used to encode documents for
copyright purposes. The practice of encoding copyright emerged from that of water-
marking computerized documents, which consists of creating a watermark image

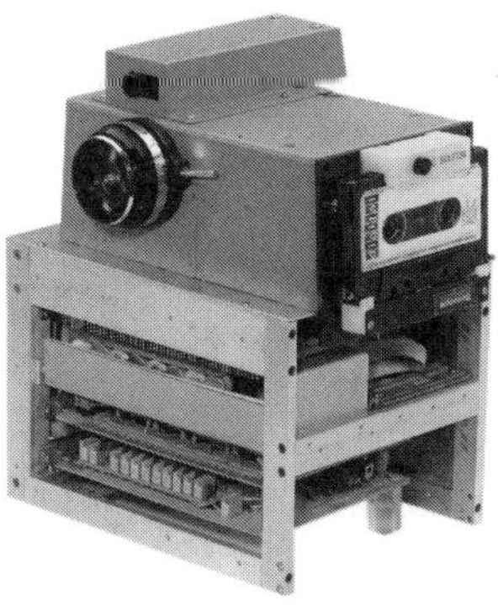

Steven Sasson's digital camera prototype.

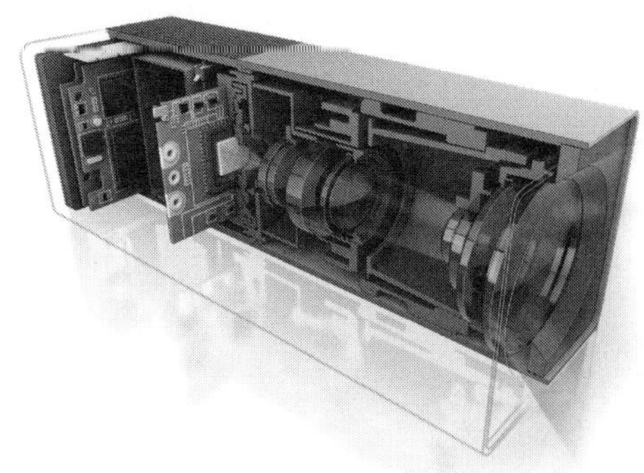

The commercially developed Lytro camera that emerged from the lightfield research.

that is printed "under" the text; the watermark may convey relevant information related to the document, such as its source, production date, and the printing house. Steganography is closely related to cryptography, a practice that produces a form of secure communication in which ordinary messages are converted into unrecognizable data that are then decoded by the intended receivers. With its origin in the Greek words *steganos* (covered or protected) and *graphein* (writing), steganography essentially means "to hide in plain sight," and suggests the presence of information that is not visible until it is revealed or unmasked. In sound samples, sonic information can be embedded into other sounds by reducing it to a low-level signal. Images can also be hidden within other images without the viewer noticing their presence.

Digital imaging technologies have generated a wide range of interdisciplinary practices, disciplines, and industries that engage with the creation, duplication, analysis, treatment, storage, classification, and authentication of images. Much of the handling of images today is based on metadata – additional information embedded in the file that gives pertinent details such as origin, production date, and other properties. There are many categories of metadata, but it can be generally defined as "data that describe data"; for instance, a person's name, gender, height, age, citizenship, and social security number are all forms of metadata.

In a paper that I wrote in the 1990s, "Image, Language, Belief and Synthesis,"[3] I explored the complex situation of the authoritativeness of the photograph in its transition from analog to digital. To this day, photographs function as authoritative evidential documents, still convincing in their transparent visual descriptions of the world even though much of our image culture and many media representations today are obvious technological enhancements or simulations. Images created through algorithmic simulations were of great interest at the time that I wrote the paper, as they replicated physical or imagined phenomena, generating discussion about the relationship of data to image. If the data were true, then the resultant image had to be believed to some degree. Photographs, once digitized, challenge notions of truth in reporting, as post-capture manipulations through digital processing increase the difficulties in identifying data transformation. Although digital photographs may be processed, manipulated, and reconstructed in post-production, the visual information in the original is limited to what was recorded at the moment of capture. For instance, a still photograph of a sports event cannot provide information about what occurred prior to or after the millisecond when the image was recorded. There is no return to the subject source, if one is limited to a standard digital camera.

Over the past six years, frenzied engineering research activities have been paving the way for a revolutionary direction in digital photography called computational photography, creating a major paradigm shift in how we are to understand the photographic image by pushing the boundaries of what a "true" photographic image may be. The evolution of this paradigm is an outcome of the confluence and synthesis of computation embedded into the camera itself so that much of the post-production work traditionally done on a computer after the image has been created is now produced at the moment, or prior to the moment, of image capture. Many of these new computation techniques enhance the image-recording process by incorporating contextual data encoded into machine vision, resulting in high-dimensional images whose properties, such as focus and spatial composition, may be adjusted in the viewing process after the image has been created. Such images expand the boundaries

3. George Legrady, "Image, Language, Belief and Synthesis," in G. Legrady, Jean Gagnon, and Pierre Dessureault, *George Legrady: From Analogue to Digital: Photography and Interactive Media = de l'analogie au codage numérique : la photographie et l'interactivité*, CD-ROM (Ottawa: National Gallery of Canada, 1998), http://www.mat.ucsb.edu/g. legrady/glWeb/publications/p/image.html.

The article was previously published in *Critical Issues in Electronic Media*, ed. Simon Penny (Albany: State University of New York Press, 1995).

of the photographic image. One of the memorable scenes in the culturally influential science fiction film *Blade Runner* (1982)[4] involves the interaction by police officer Deckard (played by Harrison Ford) with a photo-analysis machine through which Deckard manages to navigate around corners and behind walls to find the information he is looking for.

This innovative "moving around" within the visually captured space inside an existing two-dimensional photograph reveals a radical rethinking of what the photograph could be if enough additional visual information were recorded at the moment of capture. The scene in *Blade Runner* proposes the ability to discover additional information within the photograph after the fact of its original capture by recalculating the vantage point inside the flat space of the photograph.[5] What this suggests is a conflict between the still image and how it represents the world on which it is based. The nineteenth-century French sculptor Auguste Rodin (1840–1917) framed this scenario in an insightful way when he described how the artist constructs a painting in comparison to taking a photograph: "It is art that tells the truth and photography that lies. For *in reality, time does not stand still.* . . . The artist [, Rodin continues,] condenses several successive moments into a single image"[6] that then synthesizes the event more precisely than does a still frame frozen in time.

Research developments in camera optics, computational enhancement at the moment of image capture, and expansion of photographs' presence in the data cloud are some of the ways that the photograph is being redefined. Shree Nayar,[7] who directs the Computer Vision Laboratory[8] at Columbia University, one of the leading labs in the field, defines four research directions for his team, starting with digital photography, through which image processing is applied to existing images to enhance them. "Computational photography" involves computational processing during exposure to create multiple views, multiple foci through light field applications, and high-dynamic range exposure. "Computational imaging/camera" expands on the hardware through various new optics, such as multiple lenses, fish-eye panoramic imaging, and a radial catadioptric[9] system that captures a scene from a large number of viewpoints using mirrors to recover 3D information. At the receiving end of the light photons, Nayar's lab is experimenting with new types of detector sensors to push the boundaries of how pixels can be further enhanced. Finally, the "corneal imaging system" is an unusual experiment in which information within a scene is gathered on the basis of visual

4. *Blade Runner* (1982), directed by Ridley Scott, Warner Bros., http://bladerunnerthemovie. warnerbros.com.
5. Elissa Marder, "*Blade Runner*'s Moving Still," *Camera Obscura* 9, no. 27 (September 1991), 88–107, doi:10.1215/02705346-9-3_27-88.
6. Quoted in Paul Virilio, *The Vision Machine* (Bloomington: Indiana University Press, 1994), 2.

7. http://www.cs.columbia.edu/~nayar.
8. http://www1.cs.columbia.edu/CAVE.
9. "A catadioptric optical system is one where refraction and reflection are combined in an optical system, usually via lenses (dioptrics) and curved mirrors (catoptrics)." See http://en.wikipedia.org/ wiki/Catadioptric_system.

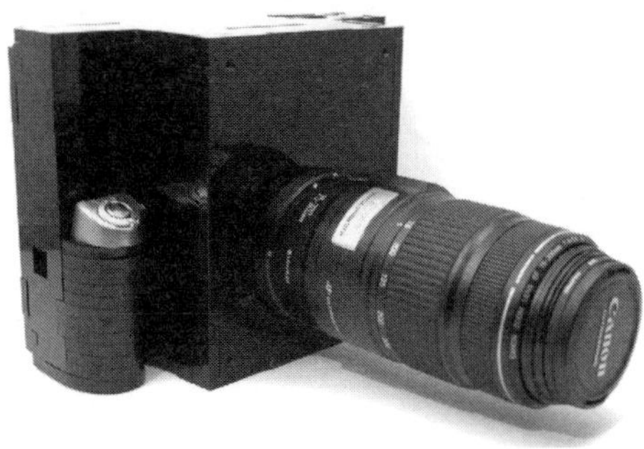

The Frankencamera from Marc Levoy's Computer
Graphics Lab at Stanford University, California.

data reflected in a subject's eye. This information can then be computationally
reformulated to accurately represent what the subject may be seeing while looking
at the photographer.

Images recorded through a set of multiple lenses positioned in a two-dimensional
matrix result in enhanced views as each lens returns a slightly different vantage
point, which can then be correlated to explore variances in depth of field and 3D
sampling of a scene. This research, initiated in the mid-1990s at the Stanford Computer
Graphics Lab directed by Marc Levoy,[10] has led to computer graphics experiments in
the light-field camera, a system that uses a microlens array to capture 4D light field
information in a scene resulting in an image with variable focus that can be adjusted
during the viewing process.

The Lytro camera[11] is a commercial product developed by Stanford graduate
student Ren Ng in Levoy's lab. The Frankencamera, also from Levoy's lab, was
designed as an experimental platform for computational photography research. It

10. http://graphics.stanford.edu/~levoy.   11. https://www.lytro.com/camera.

has a somewhat cumbersome look, reminiscent of Sasson's first digital camera, as its design is intended for programmable multifunctionality. The lab produced an application-programming interface software package (FCam)[12] to provide capture and post-processing functionalities for the camera on the Nokia N900 Smartphone.

Daniel Vaquero, a computer science doctoral researcher at the University of California, Santa Barbara, who was fortunate to collaborate with labs at Stanford, Nokia, and IBM Watson, worked with the Frankencamera and Nokia software to develop a research project called "Composition Context Photography," for which he developed software for the Nokia that would record preliminary compositions that an image maker might choose to make prior to capturing the image. Recording of and feedback on preliminary compositions may enhance the ability to create images.

As artists know, assessment of aesthetic value is a complex and challenging question, and the idea of quantifying it in photographic images to be translated into machine vision seems unrealistic. Nonetheless, researchers Ritendra Datta, Dhiraj Joshi, Jia Li, and James Z. Wang[13] at Pennsylvania State University have taken on the challenge of formulating measurable, quantifiable ways to evaluate what is a good photograph, with the intention of developing software that will be embedded into cameras to guide image makers to create better compositions. To perform their research, Datta and his colleagues have identified various image primitives, such as colour relationships, hue, the rule of thirds, familiarity measure (defined as learning to rate images from the experience gathered by seeing other images), texture, size and aspect ratio, region composition, depth of field, and other image components that they have computationally analyzed from large online photo collections such as Flickr. Large datasets may be a noisy statistical resource if compared to a sampling of what experts in the field may agree on, but it does provide a basis by which to begin to understand whether large communities use universal aesthetic standards when they assess images. Once these and other, similarly ephemeral, properties of images are quantifiably defined, our cameras will be able to tell us what to photograph, thus raising the questions of whether aesthetic analysis of the image is still within the domain of the arts and whether science can quantitatively measure what may be an aesthetic solution and implement this as a camera function. Artists find the proposition questionable, as they know that aesthetic value is a continuously changing process, based on the culture's continuous absorption and rejection of norms. Nonetheless, the project is intriguing.

12. https://graphics.stanford.edu/papers/fcam/html.

13. http://infolab.stanford.edu/~wangz/project/imsearch/Aesthetics/ECCV06/datta.pdf.

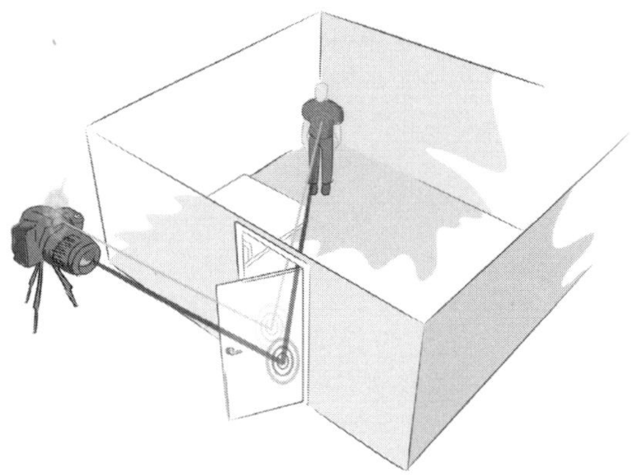

"Looking Around Corners using Femto-Photography."
Research at Ramesh Raskar's Camera Culture Group
of the MIT Media Lab, Cambridge, Massachusetts.

Photosynth,[14] a software application from Microsoft, originally developed at the University of Washington, provides the most immediate experience of connecting one's images with others in the Internet data cloud in such a way that the image becomes an information node in relation to the multitude of other images that can be correlated to it. Its visual and informational properties are sufficiently extended in detail to be viewed from many different angles, positioned in a three-dimensional volumetric space with other photographs taken at that scene at different times. With more than a billion people now using networked mobile cameras, there is tremendous real-time synchronization of any image taken with all others that were produced in the same geospatial location. Photosynth provides an expanded platform in which to contextually explore one's image in relation to others, reminiscent of *Blade Runner*'s Esper machine, as we now can navigate around our image in its visual space, surrounded by other images accessed in real-time from the cloud.

To penetrate the flat dimensions of a photograph on its own is not a realistic possibility but, as *Blade Runner*'s Esper Machine implies, a photograph may potentially represent a broader range of its spatial environment if the capture technology can record it. The technique of ray-tracing was introduced a few decades ago to enhance realism

14. http://photosynth.net.

in computer graphics. The technique consists of tracing the path of light between virtual objects in a virtual space, and simulating on the surface of these objects how the light rays bounce around and reflect off each other. Some rays are absorbed, others are reflected to varying degrees, and still others are refracted due to surface variability and environmental conditions (think of how water in a glass will bend visual information perceived through it). The process of calculating each point in a 3D simulated scene is computationally expensive, but, given the continuous increase in computational performance, a next step in computational photography is to further explore how to harvest visual information beyond the limitation of incidental light rays received by a directional lens. A paper titled "Dual Photography"[15] by Pradeep Sen,[16] a researcher in image synthesis – a field that explores simulating realistic, photographic-looking images that integrate complex renderings of lighting, texture, shading, and occlusion – exploits the "reciprocity principle" phenomena discovered in the nineteenth century by the German physicist Hermann von Helmholtz, known for his work in physics and visual perception. The reciprocity principle of "If you can see me I can see you"[17] is realized in the "Dual Photography" research by pointing a camera at a scene, and then lining up a projector that provides structured illumination at a different angle facing a scene so that two vantage points can be computationally calculated – one from the camera's point of view and the other from the projector's – resulting in two variable representations of a scene.

Another project that explores the seemingly impossible task of recording what is beyond the line of sight has been proposed by Ramesh Raskar's[18] team at the Camera Culture Group[19] at the Massachusetts Institute of Technology (MIT). The group calls its research "Femto-Photography," referring to a superfast camera that can record at a rate of one trillion exposures per second. The research involves the release of laser pulses into a multidimensional space beyond the direct sight of the camera lens. As the pulses bounce around the space, reflecting off objects near openings such as slightly ajar doors, and return to the camera lens, the camera records the incoming information and translates the sum of pulses into a visual-spatial dimension, not unlike the mechanism for sonar detection of sunken ships undersea, to sketch out the hidden geometry of surrounding spaces beyond the sight of the camera lens. With this project and the "Dual Photography" project, the barrier to representation beyond the camera's vantage point has been broken, and we can expect images to have further dimensionality as research advances.

15. P. Sen et al., "ACM Transactions on Graphics (TOG)," *Proceedings of ACM SIGGRAPH 2005* 24, no. 3, (July 2005), 745–55, http://graphics.stanford. edu/papers/dual_photography.
16. http://www.ece.ucsb.edu/~psen.
17. http://graphics.stanford.edu/papers/dual_ photography.
18. http://www.media.mit.edu/people/raskar.
19. http://web.media.mit.edu/~raskar.

My goal in this essay has been to give a brief overview of the breadth of activity in current engineering research that focuses on next-step expansions and reinventions of the camera and photography. I am particularly interested in the promise of multi-dimensional photography as suggested some three decades ago by the science fiction movie *Blade Runner*. Computational photography involves advances in optics, sensors, and computer vision applications within the camera so that multiple layers of information with changing scene parameters can be recorded and then fused to enhance the representation. In contrast to the rapid pace of technological innovations, Western culture's understanding of the photographic image's transformation into a greater "something else" is evolving at a much slower pace, widening the gap between the cultural meaning of images and the technological instruments that create them.

\ **George Legrady** is a digital media arts installation artist whose current work engages with data visualization, swarm robotic camera interaction, and creation of multi-image narratives in static lenticular displays. In the early 1990s, he began to explore the potential of computer processing for narrative-based digital interactive installations, which have been exhibited internationally. He is director of the Experimental Visualization Lab and a professor in the Media Arts & Technology PhD program at the University of California, Santa Barbara (UCSB). He is also a member of the ExpVisLab artists' collective participating in Le Mois de la Photo à Montréal 2013. His work is currently funded by two National Science Foundation grants and the Robert W. Deutsch Foundation. \ www.georgelegrady.com

APPENDIX

Selected Bibliography

Abercrombie, Nicholas, Stephen Hill, and Bryan S. Turner. *Sovereign Individuals of Capitalism*. London: Allen & Unwin, 1986.

Baert, Renee. *Max Dean*. Texts in English and French. Ottawa: The Ottawa Art Gallery, 2005.

Barad, Karen. *Meeting the Universe Halfway: Quantum Physics and the Entanglement of Matter and Meaning*. Durham, N.C.: Duke University Press, 2007.

Benjamin, Medea. *Drone Warfare: Killing by Remote Control*. New York and London: OR Books, 2012.

Bennett, Jane. *Vibrant Matter: A Political Ecology of Things*. Durham, N.C.: Duke University Press, 2010.

Berger, John. "Why Look at Animals." In *About Looking*, 3–28. New York: Vintage Books, 1991.

Bergson, Henri. *Matter and Memory*. Translated by Nancy Margaret Paul and W. Scott Palmer. London: Allen & Unwin, 1911.

Brin, David. *The Transparent Society: Will Technology Force Us to Choose Between Privacy and Freedom?* Reading, Mass.: Perseus Books, 1998.

Brotherus, Elina. *Elina Brotherus: Artist and Her Model*. Texts in English, French and Finnish. Brussels: Le Caillou Bleu, 2012.

Colebrook, Claire. *Deleuze and the Meaning of Life*. London and New York: Continuum, 2010.

Crary, Jonathan. *Suspensions of Perception: Attention, Spectacle, and Modern Culture*. Cambridge, Mass.: MIT Press, 2001.

Debord, Guy. *The Society of the Spectacle*. Translated by Donald Nicholson-Smith. New York: Zone Books, 1994.

De Landa, Manuel. *War in the Age of Intelligent Machines*. New York: Zone Books, 1991.

Dufaux, Pascal. *Le cosmos dans lequel je suis*. Quebec City: Éditions J'ai VU, 2010.

Durkheim, Émile. *The Division of Labor in Society*. Translated by George Simpson. New York: The Free Press, 1947.

Dyens, Ollivier. *Metal and Flesh: The Evolution of Man: Technology Takes Over*. Translated by Evan J. Bibbee and Ollivier Dyens. Cambridge, Mass.: MIT Press, 2001.

Ellul, Jacques. *The Technological Society*. Translated by John Wilkinson. New York: Knopf, 1964.

Flusser, Vilém. *Towards A Philosophy of Photography*. Translated by Anthony Matthews. London: Reaktion Books, 2000.

Foucault, Michael. *Discipline and Punish: The Birth of the Prison*. Translated by Alan Sheridan. New York: Vintage Books, 1995.

Frazer, James George. *The Golden Bough: A Study in Magic and Religion, Part II, Taboo and the Perils of the Soul*, 3rd edition, vol. 3. London: MacMillan, 1919.

Gray, John. *Straw Dogs: Thoughts on Humans and Other Animals*. London: Granta Books, 2002.

Hannay, Alastair. *On the Public: Thinking in Action*. New York and London: Routledge, 2005.

Haraway, Donna. "A Cyborg Manifesto: Science, Technology, and Socialist-Feminism in the Late Twentieth Century." In *Simians, Cyborgs, and Women: The Reinvention of Nature*, 149-81. New York and London: Routledge, 1991.

Haslinger, Josef. *Opernball*. Frankfurt: Fischer, 2003.

Henner, Mishka. *Dutch Landscapes*. N.p.: Print-on-demand book, open edition, 2011. http://www.mishkahenner.com/Bookshop.

Kember Sarah, and Joanna Zylinska. *Life After New Media: Mediation as a Vital Process*. Cambridge, Mass.: MIT Press, 2012.

Kittler, Friedrich A. *Gramophone, Film, Typewriter*. Translated with an introduction by Geoffrey Winthrop-Young and Michael Wutz. Stanford: Stanford University Press, 1999.

———. *Optical Media*. Translated by Anthony Evans. Cambridge, U.K.: Polity Press, 2010.

Kivland, Sharon, and Cheryl Sourkes. *Tons of Webcammer Babes / Des beautés webcam à la tonne*. Quebec City: Éditions J'ai VU, 2009.

Lake, Suzy. *Suzy Lake: Political Poetics*. Toronto: University of Toronto Art Centre and Scotiabank Contact Photography Festival, 2011.

Legrady, George, Jean Gagnon, and Pierre Dessureault. *George Legrady: From Analogue to Digital: Photography and Interactive Media / George Legrady : de l'analogie au codage numérique : la photographie et l'interactivité*. CD-ROM. Ottawa: National Gallery of Canada, 1998.

Nye, David E. *American Technological Sublime*. Cambridge, Mass.: MIT Press, 1994.

Paglen, Trevor. *Invisible: Covert Operations and Classified Landscapes*. New York: Aperture, 2010.

———. *Trevor Paglen: Secession: Visiting the Planetarium, Images of the Black World*. Texts in English and German. Vienna: Secession; Berlin: Revolver Verlag, 2010.

Pellicer, Raynal. *Photobooth: The Art of the Automatic Portrait*. New York: Abrams, 2010.

Potts, John, and Edward Scheer, eds. *Technologies of Magic: A Cultural Study of Ghosts, Machines and the Uncanny*. Sydney: Power Publications, 2006.

Probst, Barbara. *Exposures*. Göttingen: Steidl/ Museum of Contemporary Photography, 2007.

Rafman, Jon. *The Nine Eyes of Google Street View*. Texts in English and French. Paris: Jean Boîte Éditions, 2011.

Royle, Nicholas. *The Uncanny*. Manchester and New York: Manchester University Press, 2003.

Ruff, Thomas. *Thomas Ruff: ma.r.s.* Málaga: Centro de Arte Contemporáneo de Málaga, 2011.

Sawada, Tomoko. *ID400*. Kyoto: Seigensha Art Publishing, 2004.

Sconce, Jeffrey. *Haunted Media: Electronic Presence from Telegraphy to Television*. Durham, N.C.: Duke University Press, 2000.

Seers, Lindsay. *Human Camera*. Birmingham: Article Press, 2007.

Sellars, Simon, and Dan O'Hara, eds. *Extreme Metaphors: Selected Interviews with J. G. Ballard, 1967–2008*. London: Fourth Estate, 2012.

Sontag, Susan. *Regarding the Pain of Others*. New York: Picador, 2003.

Sourkes, Cheryl. *Public Camera / Caméra publique*. Ottawa: Canadian Museum of Contemporary Photography; Lethbridge: Southern Alberta Art Gallery; Owen Sound (Ont.): Tom Thomson Art Gallery, 2007.

Spinatsch, Jules. *Jules Spinatsch*. Texts in English and German. Zug, Switzerland: Kunsthaus Zug/ Kodoji Press, 2009.

Sterbak, Jana. *From Here To There*. Texts in English, French and Italian. Montreal: Musée d'art contemporain de Montréal, 2003.

———. *Jana Sterbak: Condition contrainte*. Arles, Actes Sud; Nîmes: Carré d'Art, 2006.

Sykes, Charles J. *The End of Privacy: The Attack on Personal Rights at Home, at Work, On-Line, and in Court*. New York: St. Martin's Press, 2000.

Umbrico, Penelope. *Penelope Umbrico (photographs)*. New York: Aperture, 2011.

Virilio, Paul. *The Original Accident*. Translated by Julie Rose. Cambridge, U.K.: Polity Press, 2007.

———. *The Vision Machine*. Translated by Julie Rose. Bloomington: Indiana University Press; London: British Film Institute, 1994.

Waddell, Laurence Austin. *Among the Himalayas*. New York: Amsterdam Book Co.; Westminster: A. Constable & Co., 1899.

Wallach, Wendell, and Colin Allen. *Moral Machines: Teaching Robots Right from Wrong*. Oxford and New York: Oxford University Press, 2009.

Warner, Marina. *Phantasmagoria*. Oxford and New York: Oxford University Press, 2006.

Wassink, Thijs groot / WassinkLundgren. *Don't Smile Now… Save it for Later!* London: Archive of Modern Conflict, 2008.

Wesely, Michael. *Michael Wesely: Open Shutter*. New York: The Museum of Modern Art, 2004.

Wiener, Norbert. *The Human Use of Human Beings: Cybernetics and Society*. Cambridge, Mass.: Da Capo Press, 1988.

Winner, Langdon. *Autonomous Technology: Technics-out-of-Control as a Theme in Political Thought*. Cambridge, Mass.: MIT Press, 1977.

Whitaker, Reginald. *The End of Privacy: How Total Surveillance is Becoming a Reality*. New York: New Press, 1999.

Zielinski, Siegfried. *Deep Time of the Media: Toward an Archaeology of Hearing and Seeing by Technical Means*. Translated by Gloria Custance. Cambridge, Mass.: MIT Press, 2006.

Acknowledgments by the Guest Curator

It was a great and unexpected honour to be given the opportunity to be the guest curator of Le Mois de la Photo à Montréal 2013. The rewards of being an independent curator based in London are many, including setting one's own direction and working schedule. However, as guest curator of Le Mois de la Photo à Montréal I soon realized that I was a member of a team, a highly professional one living and working over 3,200 miles away. This may be the most rewarding aspect of this project: knowing that you have people on your side – or should I say, on the other side of the Atlantic – ready to help produce this large and complex biennale involving many artists and venues across Montreal.

Working on such a project as *Drone: The Automated Image* is a rare privilege. Not many other events or biennales would take on a theme that, at first reading, might seem eccentric. Le Mois de la Photo à Montréal is unique in this respect, as it gives the guest curator a chance to develop a theme over an extended period of time, with the support to realize a range of exhibitions with substantial publication and associated activities.

On my visits to Montreal and elsewhere in Canada, I was fortunate to meet some old acquaintances and, more importantly, to develop many new friendships with artists and with colleagues working in galleries and museums. These meetings, discussions, and studio visits made my time in Montreal extremely pleasurable and rewarding, and I am sure that they will be useful in my future projects.

First, let me thank the artists who agreed to participate in this journey and the writers for producing excellent and thought-provoking texts. I also thank the visual arts institutions that agreed to be part of the biennale. To have the support of these partners gave me the confidence to continue with the project. I will mention only a few key names here. The core team of Chuck Samuels, Yasmine Tremblay, Marie-Catherine Leroux, Isabelle Aubut Gimmig, Katia Meir, Hugues Dugas, and Corina Ilea at Le Mois de la Photo à Montréal should take all the credit for realizing this project. I thank them for their care, advice, and friendship. Last but not least I should mention Tricia Wombell, my team player back in London. She played an important role in keeping me focused on the drone.

Thank you Montreal.

Paul Wombell
Guest Curator 2013

Acknowledgments by the Director General

We are proud to produce, for each event, a publication of lasting value that is the result of the creativity and hard work of many collaborators. First and foremost, I must congratulate Paul Wombell, our 2013 guest curator, for his timely and inspired theme, *Drone: The Automated Image*. I would like to thank Marie-Catherine Leroux, our publications coordinator; Corina Ilea, Paul's curatorial assistant; and graphic designer Dominique Mousseau for her striking layout; the result is a book that is both a visual and an intellectual delight. It was a great pleasure working with our German co-publisher, Kerber Verlag – especially the project manager, Martina Kupiak – for co-producing and distributing this book worldwide. With regard to the Canadian distribution, I would like to thank Pascal Chamaillard of Édipresse and Jean Lalonde from the Regroupement des centres d'artistes autogérés du Québec.

I would like to thank all the participating artists, their representatives, and their technicians, as well as the authors, speakers, and lenders. In particular, we are indebted to our exhibition partners, which provide essential and ongoing contributions to the success of each event, enabling Le Mois de la Photo à Montréal to thrive after 25 years of existence.

I would like to acknowledge the following individuals and organizations for their contributions: Caroline Andrieux and Alfonso Esparza and the rest of the team at the Darling Foundry; Christine Autate from Publicité Sauvage; Caroline Buchwalter and Gwenaël Le Bodic of Greencopper; Michèle Cantin and the team at Hotel ZERO1; David Lavoie of the Festival TransAmériques; and Claude Belanger and the Manifestation internationale d'art de Québec.

Regarding the preparation of the exhibitions, I must express my appreciation to Michel Séguin (Atelier M Séguin); Marcel Pelletier (Les Encadrements Marcel Pelletier); Louis Lussier (Atelier Louis Lussier); François Hébel and Pascale Giffard (Les Rencontres d'Arles); Marloes Krijnen, Kim Knoppers, and Karin Bareman (Foam Museum Amsterdam); Wayne Maugans (Joy of Giving Something Inc.); Claudia Altman-Siegel (Altman Siegel); and Manuela Mozo (Metro Pictures). In addition, we are grateful for the input of Hélène Samson (McCord Museum) and of Fabrizio Gallant and Louise Désy (Canadian Centre for Architecture) for the two projects featuring works from their respective collections.

From the government and institutional partners that lend their support to MPM, I would like to thank: Réjean Perron, Françoise Jean, and Gilles Pettigrew (Conseil des arts et des lettres du Québec); Michel Gaboury, Filipe Diaz, and Koba Johnson (Canada Council for the Arts); Danielle Sauvage, Marie-Michèle Cron, and Iulia-Anamaria Salagor (Conseil des arts de Montréal); Irina Vatchkova (Emploi-Québec); Sylvie Laniel and François-Olivier Labrie (Sécrétariat à la région métroplitaine); Alain Petel, Diane Régimbald, and Danièle Racine (Ville de Montréal); Renée Ouellet (Ministère de la Culture et des Communications du Québec); Stéphanie Laurin (Tourisme Montréal); Nathalie Gingras and Ève Line Lafond (Les Offices jeunesse internationaux du Québec > LOJIQ); Karen Temple, Marie-Josée Taillon, and Alain Fisette (Canadian Heritage); Jelena Delic (Pro Helvetia); Coby Reitsman (Mondriaan Fund); Alain Reinaudo and Sophie Robnard (Institut Français); Anne-Lorraine Vigouroux and Laurence Moiroux (Consulat général de France à Québec); Petra Havu (Frame Visual Art Finland); Toshi Aoyagi (The Japan Foundation, Toronto); Ingrid Klenner (Institut für Auslandsbeziehungen); and Sarah Dawbarn (British Council).

I would like to thank the members of the board of directors, Diane Charbonneau, Annie Gauthier, André Gilbert, Jean-François Bélisle, Serge Clément, and Marie-Justine Snider, for their outstanding support, as well as our generous donors, including Stéphane Aquin, François Babineau, Marta Braun, Yolanda Cespedes, Alain Chagnon, Diane Charbonneau, Daniel Fillion, Galerie Simon Blais, Robert Graham, Madeleine Poulin, George Steeves, Ewa Zebrowski, and anonymous donors.

I must, in the strongest of terms, congratulate the team at MPM, including interns and volunteers, for their hard work and unwavering commitment to the event. I am especially indebted to our incomparable assistant director, Yasmine Tremblay, without whom this and the last five events would not have been possible.

I would like to express my gratitude to friends and loved ones for their encouragement and support.

Finally, my thanks go out to all those who have contributed to our 13th edition, including those whose names came to my attention after the writing of this text.

MPM is a member of Festivals et Événements Québec and Festival of Light, an international organization of photography events.

Chuck Samuels
Director General
June 26, 2013

Le Mois de la Photo à Montréal

Team

Director General
Chuck Samuels

Assistant Director
Yasmine Tremblay

Guest Curator 2013
Paul Wombell

Curatorial Assistant
Corina Ilea

Publications Coordinator
Marie-Catherine Leroux

Exhibitions Coordinator
Hugues Dugas

Communications and Marketing Coordinator
Sandra D'Angelo
(in collaboration with Isabelle
Aubut Gimmig and Katia Meir)

Administrative Assistant
Majorie Paré

Educational Programs and Audience
Development Coordinator
Pascale Tremblay

Special Events Coordinator
Amélie Aumont

Press Relations
François Bernier

Graphic and Web Designer
Myriam Belley

Hospitality
Jade Larochelle

Educational Programs Interns
Nantou Soumahoro
Gina Cortopassi

Publication Intern
François Carl Duguay

Special Events Interns
Sandrine Briand-Milette
Marie-Philippe Mercier Lambert

Publication Design/Visual Identity
Dominique Mousseau

Board of Directors

President
Diane Charbonneau

Vice-President
André Gilbert

Treasurer
Annie Gauthier

Secretary
Jean-François Bélisle

Administrators
Serge Clément
Marie-Justine Snider

Partners

Exhibition Partners
Canadian Centre for Architecture; Centre des arts
actuels Skol; Darling Foundry; Galerie B-312;
MAI (Montréal, arts interculturels); Maison de la
culture Frontenac; Maison de la culture Marie-Uguay;
Maison de la culture du Plateau-Mont-Royal;
Make Art Public; The Montreal Museum of Fine Arts;
McCord Museum; OPTICA, a centre for contemporary
art; SBC Gallery of Contemporary Art; VOX, centre de
l'image contemporaine.

Governmental and Institutional Partners
Conseil des arts et des lettres du Québec; Emploi-
Québec; Secrétariat à la région métropolitaine;
Ministère de la Culture et des Communications
du Québec; Canada Council for the Arts; Conseil
des arts de Montréal; Ville de Montréal; Canadian
Heritage; Tourisme Montréal; Pro Helvetia;
Mondriaan Fund; Institut français; Consulat
général de France à Québec; Frame Visual Art
Finland; Japan Foundation; Institut für
Auslandsbeziehungen e. V.; British Council.

Sponsor Partners
Atelier M Séguin; Hotel ZERO1;
Publicité Sauvage; Greencopper;
National Bank Insurance.

Media Partners
Aesthetica Magazine; Afterimage; Aperture;
BlackFlash Magazine; Border Crossings; Ciel
variable; Daylight Books; ETC revue de l'art actuel;
Next Level; Prefix Photo; Rats de ville.

Cultural Partners
Dazibao; Festival of Light; Festival du Nouveau
Cinéma; Manifestation internationale d'art de
Québec; Regroupement des centres d'artistes
autogérés du Québec.

Donors
Stéphane Aquin; François Babineau;
Marta Braun; Yolanda Cespedes; Alain Chagnon;
Diane Charbonneau; Daniel Fillion;
Galerie Simon Blais; Robert Graham;
Jocelyn Philibert; Madeleine Poulin;
George Steeves; Ewa Zebrowski;
and anonymous donors.

This publication was published to accompany the event

Le Mois de la Photo à Montréal – 13th edition
Drone: The Automated Image \ Guest curator: Paul Wombell
September 5 – October 5, 2013

Editor
Paul Wombell

Publication Coordinator
Marie-Catherine Leroux

Research and Writing
Corina Ilea

Copyediting and Proofreading
Käthe Roth, Colette Tougas, Pascale Tremblay

Translation
Francine Dagenais (her essay)
Nathalie De Blois (Paul Wombell)
Francine Delorme (Paul Wombell, Jordan Crandall,
George Legrady, Joanna Zylinska, and various texts)
Käthe Roth (various texts)
Colette Tougas (Melissa Miles, and various texts)
Marine Van Hoof (various texts)

Design
Dominique Mousseau

Technical Verification of the Images
Pierre Blache

Project Management, Kerber Verlag
Martina Kupiak

Bibliothèque et Archives nationales du Québec
and Library and Archives Canada cataloguing
in publication

Mois de la photo à Montréal
(13th : 2013 : Montréal, Québec)

Drone : the automated image

Catalogue of twenty-five exhibitions of the
13th edition of Le Mois de la photo à Montréal
held in 14 sites across Montréal from
September 5 to October 5, 2013.
Issued also in French under title :
Drone : l'image automatisée.
Co-published by Kerber.
Includes bibliographical references.

ISBN 978-2-9808020-5-8
(Mois de la photo à Montréal)
ISBN 978-3-86678-803-9 (Kerber Verlag)

1. Photography, Artistic - Exhibitions.
2. Photography, Artistic.
I. Wombell, Paul.
II. Mois de la photo à Montréal (Organization).
III. Title.

TR646.C32M6 2013b
779.074'71428
C2013-940967-X

The Deutsche Nationalbibliothek lists this
publication in the Deutsche Nationalbibliografie;
detailed bibliographic data are available on the
Internet at http://dnb.d-nb.de.

ISBN 978-3-86678-803-9
(Kerber Verlag)
www.kerberverlag.com

ISBN 978-2-9808020-5-8
(Le Mois de la Photo à Montréal)
www.moisdelaphoto.com

Legal Deposit, 2013
Bibliothèque et Archives nationales du Québec
Library and Archives Canada

Printed in Germany

Printed and published by
Kerber Verlag, Bielefeld
Windelsbleicher Str. 166–170
33659 Bielefeld
Germany
Tel. +49 (0) 5 21/9 50 08-10
Fax +49 (0) 5 21/9 50 08-88
info@kerberverlag.com
www.kerberverlag.com

Edited by
Le Mois de la Photo à Montréal
661 Rose-de-Lima St., #203
Montréal, Québec
H4C 2L7 Canada
Tel. +1 (514) 390-0383
Fax +1 (514) 390-8802
info@moisdelaphoto.com
www.moisdelaphoto.com

Kerber, US Distribution
D.A.P., Distributed Art Publishers, Inc.
155 Sixth Avenue, 2nd Floor
New York, NY
10013 United States
Tel. +1 (212) 627-1999
Fax +1 (212) 627-9484
www.artbook.com

KERBER publications are available in
selected bookstores and museum shops
worldwide (distributed in Europe, Asia,
South and North America).